Y0-BQS-595

Sex and the Penitentials:
The Development of a Sexual Code
550–1150

SEX and the Penitentials

The Development of a Sexual Code 550-1150

BX /
1939
P45
P39

BT
708
·P39
1984

PIERRE J. PAYER

REGIS COLLEGE TORONTO WITHDRAWN LIBRARY

University of Toronto Press

Toronto Buffalo London

92244

© University of Toronto Press 1984
Toronto Buffalo London
Printed in Canada
ISBN 0-8020-5649-0

Canadian Cataloguing in Publication Data

Payer, Pierre J., 1936–
Sex and the penitentials

Bibliography: p.
Includes index.
ISBN 0-8020-5649-0
1. Penitentials. 2. Sex – Religious aspects –
Christianity. I. Title.
BX1939.P45P39   1984   241'.66   C84-098883-4

Sections of the introduction have appeared previously in
P. Payer 'Penance and Penitentials,' in *Dictionary of the
Middle Ages* ed Joseph R. Strayer, copyright © 1983
Charles Scribner's Sons, New York, and are used and
reprinted with the permission of the publisher.

This book has been published with the help of a grant
from the Canadian Federation for the Humanities, using
funds provided by the Social Sciences and Humanities
Research Council of Canada, and a grant from the Andrew
W. Mellon Foundation to the University of Toronto Press.

Contents

Acknowledgments

This book would not have been possible without the help of a number
of people whose generous assistance I welcome the opportunity to
acknowledge. For information about the penitentials and ongoing research in their regard I am grateful to Franz B. Asbach, Allen J. Frantzen,
and Franz Kerff, and to Raymond Kottje, who graciously responded to
my many epistolary queries. I owe a special debt of thanks to Leonard E.
Boyle, Michael Sheehan, and Roger Reynolds for helpful conversations
and for invaluable comments on earlier stages of the manuscript. I should
like to thank the Rev. D.A. Finlay for making the resources of the library
of the Pontifical Institute of Mediaeval Studies available to me.

Readers' comments solicited by the University of Toronto Press and
the Canadian Federation for the Humanities were insightful and most
helpful. I am grateful to Mount Saint Vincent University and to the
Social Sciences and Humanities Research Council of Canada for the financial assistance to bring this study to completion.

Abbreviations

Mansi	J.D. Mansi *Sacrorum conciliorum nova et amplissima collectio*
NRHDFE	*Nouvelle revue historique de droit français et étranger*
PL	Patrologia latina, ed J.P. Migne
RDC	*Revue de droit canonique*
RHE	*Revue d'histoire ecclésiastique*
RHLR	*Revue d'histoire et de littérature religieuses*
S 1	H.J. Schmitz *Die Bussbücher und die Bussdisciplin der Kirche*
S 2	H.J. Schmitz *Die Bussbücher und das kanonische Bussverfahren*
W	H. Wasserschleben *Die Bussordnungen der abendländischen Kirche*
Wasserschleben	Regino of Prüm: H. Wasserschleben *Reginonis abbatis Prumiensis*
ZSavRG.KA	*Zeitschrift der Savigny-Stiftung für Rechtsgeschichte. Kan Abt*

PENITENTIALS

The following are the conventional English or Latin titles to be used most frequently in this study and the corresponding editions used for each work, as listed in the Bibliography.

Bede-Egbert (Albers)	B. Albers 'Wann sind die Beda-Egbert'schen Bussbücher verfasst worden?' 399–418
Bede-Egbert Double Penitential	S 2.679–701
Buchard of Worms *Decretum* 19.5	S 2.409–52
Burgundian Penitential	S 2.320–2
Canons of Theodore U	Finst 285–334 (and see page 157, n 18)
Capitula iudiciorum	S 2.217–51
Excarpsus of Cummean	S. 2.597–644
Halitgar 6	S 2.290–300
Merseburg Penitential	S 2.358–68
Penitential of Bede	W 220–30

Penitential of Colum- *banus*	Bieler 96–107
Penitential of Cummean	Bieler 108–35
Penitential of Egbert	W 231–47
Penitential of Vinnian	Bieler 74–95
Reims Penitential	F.B. Asbach *Das Poenitentiale Remense* appendix, 4–77

Sex and the Penitentials:
The Development of a Sexual Code
550–1150

Introduction

The confessional manuals known as the penitentials, whose origins can be traced back to the sixth century and which were used up to the twelfth century, have long been recognized as valuable sources in the study of the economic, social, legal, and moral institutions of the early Middle Ages.[1] They were mediators between the general, theoretical ideas they sought to apply and the level of actual practice that was their sphere of immediate concern. One of the most striking features of the penitentials is the breadth and detail of their treatment of human sexual behaviour.[2] While this aspect of the tradition was not always appreciated by earlier writers, many recent works make some use of these manuals in the study of different facets of sexual behaviour. Whether they are general studies of sexuality or examinations of more particular subjects such as contraception or homosexuality, such studies indicate a growing recognition of the value of the material contained in the penitentials.[3]

Given the wealth of this material, it is curious that no one has undertaken to study in their own right the sexual contents of the penitentials. Perhaps the poor state of research into the manuals, the sometimes faulty editions, and the sheer mass of unorganized data have conspired to relegate them to being sources for researchers who were not concentrating on the penitentials themselves. But I suspect that one of the reasons for their neglect has been a failure to recognize the central role the penitentials played in the development of the medieval sexual ethos.[4]

Of course, well before the sixth century, the general theoretical principles of the Christian sexual ethic had been worked out. St Augustine had elaborated what was to be the fundamental principle governing sexual behaviour: sexual intercourse was permissible only between a man and a woman who were legitimately married to one another and then only when done for the sake of procreation. All forms of sexual expression not meeting these marital and procreational conditions were to be considered immoral and seriously sinful.[5] However, this general principle, with its roots in Stoic teaching, said nothing about who could or could not marry, who should or should not marry. A second, characteristically Christian principle was elaborated at the end of the fourth century in response to Iovinian, who had claimed that *as states* the married state and the state of virginity were equal. Out of Jerome's vitriolic attack on Iovinian and out of Augustine's more nuanced treatment of the issue there emerged a standard for evaluating the status of various kinds of sexual behaviour, a standard that set a higher priority on asexual ways of life and realized itself in the exhortation to virginal chastity, in the encouragement of monasticism, in the discouragement of second marriages for widows, and in the introduction and extension of priestly celibacy.[6] The relation between the two principles is well expressed by John Noonan: 'Virginity is preferred, but intercourse in marriage, for procreation only, is permissible.'[7]

Attention to questions of sexual behaviour was pervasive in the early Middle Ages, evident, for example, in the repeated efforts to establish and extend the rule of clerical celibacy, to safeguard monastic chastity, and to curb adultery and concubinage. The very institution of marriage raised important questions about adultery, divorce, remarriage, and prohibited degrees of consanguinity that prompted attention from popes, bishops, and ecclesiastical councils. Concern with its institutions and its established members was not the only spur to the Church to deal with questions of sexuality. The Church at this time was also attempting to spread the faith among the unconverted peoples of Europe, and the implementation of its moral positions was very much part of those efforts. An important part of the moral teaching was a sexual ethic which was not easy to impose on new converts. The difficulty and the attention to questions of sexual behaviour it occasioned are eloquently demonstrated, for example, in the sermons of the sixth-century bishop Caesarius of Arles.[8]

What were the sexual concerns of the early medieval church? What was its perception of the gravity of specific forms of proscribed sexual behaviour? How was such behaviour penalized? Were there restraints and controls placed even on permissible sexual activity within marriage? Isolated answers to some of these questions can certainly be found in the works of early ecclesiastical writers and in the official pronouncements of popes and councils.[9] However, these sources fail to treat the full range of sexual behaviour, addressing themselves largely to questions of principle and to the elaboration of answers to basic institutional problems.[10] The most ample answers to questions concerning actual behaviour are, rather, to be found in the penitentials.

From their early Irish origins the penitentials spread into Anglo-Saxon England and throughout western Europe, providing a broadly based and relatively homogeneous code of sexual behaviour. For five hundred years the penitential literature continued to be the principal agent in the formation and transmission of a code of sexual morality. Umbrage should not be taken at the expression 'code of sexual morality.' There is no suggestion that the term 'code' is to be used in the sense in which it is used to refer to the collections of Theodosius, Justinian, or Napoleon. Nor does the use of the expression imply that the penitential authors or compilers consciously set out to devise structured codes of sexual behaviour. In effect, however, many penitentials came to embody a virtually all-inclusive register of proscribed sexual acts. The penitentials were central to the compilation and transmission of a comprehensive code of sexual ethics in the early Middle Ages, and their study must form an important chapter in the history of sexuality during that period.

There is no adequate history of sexuality in the early Middle Ages, an important formative period in the development of Western civilization. Perhaps the best work to date is John Noonan's book on contraception, whose title belies its wealth of information and suggestive insights into matters other than its relatively narrow subject-matter. Rattray Taylor's work attempts to cover the whole history of sexuality in the West but is highly interpretative from a psychological point of view and is largely uncritical in regard to sources. Taylor, however, is conscious of the need for primary research in the history of sexual mores before an adequate interpretation can be written.[11] A careful examination of the sexual content of the penitentials would make a useful contribution to this primary research. The relative completeness of their treatment of sexual behaviour, their wide geographical distribution, their temporal span of influence, and their contribution to later collections of ecclesiastical law make the penitentials key witnesses to the concerns of the early Middle Ages.

The following study sets out to accomplish four tasks: 1/ to survey and analyse the sexual contents of representative Welsh, Irish, Anglo-Saxon, and Frankish penitential texts which originated during the creative, formative period prior to 813; 2/ to trace out the traditions of borrowing and transmission of these penitential canons; 3/ to examine the reception and development of the penitential tradition in the ninth century; and 4/ to identify the sexual material taken over from the penitentials which was incorporated into several later collections of ecclesiastical law up to the twelfth century. If these goals are met, the result should be a reliable mapping of the handling of sexual behaviour during an important phase of the development of Western culture. Certainly a map does not capture the rich detail of a region, but by indicating the main routes and major centres it enables a person to make his way about without fear of getting lost. The study does not pretend to be an exhaustive treatment of the sexual contents of the penitentials, which is probably more suited to individual studies of particular themes. However, it is designed to illuminate the broad context in which studies might intelligently be undertaken. Although frequent reference is made to parallel non-penitential literature and to problems of sources and interpretation, no attempt has been made to place the penitential canons in their full ecclesiastical, liturgical, social, and legal context. Given the almost total absence of studies of the sexual content of the penitentials, a detailed survey seems more desirable at this time. It is hoped that such a survey will prepare the ground for an examination of the sexual content of the penitentials against their full historical and anthropological background.

The three chapters and the appendixes of this book might be seen to comprise a collection of studies on sex in the penitentials rather than a synthetic, unified composition. Because of the lack of an adequate history of sex in the medieval period and because of the state of research into the penitentials generally, it would be fruitless to attempt an interpretative, synthetic work. The three chapters block out major areas of concentration, and the appendixes provide structured overviews of selected problems and questions relating to the subject. There is, however, a unity provided by the theme of sex and the penitentials, and the book is meant to be read as a whole.

The rationale for my choice of individual early penitentials and certain general methodological questions touching on my approach will be discussed below, but it would be useful at this point to say a word about the penitentials themselves.

THE PENITENTIALS

From the beginning, the early Christian Church acknowledged that sinners could obtain forgiveness for sins committed after baptism. However, forgiveness for the major or capital sins (for example, adultery, murder, idolatry) could only be obtained through the rite of public penance, which began on Ash Wednesday with the excommunication of penitents from the church and the Eucharist, prayers for their forgiveness, and the imposition of penance. The penance was carried out during Lent and ended on Holy Thursday with reconciliation and readmission to the Eucharist. The discipline of public penance was the one chance open to ordinary Christians to obtain remission of their serious sins. However, it was a severe practice which could only be undertaken once in a lifetime and which carried heavy disabilities. Those who underwent public penance could not marry afterwards if they were single, could not engage in sexual relations during and after public penance if they were already married, could not enter military service, and were barred from becoming clerics in the future. To undergo public penance was a serious decision not to be made lightly.

By the sixth century there were signs that a new form of penance was developing which was more accommodating to human failings. This new form was private (between an individual sinner and a priest to whom he confessed his sins and who levied an appropriate penance), repeatable, and did not entail the harsh disabilities which were associated with public penance. It would seem that the practice of private penance began in Ireland and was originally associated with the tradition of a soul-friend or personal spiritual director, a monastic tradition which encouraged the confession of faults to a superior, who imposed appropriate penances. At this time the principal ecclesiastical centres were monasteries, and the principal ecclesiastical leaders were abbots, not bishops. It is easy to imagine how private penance could, in such a context, develop out of the monastic tradition of the confession of faults and how it would be extended to both the monks and the laity who were the charges of monastic houses.

It was within this setting that there began to appear in Ireland in the second half of the sixth century religious works commonly referred to as 'penitentials' which reflected and reinforced the developing practice of private penance.[12] The purpose of the penitentials was to aid the priest or spiritual guide by providing descriptions of various sins and by specifying correspondingly appropriate penances. No doubt the sins and their penances are the most striking features of the penitentials, and some penitentials are simply lists of penanced sins. However, many of these manuals are far more ample, containing introductions and conclusions for the instruction of the confessor which remind him of his role as spiritual physician of souls and counsel him to give due consideration to the subjective dispositions of the penitent. It is this material which is often overlooked by those who see the penitentials simply as tariffs for sins.[13]

One of the unfortunate gaps in our knowledge of the penitentials is our ignorance of how these manuals were used in practice. However, their structure and contents permit some educated speculation. It would be to caricature their use to suggest that they were used by the priest while actually hearing confession. It is more likely that they served as reference works and guides, informing the priest of the different kinds of sin, of aggravating and mitigating circumstances, and providing suggestions for appropriate penances. All of the penitentials, even the slimmest, have catalogues of penanced sins that would serve these purposes well. It must be remembered that few of the penitentials are so lengthy that a priest would not, as a matter of course after several readings and numerous applications, tend to commit their strictures to memory. Once memorized, this material would also help the priest in questioning the penitent, which was an important aspect of early medieval private penance. Such interrogation was designed to ensure that penitents confessed all of their serious sins and, at the same time, would serve to instruct them about what the serious sins were. In fact, in the ninth century Theodulf of Orleans, among others, warned his priests to be careful in their questioning lest they make penitents worse off by suggesting sins to them which they had never even imagined (see below, page 56).

Many of the developed penitentials (for example, the *Excarpsus of Cummean*, the *Reims Penitential*, and the *Bede-Egbert Double Penitential*) do contain much more than catalogues of tariffed sins. They include discursive material aimed at instructing the confessor in his office of physician of souls, reminding him of the discernment that is necessary in the imposition of penances and of how he must carefully weigh the subjective dispositions of penitents on the scales of justice. This kind of instruction would be invaluable to a new priest who was being initiated into the confessor's office and would be a constant reminder to practising confessors not to fall into the legalistic automatism which contemporary scholars often improperly accuse the penitentials of fostering. Some penitentials reflect their liturgical contexts and retain instructions on how to receive penitents, what to say to them to allay their fears and shame, and include prayers to be said before the interrogation and confession. It is likely that these types of manual would be read by the priest during the rite of private penance.

In short, the penitentials were personal handbooks of reference for the priest-confessor. They educated, instructed, guided, and exhorted him in his confessional duties. That this was how the penitentials were meant to be used is suggested by the condemnations of the ninth century. Those who reacted against what they believed to be the improper instruction provided by the penitentials felt sufficiently strongly that they condemned the penitentials on two occasions, an unlikely course of action unless the penitentials were believed to be functioning effectively in the society (see below, page 58). Finally, it should be borne in mind that, to the extent that the penitentials were successfully used by the priest for his own guidance and instruction, the benefits of such instruction would have been passed on to the laity who were the objects of his pastoral and confessional care.

The earliest penitential we possess is the *Penitential of Vinnian*, which was written before the Irish missionary Columbanus wrote his penitential (circa 591 AD), and it was through the *Penitential of Columbanus* that these manuals were introduced to continental Europe. Soon penitentials were associated with such outstanding names of the British Church as Theodore of Canterbury (d 690), the Venerable Bede (d 735), and Egbert of York (d 766). During the seventh and eighth centuries penitentials were also produced on the Continent, incorporating Irish and Anglo-Saxon sources along with their own material. When the Carolingians turned their attention to reform, they recommended that a penitential be among the books every priest should have and know. However, just as the penitentials were being fostered at the beginning of the ninth century, a reaction seems to have set in, and we find them explicitly condemned by one of the reform councils of 813, a date which marks the end of the first phase of their development. The broad outlines of this development have been, in general, reliably sketched, and the recent work of Cyrille Vogel is a convenient survey of the contemporary state of the question.[14]

The penitential canons are usually comprised of two distinct parts – the specification of an offence and the imposition of a penance. ('Canon' is used here to refer to individual statements of rule, regulation, or censure. The usage derives from the traditional use of the term for the enunciation of disciplinary rules by ecclesiastical councils.) The primary focus here will be on the offences; no attempt has been made to integrate an examination of the penances into the discussion, other than to mention penances that deviate in some manner from the common penances, which usually consist in fasting on appointed days. The resulting detailed description of the sexual contents of the penitentials perhaps lacks some perspective because the sexual sins are not seen in relation to other offences. Although the perspective cannot be completely supplied without going too far afield into a complex discussion of penances, Appendix C addresses the methodological problems attendant on using penances as indicators of the gravity of sins and discusses the problems of attempting to determine the comparative gravity of different kinds of sin by using their respective penances.

CHOICE OF EARLY PENITENTIALS

In choosing which penitentials to examine systematically I have been guided by two considerations – that the selection should be exhaustive in regard to the early penitentials and that it should be representative of the later transmission stage.

The original body of texts is composed of several early Welsh pieces and the first Irish penitentials. The *Preface of Gildas*, Synod of North Britain, Synod of the Grove of Victory, and *Excerpts from a Book of David* are not, strictly speaking, penitentials, but these Welsh works contain penitential-like prescriptions which were incorporated into the early Irish manuals.[15] All of the texts dealing with sexual behaviour in the penitentials of Vinnian, Columbanus, and Cummean will be examined. These three original Irish penitentials, written in Latin, provided a core of canons dealing with sexual matters and became part of the penitential tradition up to the twelfth century and even after. The *Penitential of Vinnian*, the earliest of the penitentials, had to be written before 591 AD, since by that date Columbanus had written his own penitential and he obviously used material from Vinnian. As far as authorship of Vinnian is concerned, Ludwig Bieler is of the view that a decision between Finnian of Clonard (d 549) and Finnian of Moville (d 579) seems impossible.[16]

Bieler does not suggest a date for the most comprehensive of the three Irish penitentials, the *Penitential of Cummean*, but he seems to accept the authorship of Cummaine Fota, who is reported to have died in 662.[17]

A second core of basic early penitential canons was supplied by works associated with the names of Theodore of Canterbury, Bede, and Egbert. Several different collections are traditionally associated with the name of Theodore. I shall use only the penitential in two books, which was probably completed in its present form about 741 AD.[18] Reference will also be made to the individual penitentials attributed to Bede and Egbert.[19]

Given the number of penitentials composed on the Continent, one must choose among them.[20] Many of these penitentials contain a core of canons coming almost entirely from minor early Frankish penitentials. I have chosen as representative of this core the *Burgundian Penitential* (S 2.319–22).[21] Since the appearance of the second volume of H.J. Schmitz's editions of the penitentials, the existence of tripartite Continental penitentials has been recognized.[22] These manuals incorporate materials from 'canonical' sources (primarily from Frankish sources such as the *Burgundian Penitential*), Irish sources, and Anglo-Saxon sources. Schmitz identified two, the *Tripartite of St Gall* (S 2.177–89) and the *Capitula iudiciorum* (S 2.217–51). Later, Paul Fournier noted the tripartite structure of the *Vallicellian Penitential* (S 1.239–342) as well as the *Merseburg Penitential* (S 2.356–68), which is the probable source for virtually all the canons of the former.[23] More recently, Franz Asbach has argued for the tripartite structure of the *Excarpsus of Cummean* and the *Reims Penitential*.[24] I have chosen to examine the *Excarpsus of Cummean* because of its central importance for the subsequent history of the penitentials. The *Capitula iudiciorum* and the *Merseburg Penitential* will represent the tripartite penitentials of the second half of the eighth century: the former is a well-planned and orderly work; the latter is a rather disorganized piece.[25]

One of the striking characteristics of the penitential tradition is the transmission of the prescriptions of earlier penitentials through borrowings by later penitentials. In order to indicate this feature, I have included references of the following sort: *Canons of Theodore U* 2.11.9 (Finst 326) = *Excarpsus of Cummean* 1.28 (S 2.607), *Merseburg P* 143 (S 2.367); cf *P of Bede* 3.26 (W 223). The equal sign indicates that the canon of Theodore is also found in the penitentials that follow. The 'cf' means that the substance of Bede's canon is the same as that of Theodore but the wording is modified. Such a reference is not meant to imply that the text was transmitted along the precise lines suggested by the reference. The compiler of the *Excarpsus of Cummean* or of the *Merseburg Penitential* may never have directly used the *Canons of Theodore*. The reference simply indicates that a particular text is also found in later works.

The penitentials thus selected have been systematically studied, and all of their sexual regulations will be included in the following analysis. Occasionally, reference will be made to other penitentials, but their sexual material will not be included in a systematic way. Consideration of the Spanish penitentials has been ruled out. While these works show a strong influence from traditional penitential sources, they also demonstrate the influence of Spanish conciliar legislation, particularly from the Council of Elvira. In view of this, they deserve separate study within the context of the development of the Spanish Church.[26]

It should be noted here that several of the penitential texts chosen for particular study in the first chapter exist in English translation. The Welsh literature and the penitentials of Vinnian, Columbanus, and Cummean may be found translated in Bieler's edition of the Irish penitentials, along with the *Bigotian Penitential*, which will be cited occasionally. The *Burgundian Penitential* and the *Canons of Theodore* are translated in their entirety in J.T. McNeill and H.M. Gamer's discussion of the penitentials.[27]

METHODOLOGICAL OBSERVATIONS

Assumptions

I assume that the penitentials were actually used in the pastoral ministry and that they reflect what people were doing sexually – doing sufficiently frequently to warrant inclusion in these manuals. The persistence of certain regulations, selective borrowings, modifications made to previous canons, and new additions all indicate that the penitentials were living documents used for the practical ends which they frequently claim for themselves. Both the recommendations and the condemnations encountered in the ninth century suggest that these manuals were being used. If they were used, then it is reasonable to believe that their contents reflect what was in fact being done. This is a modest claim, suggesting no more than that the sexual content of these manuals is not the result either of prurient imagination or of legalistic distinction-spinning. Vogel insists that the penitentials are not legal or juridical works, nor are they even primarily of a didactic or instructional nature. They were destined for the daily practice of confession.[28] In his discussion of marriage Raymond Kottje on several occasions remarks on the practical purpose of the penitentials.[29]

However, there does seem to be a resistance on the part of some authors to see the penitential prescriptions as reflecting the actual concerns of their authors or compilers. There are commentators who seem more ready to believe that the penitential canons dealing with some types of sexual behaviour are quite unrelated to practice. Nora Chadwick attributes those canons to the wild imagination of their authors but offers no evidence for her position:

We may be sure that many of these cases are the webs spun in the casuistry of the monkish brain. They form an abstract compendium of *supposititious* crimes and unnatural sins, thought up in the cloister by the tortuous intellect of the clerical scribe.[30]

Bieler is even more explicit in his denial of the real-life context of some of the canons. When speaking about references to incest and sodomy in the Irish penitentials, he says, 'I feel sure that the frequency of these references with their detailed specifications of obscene acts bear little if any relation to reality.'[31] The author provides no reason for this claim except that 'A great deal of all this would seem to owe its existence to a desire for material completeness and a delight in subtle distinctions and classifications, which is a notorious weakness of the legal mind.'[32] Why does Bieler take as factual a statement from the *Table of Commutations* which says, 'There is hardly a single layman or laywoman who has not some part in manslaughter,'[33] but seem unwilling to take as factual the claim that sodomy is among the common sins? Columbanus says, 'But if anyone has sinned in act with the common sins, if he has committed the sin of murder or sodomy ... ' (*P of Columbanus* A.3; Bieler 97). The very existence of such prescriptions over centuries would seem to be sufficient grounds for the assumption of their practical nature – that they represent responses to actual experience.

A second assumption is that penances are at least rough indicators of the perceived gravity of the various offences. For example, if one finds a consistent tradition of a five-year 'base penance' for act x and a ten-year base penance for act y, it is reasonable to assume that y was considered to be more grave than x.[34] Whether or not the penances were actually carried out in the way laid down in the penitentials is a moot question which need not concern us here. [35] Even in alternate systems of commutations or redemptions the same proportionality is maintained, so that the commutation of a five-year penance would be less severe than that of a ten-year penance.[36] These remarks are not intended to contradict the discussion in Appendix C. They are meant simply to suggest a rule of thumb which seems reasonable in the circumstances.

Terminology

The discussion of the sexual content of the penitentials poses a serious methodological problem at the outset. The Latin vocabulary of these works is poor in its stock of common nouns connoting general classes of sexual acts, and it does not have counterparts to the English *sex, sexuality*, or *sexual*. The following are some of the nouns I use in this study for which there are no Latin counterparts: *aphrodisiac, bestiality, contraception, fornication* (in the strict sense of heterosexual relations between two unmarried people), *homosexuality, lesbianism, masturbation*. The practice of the penitentials is to employ a general-duty verb such as *fornicare* (literally, 'to fornicate') in conjunction with a word or phrase which usually succeeds in identifying the act.

The question of terminology is a problem because it is not simply a matter of the penitentials' lack (or that of other literature of the period) of a store of common nouns. Class nouns indicate a particular way of conceptualization; the absence of class nouns is a fair indication of the absence of the corresponding concepts and ideas. For example, the concept of sex or sexuality referring to a more or less morally neutral dimension of human persons is not encountered in the Middle Ages. Strictly speaking, the medievals did not speak about sex as such. To use terms such as *sex* and *sexuality*, to say nothing of the other nouns mentioned above, is to use a vocabulary and a conceptual scheme that is foreign to the penitentials throughout the period we shall be studying.

On the other hand, it is virtually impossible to divorce oneself from one's own conceptual schemes. There is a danger of leaving the reader with the wrong impression, of suggesting that the penitentials addressed themselves to questions which really did not exist for them and that they used a language which was not available to them. However, I see no alternative to this if one wishes to gain an understanding of the penitential treatment of what we call sexual behaviour. I can only hope that these remarks, the frequent citation of penitential texts, the occasional observations about language and meaning, and the appendix on the language that the penitentials use to speak about sexual acts will guard readers against importing modern categories into these ancient documents. But I see no reasonable way for a contemporary writer to avoid employing such categories. Perhaps forewarned is forearmed.[37]

The Subject of the Canons

Before the ninth century, penitential canons were usually addressed to one person, most frequently to the male in a heterosexual union. In the absence of general rules of interpretation I have assumed that such canons applied solely to the person to whom they were addressed. For example, one of the features of the penitential system is that the penances are graded according to ecclesiastical rank. Unless otherwise stated, it should not be assumed that women in illicit sexual unions with ecclesiastics of different ranks were to perform the penances of their male partners.[38]

THE PENITENTIALS: ADDITIONAL REMARKS

The following remarks are not essential for the comprehension of the material in this book. They are added for those who might have a particular interest in the penitentials and the state of contemporary research.

While we have a fairly good idea of the general history of the penitentials, a great deal of uncertainty remains in regard to the manuscript traditions, and good editions are largely lacking. Until very recently the best editions have been the nineteenth-century works of F.W.H. Wasserschleben and H.J. Schmitz. The former was generally more accurate in his transcriptions but incomplete; the latter supplied editions of many more penitentials and often provided much useful comment. Unfortunately, however, the two volumes of Schmitz are skewed by the author's peculiar theory about the existence of an early Roman penitential which formed the base of the penitential tradition. This virtual obsession with a Roman penitential makes the work of Schmitz less valuable than it might have been and creates in the reader a sense of mistrust which then tends to extend to everything Schmitz says. None the less, we are still dependent on him for the editions of many penitentials.

P.W. Finsterwalder's edition of the material attributed to Theodore

began a new era of editions which has, however, been slow in developing. Bieler's edition of the Irish penitentials is really the only entirely
trustworthy edition to date. The study of the penitentials which is currently being undertaken under the direction of Professor Kottje of the
University of Bonn has progressed sufficiently that new editions will
soon be forthcoming in the Corpus Christianorum series. In studies of
the contents of the penitentials, however, nothing is to be gained by
waiting until the critical study of the manuscript traditions is more
advanced. In fact, it might be argued that the serious study of the contents of the penitentials will give impetus to the examination of their
manuscript traditions. It is only when they are used that the inadequacies of the available editions stand revealed. Still, a careful use of the
penitentials demands an awareness of and considerable acquaintance
with the current scholarship, to safeguard against abusing the evidence.
This study of sex in the penitentials has been undertaken in the full
realization of the inadequacy of many of the available texts, and I have
tried in what follows to fortify my use of the penitential texts with the
best and most current work done on the manuscripts.

Even with the best of intentions one is sometimes still left with unre-
solved problems in regard to the use of important texts. For example, it is
impossible to chart an entirely safe course through the works attributed
to Bede and Egbert. Let me illustrate with a survey of the editions.
Wasserschleben based his editions of Bede and Egbert on Vienna Österreichische Nationalbibliothek ms 2223, s ix$^{1/2}$.[39] In his first volume Schmitz
based his edition of Bede and Egbert on Munich Staatsbibliothek Cod lat
12673, s x.[40] In his second volume Schmitz used Vatican Pal lat 294, s xi,
for the edition of Bede[41] and Vat Pal lat 485, s ix$^{3/4}$ (before 875),[42] for his
edition of Egbert. The texts of all of these editions are virtually identical.
However, little effort was made by either editor to provide a careful
study of his base manuscripts, nor did either attempt to relate the base
manuscripts to the variant readings which are provided from other
manuscripts. It is impossible to make a fully justifiable choice of editions
given this state of affairs, short of doing the palaeographical work oneself or working from single manuscript copies. I have decided to use the
editions of Bede and Egbert prepared by Wasserschleben since he used
the Vienna manuscript, the oldest of the manuscripts containing both
penitentials. It is important to recognize, however, that although the
Vienna texts are the oldest, they do not necessarily represent the most
primitive state of the penitentials. It is entirely possible that a later manu-

script could represent a more primitive state of the text because it was based on an even older and more primitive exemplar. However, the use of Wasserschleben's edition seems reasonable in the absence of better editions.

The situation with the texts attributed to Bede and Egbert is further complicated because there were at least two versions of a double penitential in circulation in the ninth century, made up principally of material from the individual penitentials attributed to Bede and Egbert. Wasserschleben based his edition of this composite work on the earlier edition of F. Kunstmann, who had used Munich Staatsbibliothek Cod lat 3853, s x^2, which is the manuscript used by Schmitz.[43] An apparently less developed version of this double penitential was later edited by Albers from Vatican Barb lat 477 (xi 120), s xi in.[44] This version of the Bede-Egbert material will not concern us until we come to deal with Regino of Prüm.

Another possible source of confusion in using Wasserschleben and Schmitz is the different conventions they used for their editions of several Vallicellian manuscripts. In regard to the editions of these manuscripts the following should be noted:

- Schmitz (S 1.239–342): *Poenitentiale Valicellanum* I, based on Rome Bibl Vallic, Codex E 15, s $x^{1/2}$; no corresponding edition in Wasserschleben[45]
- Schmitz (S 1.350–88): *Poenitentiale Valicellanum* II, based on Rome Bibl Vallic, Codex C 6, s $xii^{1/2}$; partially edited by Wasserschleben as *Poenitentiale Valicellanum* I (W 547–50)[46]
- Schmitz (S 1.774–86): *Poenitentiale Valicellanum* III, based on Rome Bibl Vallic, Codex B 58, s xi; no corresponding edition in Wasserschleben[47]
- Wasserschleben (W 550–66): *Poenitentiale Valicellanum* II, based on Rome Bibl Vallic, Codex E 62, s xii in; no corresponding edition in Schmitz[48]
- Wasserschleben (W 682–8): *Poenitentiale Valicellanum* III, based on Rome Bibl Vallic, Codex F 92, s xi ex; no corresponding edition in Schmitz.[49]

There is a facet of the manuscript tradition of the penitentials which, although not exploited in this study, should be noted. One of the criticisms a later period will level against the penitentials is their lack of authority. More will be said about this in the discussion of the ninth-century attacks on the penitentials. For now, however, it is enough to note that penitential materials are frequently found in manuscripts which also contain important collections of ecclesiastical law. A fine example of this phenomenon is the manuscript Paris BN lat 3182, s x, which has

parallels in the manuscript Cambrai 625 (576), s ix ex. In the sections
common to both manuscripts there are several Welsh and Irish penitential texts and the *Bigotian Penitential* in conjunction with the authoritative
Dionysio-Hadriana Collection.[50] The manuscript Brussels Bibl Royal, Bur-
gund 10127–44, s viii ex, has the *Collectio Vetus Gallica* along with part of
the *Canons of Theodore U* and the *Reims Penitential*.[51] Cologne Dombibliothek, Cod 91, s viii–ix, has the *Collectio Vetus Gallica* with the *Canons of
Theodore U* book 1, chapter 13, and book 2, and the *Excarpsus of Cummean*.[52]
The manuscript Paris BN lat 1603, s viii–ix, has the *Scarapsus of Pirmin*
and the *Collectio Vetus Gallica* with the *Canons of Theodore U* book 1,
chapter 13, and book 2, in addition to the *Reims Penitential*.[53] These
manuscripts might be seen to represent a compendium of texts which
were addressed to different needs of the compiler. The penitentials in
the manuscripts would serve the practical needs of a confessor and would
gain a certain amount of authority from their close association with other
acknowledged authoritative texts such as the *Dionysio-Hadriana* and the
Vetus Gallica. This juxtaposition of penitentials with other works of a
different kind in the same manuscript will give way, as we shall see in
the third chapter, to the integration of penitential texts into the body of
canonical collections.

1

The Penitentials to 813

All of the penitentials contain a great many canons censuring various types of sexual behaviour. Although some of these works divide their subject-matter topically, the divisions are neither uniformly adopted nor sufficiently discriminatory for purposes of this analysis. Consequently, in order to provide a more intelligible distribution, the material has been grouped into the following categories: the heterosexual life of the married; the heterosexual life of the unmarried; homosexuality and lesbianism; bestiality; masturbation; safeguards of chastity; and seminal pollution. The categories are mutually exclusive, involving no significant overlap except possibly for some items in the first two categories. A number of canons censure unlawful sexual intercourse without making it clear whether they mean to include adulterous relations within their scope. Those ambiguous canons will be discussed under the heterosexual life of the unmarried.[1] Some consideration of the chapter headings actually used by the penitential compilers will be given in Appendix E, which deals with the sexual language of the penitentials. These headings throw valuable light on the early conceptualization of sexual behaviour and the various standpoints taken to categorize such activity.

THE HETEROSEXUAL LIFE OF THE MARRIED

In addition to addressing the topic of adultery the penitentials are also concerned with a wide range of marital sexual behaviour. This study will consider their treatment of each of the following subjects: adultery, periods of sexual abstinence, the proper form of intercourse, sexual incest, aphrodisiacs, sterility and impotence, and contraception.[2] Certain subjects having to do more directly with the institution of marriage than with sexual behaviour – subjects such as divorce, separation, desertion, remarriage, and clerical marriage – will not be examined.

Adultery

Adultery will be understood to be sexual intercourse between two people of whom at least one is married. Sometimes canons dealing with this subject use the term *adulterium* ('adultery') or *adultera* ('adulteress'), but more frequently they use expressions such as *cum uxore alterius* ('with another's wife') or *qui uxorem habens* ('whoever has a wife') to designate that one of the partners is married. In still others, no linguistic clues are present in the statement of the offence but it is clear from the penance that adultery is in question, since the penance includes sexual abstinence from his own wife for the offending male. The problem posed by penitential use of the word for adultery is particularly knotty and calls for an extended digression before the subject-matter of adultery may be discussed.

For the writers of the penitentials *adulterium* seems not to have been a univocal term but to have had a wider extension than the word *adultery* has today. There are two series of canons in the penitentials which deal with ecclesiastics who return to the lay state or who marry. A first series, perhaps beginning with the *Burgundian Penitential* (30; S 2.321), seems to depend on a canon of the Council of Agde (506 AD).[3] No mention is made of adultery in this first series of canons, but it is found alongside a similar series which deals with clerics who have been married before becoming clerics and who subsequently return to their wives. Vinnian remarks that such a cleric should realize that 'he has fallen to the depths of ruin.'[4] This canon is also found in the *Penitential of Columbanus* (B.8; Bieler 101), where Vinnian's phrase is changed to 'let him know that he has committed adultery.'[5] Here the notion of adultery is understood to include sexual intercourse between a husband and wife if it occurs after the husband has become a cleric and then returns to his wife.

There is a text in the *Excarpsus of Cummean* which appears to extend the class of adulterous relations even further. Unfortunately, however, the beginning of the Latin text in Schmitz poses problems of interpretation and grammar.[6] The canon begins, 'If anyone commits adultery, that is, with another's wife or ...' There then follows reference to a fiancée, a virgin, and a nun or a woman dedicated to God, apparently in relation to the verb 'corrupts.' However, the nouns are all in the ablative case, which would associate them with the preposition 'with' in the introductory clause and would leave the verb 'corrupts' without a direct object. In variants noted by Schmitz these nouns are all direct objects of 'corrupts,' suggesting that only 'another's wife' is covered by the reference to adultery. Other penitentials include this canon in slightly different versions.[7]

The problem is to determine whether sexual intercourse with each class of woman is to be understood as adultery or whether 'adultery' governs only the expression 'with another's wife' while 'corrupts' governs the other terms, which should be rendered in the accusative. Without access to the intentions of the compilers it is virtually impossible to resolve these interpretative and grammatical questions. However, there is a text in a ninth-century penitential which lends some support to an interpretation that understands adultery to include sexual relations with a nun or a woman dedicated to God: 'It is said to be adultery when someone violates another's wife or a nun.'[8] Given this interpretation, the text of the *Excarpsus of Cummean* might be understood to read, 'If anyone commits adultery with another's wife or fiancée, or corrupts a virgin, or with a nun or a woman dedicated to God ...' The *Paris Penitential* covers the classes of women in two canons; in the second, which refers to nuns, it retains the reference to adultery: 'If anyone commits fornication with a nun or with a woman dedicated to God, he should know that he has committed adultery. Let each one do penance as laid out in the above judgment in accord with his ecclesiastical order.'[9] Penitential usage, then, suggests that sexual relations with another's wife or fiancée or with a nun were viewed as coming under the descriptive term *adulterium*. Bestiality and relations between a priest and his 'spiritual daughter' are also called adultery.[10]

Many of the canons dealing with adultery derive from the *Penitential of Vinnian* mediated through Cummean, who usually shortens and reformulates his source.[11] The canons are addressed to married men and cover the cases of adultery with another's wife or virgin daughter, with a vowed virgin, or with his own female slave.[12] Additional stipulations are made in the event that the vowed virgin or the female slave gives birth to a child.[13] The longer version of the canon dealing with the female slave who begets a child indicates that the slave was actually serving as a concubine:

But if he begets by this female slave one, two, or three children, he is to set her free, and if he wishes to sell her it shall not be permitted to him, but they shall be separated from each other, and he shall do penance an entire year on an allowance of bread and water; and he shall have no further intercourse with his concubine but be joined to his own wife.[14]

The penances, which range from one to three years in Vinnian, are usually retained by the subsequent penitentials, although sometimes they are lengthened. For cases of adultery with another's wife and with a vowed virgin Vinnian also stipulates that the offender is not to have sexual relations with his own wife during the time of his penance. This provision is perhaps a reflection of a more general principle formulated by Columbanus:

For the laity must know, that in the period of penance assigned to them by the priests it is not lawful for them to know their wives, except after the conclusion of the penance; for penance ought not to be halved.[15]

The implication, which is clear in Vinnian, is that in the case of a married couple the innocent party is to refrain from having sexual relations with the guilty party during the latter's time of penance.[16] This provision of Vinnian is not found in later penitentials, but there is a canon in Theodore which is closely related to it. According to Theodore, should a man discover that his wife has been guilty of adultery, he is to refrain from sexual relations with her during her penance, and if he does not, he himself is to do penance for two years.[17]

The *Penitential of Columbanus* addresses two situations not covered by Vinnian, adultery with another's wife resulting in the birth of a child, and adultery with widows or young women (*puellae*). In the former case, monetary restitution is to be made to the offended husband[18]; in the case of a young woman or a widow, compensation is to be made to her parents.[19]

Censures of adultery by the penitentials are rarely supported by the citation of biblical or other authorities. In one canon in which Theodore provides seven years' penance for an adulteress, he adds, 'and this matter is stated the same way in the canon.'[20] Finsterwalder suggests St Basil's canonical epistles as the source, but it could as well be the Council of Ancyra, which is quoted later without acknowledgment by the *Excarpsus of Cummean*.[21]

The *Merseburg Penitential* has a canon which is not found in any other penitential at this time. It is directed to married men who have illicit sexual relations when their wives are present, imposing a penance of a forty-two-week fast. There then follows a lengthy discussion of the monetary substitution that is allowed should the man be unable to fast.[22] This discussion is found in several liturgical penitential rituals in later collections.[23]

The treatment of adultery in these manuals frequently follows the lines of development suggested by Vinnian's canons as modified by Cummean. Except in cases where either Ancyra or St Basil may be the underlying source, the base penances are relatively short; in the penitentials which include lists of graded penances, the longer times are reserved for higher ecclesiastical offenders. The following canon from the *Capitula iudiciorum* is representative of such gradations:

If a bishop commits adultery with another's wife [he shall do penance] for twelve years, three of these years on bread and water, and is to be deposed; a priest, for ten years, three of these years on bread and water, and is to be deposed; a deacon and a monk, for seven years, three of these years on bread and water, and is to be deposed; a cleric and a layman, for five years, two of these years on bread and water. The aforementioned are to be deprived of communion. After the penance has been completed, they are to be reconciled to communion, for they shall never approach the priesthood.[24]

The *Bobbio Penitential* alone has no canon on adultery in the strict sense, although it does have one for clerics returning to their wives.[25]

Periods of Sexual Abstinence

The Bible recommends sexual abstinence for various reasons. Moses commanded the people to abstain from sexual intercourse in preparation for the revelation of God on the third day (Exod 19:15). In several passages the Old Testament prohibits sexual relations with a woman during her menstrual period (Lev 15:24, 18:19, 20:18; Ezek 18:6). The Levitical law of purification after childbirth is premised on the notion that the woman is unclean during that time (Lev 12:1–5). The priest Abimelech agreed to relieve the hunger of David and his soldiers with the holy bread if they had not had sexual relations for the previous three days (1 Sam 21:4–5). The Vulgate Latin version of Tobit has Tobias and his new wife remaining continent for the first three days after they are married (Tobit 6:18, 8:4). Finally, there is the well-known passage in which St Paul counsels sexual abstinence for a time to enable married couples to give themselves over to prayer (1 Cor 7:5).

Frequent allusions to the desirability of sexual abstinence are found in Christian authors prior to Vinnian.[26] The penitentials, in specifying the times when sexual intercourse would be considered improper, perpetuated and added to these more ancient traditions. To avoid needless repetition I will simply indicate cumulative additions to the list of times when sexual relations were forbidden, indicate apparent borrowings, and point out any allusions to a rationale for the various prohibitions.[27]

Vinnian is the first to recommend certain times of sexual abstinence, in a canon which is a virtual treatise on the subject. His basic premise is that marriage without continence is not lawful but sinful and that marriage was not granted by God for lust but for the sake of children.[28] The abstinence periods proposed are the three Lents (that is, the three forty-day periods before Christmas, before Easter, and after Pentecost), Sunday night or Saturday night, and from conception up to the birth of the child. The presentation is woven into an oft-quoted passage of St Paul:

For they should mutually abstain during the three forty-day periods in each single year, by consent for the time being, that they may be able to have time for prayer for the salvation of their souls: and on Sunday night or Saturday night they shall mutually abstain; and after the wife has conceived he shall not have intercourse with her until she has borne her child, and they shall come together again for this purpose, as saith the Apostle.[29]

There follows an allusion to 1 Cor 11:27–9 (Vinnian says, 'then they are worthy of the Lord's body'), but there is no explicit prohibition of sexual intercourse before communion. However, the reference to Saturday night was probably made in view of communion the following day. The text closes with the hopeful announcement that those who fulfil matrimony by giving alms, by carrying out the commands of God, and by expelling vices will reign with Christ and the saints and receive the thirty-fold set aside for the married.[30] Taking his lead from St Paul, Vinnian says that abstinence is to be by mutual consent; he provides no penance for non-fulfilment.

Columbanus includes nothing about periods of sexual abstinence, but the *Penitential of Cummean* adds to the list of Vinnian. There is to be continence 'on the two appointed days,' which, Bieler points out in a note, is a reference to Wednesdays and Fridays – traditional penitential days in the ancient church.[31] Cummean makes two further additions, both of which have some scriptural justification. The first is the prohibition of intercourse during menstruation, the second, the prohibition of intercourse after the birth of a child, thirty-three days if it is a boy, fifty-six days if it is a girl.[32] Like Vinnian, Cummean does not attach any penance to his list of periods of abstinence, an indication, perhaps, that sexual abstinence at these prescribed times was viewed as a matter of recommendation and not of regulation.

Although the *Canons of Theodore* do not add substantially to the list of Cummean, their treatment is original enough to warrant particular consideration. Theodore's first mention of abstinence introduces a new period to the list. He says that the Greeks and the Romans abstained from their wives three days 'before the holy bread as it is written in the Law.'[33] This is a reference to 1 Sam 21:4–5. The rule of three nights' abstinence before communion is also found in a later canon, but without sanction.[34] Theodore first mentions abstinence during the menstrual period and after childbirth in the context of prohibiting women from entering a church during these times. After laying down those prohibitions, the penitential adds, 'But whoever has sexual relations at these times must do penance for twenty days.'[35] This is the first instance of a penance being attached to the non-observance of periods of abstinence, but there does not seem to be consistency in the regulations. In a separate canon on the menstrual period (*Canons of Theodore U* 1.14.23; Finst 309) the penance is forty days of fasting, and in the regulations concerning pregnancy no penance is attached to non-observance.[36] In regard to Sunday Theodore says, 'He who has sexual relations on the Lord's day shall ask indulgence from God and do penance for one or two or three days.'[37] Finally, there is a canon (2.12.2; Finst 326) about abstinence during the Lent before Easter and during the Easter octave to which is appended an excerpt from 1 Cor 7:5, but no penance is imposed.

In addition to its reliance on Theodore the *Excarpsus of Cummean* includes a list which is modelled on the *Penitential of Cummean* (2.30; Bieler 116).[38] It adds the period of three days before communion which is found in Theodore (2.12.1), and it changes Cummean's 'on the two appointed days' to 'on several days.'[39] However, nothing new is introduced which cannot be found in previous regulations, nor is any penance attached for the non-observance of periods on the list.[40]

The *Penitential of Egbert* adds some modifications to its recognizable borrowings. In a text which corresponds to the *Canons of Theodore U* 2.12.3 (Finst 326) Egbert adds, 'However, he who has sexual relations on these days must do penance for forty days, or thirty, or twenty' (*P of Egbert* 7.2; W 238). In both the *Canons of Theodore* and the *Excarpsus of Cummean* this sentence makes sense in the context of the immediately preceding regulations, which prohibit church entry during menstruation and after childbirth.[41] However, it is unnecessary in the *Penitential of Egbert*, since the preceding canon (7.1; W 238) has already spoken of sexual abstinence during pregnancy and after childbirth. It does, though, attach a penance to a regulation which did not previously have one in Theodore. Another canon in Egbert which is modelled on previous lists clears up any confusion about the phrase 'on the two appointed days' by substituting 'and on the fourth and sixth days which are appointed.'[42]

What is surprising about the *Penitential of Egbert* is the omission of any reference to abstinence during the menstrual period. Of the penitentials after Vinnian which include canons on sexual abstinence, Egbert's alone does not mention the menstrual period. This could be attributable to a copyist who was using a text resembling *Excarpsus of Cummean* 3.18 (S 2.614). In the *Excarpsus*, after the passage 'before they receive communion' there follows 'and after conception up to the time the blood is cleared up and at the time of menstruation he must be continent.' The two canons prior to the *Penitential of Egbert* 7.3 deal with the question of abstinence during pregnancy and after childbirth. So it is plausible that when the copyist or compiler came to 'after conception' he stopped, not realizing that in doing so he was omitting the menstrual period, which is not covered in other canons in Egbert.

The final two canons in Egbert which deal with sexual abstinence concern the Lent before Easter and are original in their wording, although they do not add to the list of times calling for abstinence. What is of note is that monetary composition is allowed as a substitution for the penance:

Whoever knows his wife during the Lent before Easter and refuses to abstain shall do penance for a year or pay his price to the church or divide it among the poor or donate twenty-six solidi.[43]

The *Penitential of Bede* includes a list of periods of abstinence whose expression is original but whose content is not. Instead of the three Lents, this work specifies forty days before Christmas and before Easter, omits Saturday, and reintroduces the Levitical rule of purgation after childbirth, which distinguishes between boys and girls.[44] The only non-observance penalized in Bede's list is in regard to the menstrual period (forty days) and Sundays (seven days).

As is evident from Appendix B, by the mid-eighth century the Irish and Anglo-Saxon penitentials had developed a substantial list of periods of sexual abstinence for married people. Each period is associated with times of penance (the three Lents, Wednesdays, Fridays) or has unmistakable Biblical justification (menstrual period, after childbirth) or is allegorically associated with a Biblical episode (before communion). None of the penitentials attempts to justify abstinence during pregnancy. There is no set pattern of penances provided for non-observance, nor do the penitentials after Vinnian establish a relationship between periods of abstinence and the procreative purpose of intercourse, even in the case of abstinence during the wife's pregnancy. Finally, there seems to be no pattern as to whom the regulations are addressed: some are addressed generally to those who are married, some to the husband, and others to the wife. In the absence of a doctrine of *conjugal debt* and of the distinction between *rendering the debt* and *demanding the debt*, no special significance should be attached to whether the prescriptions are addressed to the husband or to the wife.[45]

The Burgundian, Bobbio, Paris, and St Gall penitentials include nothing about periods of sexual abstinence in marriage. Both the *Merseburg Penitential* and the *Capitula iudiciorum* repeat previous canons.[46] In non-penitential texts of the period one seldom encounters regulations that prescribe sexual abstinence.[47]

In our examination of adultery we encountered the stipulation in Vinnian and Theodore that the offending parties were to abstain from sexual intercourse during the time that they were performing the prescribed penance (see page 22). Columbanus adds to his treatment of child abuse the more general principle that the laity are not 'to know their wives' until after they have performed their assigned penances (see page 22). Vogel frequently points out that, according to the ancient practice, married couples were to abstain during the time of penance and even after the penance had been carried out.[48] The principle enunciated by Columbanus reflects this earlier practice, but later penitentials do not take up the principle in its clear, unambiguous formulation.

Several penitentials after Columbanus have a canon which associates penance in general with sexual abstinence, but it is difficult to make out what they mean. They seem to be suggesting that those who wish to add to the assigned penances ought to practise sexual restraint during the time of penance. However, the specific times which are stipulated for these supererogatory acts are times which are laid down as a matter of precept elsewhere in the penitentials. Perhaps these canons reflect an earlier tradition when periods of sexual abstinence were more a matter of recommendation than of obligation. They certainly make little sense in the contexts in which they are found at present.[49] But some later collections of canon law include penitential canons which clearly stipulate that sexual abstinence is required during the time of penance (*tempore penitentiae*), signalling a return to the general principle enunciated by the *Penitential of Columbanus*.[50]

There is some evidence of a difference of opinion in the ninth century with regard to the practice of imposing sexual abstinence as part of a penance. The Council of Mainz (852 AD) includes sexual abstinence for the first forty days as part of the penance for the negligent suffocation of an infant and the same abstinence for inflicting deadly wounds on a man. In this same eleventh canon a certain Albigis is accused of carrying off the wife of Patrichus, and someone named Battonis is accused of having killed five men. Part of the penance for Albigis is that he remain without a wife as long as he live, and Battonis is to do likewise. In regard to Battonis, however, the expression 'a coniugio se abstinere' could mean sexual abstinence from his wife if he was married.[51]

The Council of Worms (868 AD), by contrast, insists that those undergoing penance are not to be separated from legitimate marriage lest they fall into fornication (canon 37).[52] In its penance for patricide and fratricide it says:

If they have wives they are not to be separated. However, if they do not and are not able to be continent, let them take lawful women in marriage lest they are seen to fall into the abyss of fornication.[53]

A general practice seems not to have been elaborated. In the middle of the century Pope Benedict III wrote two letters indicating the penances to be imposed for a case of parricide and one of fratricide. In the second case the man is known to have been married, but sexual abstinence is not imposed as part of his penance.[54] At the end of the century, however, the Council of Tribur (895 AD) established sexual abstinence as part of the penance for murder during the first forty days of the penance.[55]

Proper Form of Sexual Intercourse

The first indication of a concern with the proper form of marital intercourse is encountered in the *Canons of Theodore,* which condemns sexual positions that depart from what today is sometimes called 'the missionary position' and perhaps also rules against oral sex.[56] Theodore censures intercourse with one's wife 'retro,' penalizing the first occasion with forty days' penance without saying anything about subsequent occasions.[57] He also prohibits intercourse 'in tergo.' ('If he should practise anal intercourse he must do penance as one who offends with animals.')[58] 'Retro' seems to refer to intercourse from behind; 'in tergo' is an expression used regularly in homosexual contexts, as we shall see, and seems to refer to anal intercourse.[59] The only rationale given is for that of anal intercourse, which has suggestions of bestiality for Theodore.

The *Excarpsus of Cummean* (3.11–12; S 2.613–14) simply repeats the two canons of Theodore, while Egbert and Bede change Theodore's text. Egbert associates 'with animals' with dorsal intercourse (*retro*) and penalizes its habitual practice with three years' penance; anal intercourse carries a seven-year penance (*P of Egbert* 7.10; W 239). Bede, on the other hand, is content to repeat Theodore's canon regarding dorsal intercourse but drops the reference to bestiality in his canon covering anal intercourse, comparing the act to sodomy (*P of Bede* 3.39; W 224).

There are frequent references in the penitentials to oral sex, most of them relating to homosexual practices. There is a canon in Theodore which may refer to heterosexual oral sex, but the reference is certainly not clear, particularly when one considers that the canon appears under the heading 'On fornication' and not under 'On the penances of the married in particular' or 'On questions relating to spouses.' Derrick Bailey in his study of homosexuality understands Theodore's canon to refer to homosexual fellatio, while Noonan in his study of contraception seems to understand the same canon in reference to heterosexual oral intercourse. There is perhaps no way of settling the question, but the context argues for its homosexual interpretation.[60]

This canon, which is repeated with some modification by the *Excarpsus of Cummean,* in the edition of Schmitz seems to refer to the homosexual relations of natural brothers, which is mentioned in the previous canon.[61] Neither Egbert nor Bede refers to oral sex. The weight of evidence suggests that reference to heterosexual oral practices is not to be found in these early penitentials, nor is it found in the later manuals except for a canon in the *Tripartite of St Gall*, which makes the only unambiguous reference to a heterosexual oral relation in the Latin penitentials: 'He who emits semen into the mouth of a woman shall do penance for three years; if they are in the habit they shall do penance for seven years.'[62] Anticipating our discussion of homosexuality, we can say that while homosexual oral practices were of some concern to the writers of the penitentials from the time of Vinnian, heterosexual oral practices were not. Certainly, this would not have been because the practices themselves were considered less grave but probably because they were not widespread enough to warrant inclusion in the penitentials.[63]

By contrast, the concern first expressed by Theodore about dorsal and anal intercourse seems not to be foreign to the concerns of later writers. It is clear that anal intercourse was heavily penanced because of its similarity either to bestiality or to sodomy. It is not so clear why dorsal intercourse was condemned, nor from the texts examined is it entirely clear that the authors after Theodore even understood the distinction, since they sometimes seem to confuse the two. Neither the rationale of an anti-contraceptive stance nor the explicit rationale of unnaturalness is used in condemning these two types of intercourse, although the association with bestiality or sodomy suggests acts against nature.

Incest

Incest is discussed here under the heterosexual life of the married because the initial concerns of the penitential writers were with members of the immediate family unit. However, not all incestuous relations involved married people.

Incestuous relations in the early medieval period might be seen to fall into two broad categories which for our purposes will be called marital incest and sexual incest. The first refers to the problem of incestuous marriages, which preoccupied medieval legislators for nearly a thousand years. The result was a complex doctrine of disqualifying relationships based on consanguinity, affinity through marriage, and spiritual relationship arising from sponsorship at baptism or confirmation.[64] Although the penitentials address this problem, it will not concern us here.[65] By sexual incest I mean sexual relations between blood relatives and between those who are legally barred from marrying each other because of particular relationships of affinity or sponsorship. It is this form of incest that we shall examine.

Incestuous relations between members of the same family were dealt with in the earliest penitential literature. The Synod of the Grove of Victory (6; Bieler 68) condemns sexual relations with one's mother, and the *Excerpts from a Book of David* (11; Bieler 70) censures intercourse with one's sister. Neither Vinnian nor Columbanus deals with this matter, and the *Penitential of Cummean* simply repeats the canon of the Grove of Victory (*P of Cummean* 2.7; Bieler 114).

It is in the *Canons of Theodore* that one encounters for the first time a detailed account of sexual incest. Cases of incestuous relations with one's mother, with one's sister, and homosexual relations between natural brothers are covered.[66] In the first two cases there is a penance of fifteen years and a stipulation not to change (clothes?) except on Sundays. For the third, the penance is abstinence from meat for fifteen years. Finally, a mother simulating sexual intercourse with her small son is to abstain from meat for three years and to fast one day a week until vespers.[67]

The *Bigotianum Penitential* groups together the three canons of Theodore covering mother, sister, and natural brothers and penalizes all with seven or fifteen years, with no further discrimination. It concludes with the phrase, 'Another says otherwise,' which leads into the next moderating canon, 'He says that a man mating his mother or sister shall do penance for four years, and less strictly than is the rule.'[68] I am unable to suggest who this 'other' might be, nor does Bieler in his edition refer to another authority.

In addition to its reliance on Theodore, the *Excarpsus of Cummean* includes a text from the Council of Ancyra under the title 'In canonibus Anchiritanis. De incestis.'[69] Although the canon does not exactly correspond to any of the versions found in Turner, it does belong to the *Hispana* tradition, which understands Ancyra canon 16 to apply to homosexuality, bestiality, or incest.[70] This is the only explicit citation of this canon in the penitentials examined.

Bede deals with incestuous relations with a sister (3.17; W 222) and with a mother simulating intercourse with her infant son (3.29; W 223). In regard to incest with one's mother Bede adds a penance which seems to vary in the manuscript tradition. In the Wasserschleben edition there is the stipulation that the offending party is to be

continent as long as he lives. However, in the second volume of
Schmitz the stipulation is that the offending party is to do penance as
long as he lives.[71] The *Penitential of Egbert* repeats three of the canons of
Theodore and adds one dealing with the father-daughter relationship.[72]

Other penitentials extend the class of forbidden incestuous sexual
relations, perhaps reflecting the Continental concerns with marital
incest. Whereas the previous penitentials were solely concerned with
relations within the nuclear family, the treatment in the *Merseburg
Penitential* is more extensive:

If anyone commits fornication with his father's widow, or with the widow of
his paternal uncle, or with his sister, or with a female relation, or if a father
uncovers the shame of his son [see Lev 18:15], or has relations with his
step-daughter, he shall do penance for ten years on pilgrimage, two of these
years on bread and water. If he is unable to go on pilgrimage, he shall give
twelve solidi for [each?] year. If he is a layman, he is to be beaten and to set a
man free.[73]

This canon goes well beyond blood relations to include relations of
affinity; in a later canon the same penitential covers a case of spiritual
relationship: 'If anyone commits fornication with his godmother, he
shall do penance for seven years.'[74] Finally, the *Merseburg Penitential*
incorporates the case of homosexual relations between natural
brothers.[75]

Aphrodisiacs

Several canons in the penitentials reflect popular beliefs about practices
thought to have an aphrodisiac effect. Theodore introduces a canon
against the practice of mixing a husband's semen in food, imposing a
penance of three years: 'She who mixes the semen of her husband in
food so that she might receive greater love thereby shall do a similar
penance.'[76] Another practice which seems to have had some currency
was the preparation of potions which were believed to have love-
giving powers. The concocters of such potions were called 'sooth-
sayers' (*malefici* or *venefici*) and were also employed to make abortifa-
cients. Vinnian is the first to speak against this practice, in a canon
which follows the condemnation of a cleric or a woman who leads
anyone astray through magic. If the soothsayer does not lead anyone
astray but gives a potion for the sake of wanton love ('pro inlecebroso

amore'), he is to do penance for a year.[77] Columbanus reformulates Vinnian's provisions:

> But if anyone has used magic to excite love, and has destroyed no one, let him do penance on bread and water for a whole year, if a cleric; for half a year, if a layman; if a deacon, for two; if a priest, for three; especially if anyone has thus produced abortion, on that account let each add on six extra forty-day periods, lest he be guilty of murder.[78]

The text is found in the *Excarpsus of Cummean*, with 'veneficus' for 'maleficus.'[79] The *Burgundian Penitential* (10; S 2.320), which seems to have been copied by the *Merseburg Penitential* (10; S 2.360), is addressed to clerics, deacons, and priests; the *Bobbio Penitential* (10; S 2.324) includes a general condemnation without signalling any class for particular penance.

Sterility and Impotence

In the penitentials surveyed there are two early references to sterility and one to impotence. Both Vinnian and Cummean counsel continence if the wife is sterile. This is no doubt a reflection of the traditional belief that the purpose of sexual intercourse is procreation.[80]

The problem of impotence is not so much a moral problem of human sexuality as it is a legal problem concerning the possibility of re-marriage. This is probably the reason why the lone text of Theodore on the subject is not found in any of the later penitentials until it is revived by Hrabanus Maurus in the ninth century. The *Canons of Theodore* allows the woman to take another husband if it can be proved that her present husband has been unable to have intercourse with her since their marriage:

> If a man and a woman should join in marriage, and afterwards the woman says of the man that he was unable to have sexual relations with her, if anyone can prove that this is true, let her take another.[81]

Contraception

Given the procreative principle of intercourse which was generally accepted in the early Christian tradition, one might expect to find frequent condemnations of contraception in the penitentials. In discussing this subject a distinction must be made between the condemnation of contraceptive practices as contraceptive and the condemnation of practices which happen to be contraceptive. Only the former will be understood to be canons dealing with contraception. Noonan discusses the problem of contraception in the penitentials, extending his study as far as the *Decretum* of Burchard (circa 1008 AD), but does not insist on the distinction just made.[82] As a result he includes in a chart items which happen to be contraceptive (and which may be so in the intention of the participants) but which are not explicitly proscribed for their contraceptive effects – for example, anal and oral intercourse.[83] But surely it is misleading to suggest that condemnations of practices which simply happen to be contraceptive are, without additional evidence, condemnations of contraception as such.

Noonan shows that contraceptive and sterilizing potions were censured in documents contemporary with the penitentials we have examined. However, none of the condemnations of magical potions in these penitentials is directed to their contraceptive effects. Restricting our remarks to the penitentials written prior to 813 that have been selected for study here, it appears that none includes a condemnation either of contraceptive practices as such or of contraceptive potions. The only hint of this subject is in the *Penitential of Vinnian*, which remarks on the procreative purpose of marriage, using an expression reminiscent of Caesarius of Arles.[84]

Conclusion

Taken together, the early penitentials provide a comprehensive treatment of the heterosexual life of the married. It is unlikely that a confessor familiar with these works would encounter instances of sexual behaviour not covered by them. While not creative of a sexual ethic *ex nihilo*, they specified the consequences implied by the previous patristic teaching on the legitimacy of sexual intercourse and are important witnesses of the penitential practice for dealing with marital sexual offences. Because they were intended to be practical handbooks, they must also have served an important instructional function, educating confessors and, through them, the faithful. In terms of a sexual ethic of the married state this function must not be underestimated. These collections of sexual rules and regulations had no counterpart anywhere else at this time. Book 46 of the *Collectio canonum*

Hibernensis, entitled 'De ratione matrimonii,' which also circulated as a separate tract, provided a valuable complement to the penitential canons.[85] However, aside from the eleventh chapter, on the times of sexual abstinence in marriage, book 46 deals primarily with more general notions of marriage.[86]

By way of concluding this section, mention should be made of an important work which was in circulation by the middle of the eighth century. In the first book of his *Ecclesiastical History* Bede includes a letter reputed to be a set of responses sent by Pope Gregory I to Augustine of Canterbury in reply to the latter's questions.[87] The eighth response is a reply to a series of questions having to do with pregnant women, the menstrual period, and whether one must refrain from entering a church immediately after sexual intercourse. Gregory's responses are lengthy and detailed; I shall simply indicate the relevant questions and summarize the reply to each:

- 'And when the child has been born, how much time should elapse before she can enter the church?' Gregory says that the mother should not be prohibited from entering the church even if she wants to give thanks there in the very hour of birth.
- 'And after what length of time may her husband have intercourse with her?' Gregory distinguishes between those women who nurse their children after birth and those who give them up to others for nursing, the latter for reasons of incontinence. If these give up their children to others to be nursed before the time of purgation has passed, there is to be no intercourse, for the same reason that it is prohibited during menstruation, because there is no chance of procreation.
- 'And is it lawful for her to enter the church if she is in her period or to receive the sacrament of holy communion?' Gregory insists on the naturalness of menstruation and does not forbid women during their period to enter a church. He is more nuanced about the reception of communion, saying that if, out of religious fervour, women do receive communion, they are not to be censured; however, if they do not presume to approach the sacrament at this time, their judicious decision ('recta consideratio') is to be praised.
- 'Or may a man who has had intercourse with his wife enter the church before he has washed; or approach the mystery of the holy communion?' Gregory's reply to this question is a short treatise on marital intercourse and its procreative purpose. His basic answer is that

the man must wash and wait a while before entering a church. But he distinguishes between intercourse which has been solely for procreation without the rapture of pleasure and intercourse with pleasure. In the first case he leaves the judgment up to the man.

The subjects dealt with in these replies have an uncanny parallel with some texts in the *Canons of Theodore*. The latter prohibits church entry for forty days after childbirth (1.14.18; Finst 309) and forbids intercourse during the same time (1.14.19). Women are not to enter a church or to receive communion during their menstrual period (1.14.17). Finally, men are to wash after intercourse before entering a church (2.12.30; Finst 330).

It would almost seem that the replies of Gregory were designed to refute some of the regulations found in Theodore. However, if these replies of Gregory the Great are authentic, they would pre-date Theodore and presumably would have been available to him at Canterbury. Assuming their authenticity, one can only say that they were unknown to the compiler of the *Canons of Theodore* or that he knowingly departed from them. A definitive answer to this problem must await the conclusions from work currently being done on the manuscript tradition of Gregory's letter to Augustine.[88]

THE HETEROSEXUAL LIFE OF THE UNMARRIED

Throughout this study the term *fornication* is used in the restricted sense of heterosexual intercourse between two unmarried people. In the discussion of adultery only those canons were considered which dealt with cases in which it was known that at least one of the parties was married. Most of them were addressed to married men, and it was obvious that the specific offence of adultery was in question. There remain, however, numerous canons in the penitentials which deal with illicit sexual intercourse in which adultery as such is not the issue. A few of these canons are unquestionably addressed to unmarried lay people, but the majority of them are addressed to the clerical or monastic classes. Unfortunately, it is not always clear in these latter cases whether the woman (or the man in the case of canons addressed to nuns) is married or not. The writer or compiler was concerned with the sexual offences of the clergy or monks, regardless of the marital status of their partners.

What distinguishes this section from the previous section on the married is its focus on canons dealing with the unmarried. No claim is made that adulterous relations are excluded; in fact, in many cases such relations would probably be implied by the generality of the prohibitions. The governing principle in selecting canons for this category has been that they deal with heterosexual relations either between two people who are clearly not married or between two persons whose marital status is unclear. In order to highlight the ambiguity of this latter group of canons, the illicit intercourse of unmarried laity will be discussed first, followed by canons dealing with fornication in the strict sense among clerical or monastic persons and finally by the ambiguous canons which are open to the inclusion of adultery.

Lay Persons

The subject of sexual intercourse between two unmarried lay persons is virtually ignored by the penitentials. Vinnian provides a canon in regard to a young man who intends to commit fornication with a young woman and who is successful in his endeavour.[89] A canon in Columbanus which is addressed to a married layman who has sexual relations with unmarried women adds in a second part, 'Yet, if he has no wife, but has lain as a virgin with the virgin, if her relatives agree, let her be his wife, but on condition that both first do penance for a year, and so let them be wedded.'[90] Notice that the two parties are to do equal penance; this is one of the few occasions in which a penance is explicitly provided for both parties to an offence.

Bede deals with the sexual relations of male youths (*adulescens*) in a series of canons which are enigmatic in their brevity but all seem to be addressed to the same class of young men. The principal cases cover virgins, young women (*puellae*) over twenty, widows, and women who have already lost their virginity (*stuprata*). If a youth has intercourse with a virgin once and as if by chance (*fortuitu*), the year's penance that is standard in the other cases is to be lightened. Finally, if a child is born from such a union, a penance of two years is imposed, with an additional two years of a milder penance (*P of Bede* 3.1–6; W 221).

While there was some concern with the heterosexual practices of youths, there was virtually no interest in fornication in the strict sense as it applied to the general class of unmarried laity. On a priori grounds one would assume that this would not be the case since it is unlikely that illicit heterosexual relations among the unmarried laity were infrequent.[91] Perhaps such sexual activity was more tolerated when it did not involve marriage, clerical celibacy, or monastic chastity. Whatever the reason, the penitentials up to 813 show little interest in singling out for special mention the heterosexual relations of unmarried lay adults. Furthermore, during this period no mention is made in the Irish, Anglo-Saxon, or Frankish penitentials of prostitution.[92]

Before leaving this subject, we should note a series of canons which repeat the *Burgundian Penitential's* condemnation of *raptus*.[93] It is tempting to see a condemnation of rape here, and McNeill seems to suggest such an interpretation in his translation of the text 'If he violates any virgin or widow, he shall do penance for three years on bread and water.'[94] However, it is not clear whether *raptus* in the early penitential and conciliar texts had the primary connotation of sexual rape; the term seems, rather, to connote abduction. Both the Burgundian and Bobbio canons appear to be concerned with those who carry off virgins or widows either against their will or against the will of their parents. This is not to deny that sexual relations would be involved at some point; it is simply to question the focus of the canons.[95] In a canon of the Council of Chalcedon (450 A.D.) the concern is with carrying off women to make them wives.[96] A Roman council (721 A.D.) which was contemporaneous with these penitentials, echoing Chalcedon, is clearly concerned with forced marriages.[97]

Clergy, Monks, Nuns

Egbert alone of the major penitentials has a substantial number of canons addressed to monks and to the clergy in which both parties concerned are unmarried. The first two (*Egbert* 2.3–4; W 234) are from the section curiously entitled 'Of minor sins'; the others are from the fifth section entitled 'Of the penance of clerics.'[98] These canons deal with priests, deacons with and without monastic vows, monks, and clerics; the women involved are young girls and religious women. The penances are graded according to the ecclesiastical rank of the men and the religious status of the women, so that the longest penance is reserved for a priest having intercourse with a religious woman ('cum ancilla dei,' ten or eleven years), the shortest penance for a simple cleric having relations with a young girl (one year).[99]

There is an early canon in the *Burgundian Penitential*, repeated in several of the later manuals, in which both parties concerned are unmarried: 'If anyone has sexual relations with a nun or with a woman dedicated \

to God he shall do penance according to the above judgment, each according to his ecclesiastical rank.'[100] The phrase 'according to the above judgment' refers to the immediately preceding canon in each case, which in the Burgundian, Bobbio, and Merseburg penitentials deals with a member of the clergy who has been married, becomes a major cleric, and then returns to have intercourse with his wife. Since this canon is only concerned with the clergy, it follows that the one under consideration is also restricted to members of the clergy who have sexual relations with religious women. The *Capitula iudiciorum* (S 2.222–3), in its stylized manner of distributing penances over the ranks of the clergy, deals with clerics or monks who have sexual relations with consecrated women (7.2; S 2.222) or with a widow or another's fiancée (7.4). Although a 'laicus' ('layman' – married or unmarried?) is mentioned, the canons are primarily addressed to the clergy.

Except for the *Penitential of Egbert* there is little interest in the early penitential literature with specifying cases in which members of the clergy or monks are engaged in illicit sexual relations with unmarried women. As in the case of laymen, the penitentials are not concerned with fornication in the strict sense. This lack of interest is reflected in the absence of any noun used exclusively to mean fornication in the sense of heterosexual relations between two unmarried people.

Ambiguous Canons

We are left with a number of canons in the penitentials which deal with what are neither clear cases of adultery nor clear cases of fornication in the strict sense.[101] With the exception of Merseburg and St Gall all of the penitentials surveyed have a number of ambiguous canons against illicit heterosexual relations, and almost all are addressed to the clergy or to monks.[102] Some are either addressed to anyone in general (*si quis*) or, as in the case of *Bede* 3.27 (W 223), are addressed to the laity without mention of whether either party is married.[103] The *Penitential of Egbert* covers nuns who have sexual relations with laymen.[104] Finally, the *Paris Penitential* seems to impose a life-long penance for sexual intercourse in a church: 'The penance for one who commits fornication in a church is that he shall offer service to the house of God all the days of his life.'[105]

As is the general rule in other matters, these canons seldom appeal to authoritative sources in support of their censures. There is a text in Theodore which refers to canons which are otherwise unidentifiable:

The first canon judged that he who commits fornication often shall do penance for ten years, the second canon, for seven years, but because of human weakness they counselled three years' penance.[106]

Another use of an authoritative source is Egbert's explicit appeal to the *Canons of the Apostles* in his censure of clerics for capital offences.[107]

The scale of penances for clerical offenders generally ranges from a few years for simple clerics to twelve years for bishops. There is no consistent practice of imposing degradation from ecclesiastical office, but the trend is in that direction for bishops, priests, and deacons. The first clear imposition of degradation for bishops is found in the *Penitential of Cummean* (2.1; Bieler 112). In the 'Iudicium canonicum' section of the *Capitula iudiciorum* (7; S 2.222–3) deposition is a usual component of the penances.

HOMOSEXUALITY AND LESBIANISM

The penitentials throughout the whole period under consideration show a great interest in homosexuality.[108] In a religious culture which placed a high premium on virginity, celibacy, and sexual continence and which fostered institutions whose populations were sexually homogeneous, incidents of homosexuality would not be unheard of. Unfortunately, however, it is often impossible to distinguish between canons addressed to religious individuals and those meant for males generally.[109] Furthermore, the distinction between homosexual acts and people who might be called homosexuals does not seem to be operative in these manuals, whose focus is on the commission of sins. The penitentials do censure *sodomitae* ('sodomists'), but, as will become clear in what follows, this term is probably their way of referring to those who practise anal intercourse, and should not be translated 'homosexuals.'

There is a canon in Theodore which characterizes certain persons as 'molles' in a homosexual context.[110] The term figures in St Paul's list of those who will not possess the kingdom of heaven.[111] McNeill translates 'molles' as 'the effeminate man,' and Bailey believes that the term should be understood in reference to the person in a homosexual relation who takes the passive role.[112] In assigning the same penance (seven years) to *molles* as to adulterous women, a penance which is also identical to the penance assigned to sodomists, Theodore seems to consider these individuals guilty of a serious sexual offence.[113] The association with women perhaps suggests that he understood the term to refer to those who take the passive role. The reference to *molles* is found in later works but usually with the penance reduced to one year.[114] The reduced penance suggests that the compilers did not understand the term in the same way as Theodore. However, I am uncertain as to what their understanding might have been. It does not seem to have included strictly homosexual activity between adult males, which is invariably more severely penalized. In the *Excarpsus of Cummean* the canon referring to *molles* is the last of a group dealing with the homosexual practices of boys, all of which canons are characterized by rather short penances.[115]

Nevertheless, if there is no word in general usage in the penitentials for homosexuality as a category, the descriptive language employed leaves no doubt when there is a question of sexual contact between members of the same sex. As various distinctions were introduced by the early writers to differentiate among forms of homosexual contact, the linguistic expressions for these distinctions tended to become formalized and to be adopted by subsequent manuals.

The Welsh documents which antedate Vinnian mention homosexuality, three of them in the context of other sexual offences.[116] The Synod of the Grove of Victory censures three forms of homosexual practice in addition to masturbation.[117] Femoral intercourse and mutual masturbation are clearly referred to and penanced with three and two years respectively. The expression 'whoever commits the male crime as the sodomists' is ambiguous, but, since this activity is distinguished from the two forms which are subsequently mentioned, it probably refers to homosexual anal intercourse. In the following discussion expressions using the terms *sodomitae* or *sodomiticus* will be assumed to refer to homosexual anal intercourse unless there is a clear indication that they should be interpreted otherwise. 'Homosexual' is not a proper translation of *sodomita* since the penitentials seem to be careful to differentiate these from men engaged in other forms of homosexual practice.[118] Sodomy is a specific form of activity and those engaged in it are sodomists; the 'sodomitic practice' invariably receives a heavier penance. Alternate expressions will also be used by the penitentials to connote this behaviour.

Vinnian has a reference to homosexual anal intercourse couched in an alternate expression ('in terga fornicantes') and addressed to boys and men. If the offence is habitual, the penance is to be increased at the discretion of the priest.[119] There is also in Vinnian what seems to be a reference to fellatio among boys: 'Those who satisfy their desires with their lips, three years. If it has become a habit, seven years.'[120]

In the section of his penitential dealing with clerics and monks Columbanus mentions homosexuality twice. The first reference is in a canon which deals with what are called the 'common' or 'prevalent' sins (homicide, sodomy, fornication, marital desertion) and imposes a penance of ten years.[121] The second condemns those who 'fornicate as the Sodomites did,' also imposing a penance of ten years.[122] This canon is adopted by the *Burgundian Penitential* and is repeated with minor variations by later Frankish manuals.[123] A third reference in Columbanus is in the section dealing with the offences of the laity. The introductory words suggest the Biblical condemnation of homosexuality in Leviticus and provide some justification for understanding references to *sodomiticus* as references to homosexual anal intercourse. The canon begins, 'But if any layman has committed fornication in sodomite fashion, that is, has sinned *with a man as with a woman ... '*[124]

The *Penitential of Cummean* provides the most ample treatment of homosexuality of any of the penitentials.[125] Some of the material is borrowed from Vinnian, but most is original and is frequently adopted by later penitentials. In the second book, entitled 'De fornicatione' and more accurately translated 'Concerning sexual offences,' the *Penitential of Cummean* deals with fellatio, the act of the Sodomites, and femoral intercourse. The age and status of those to whom the canons are addressed are not specified.[126] The other canons dealing with homosexual acts are from the tenth book, entitled 'let us now set forth the decrees of our fathers on the playing of boys,' although males other than boys are mentioned. The penitential here is very precise in regard to the classes of males dealt with and is discriminating in regard to the types of act. Children (*minimi*), boys (*pueri*), boys (*pueri*) over twenty, the small boy (*puer parvulus*), and men (*viri*) are singled out for explicit mention. Children imitating acts of fornication and stimulating one another are to do penance for twenty days, forty if the acts are frequent.[127] Boys of twenty who practice mutual masturbation receive a penance of twenty or forty days and a hundred days for femoral intercourse. The penances are increased if the acts are repeated after confession or are frequent.[128] There is a curious canon which seems to deal with the homosexual abuse of a young boy, but it is the boy who is abused who is to do the penance: 'A small boy misused by an older one, if he is ten years of age, shall fast for a week; if he consents, for twenty days.'[129] It is reasonable to impose a penance if consent was present, but the penitentials usually do not penance an act in which consent was lacking. Perhaps this canon was meant to serve an educational function and was not simply punitive.

Men practising femoral intercourse and men and boys practising anal intercourse (*in terga*) are explicitly mentioned.[130] Finally, there is a general censure of fellatio, without specific reference to any class of males.[131]

The *Canons of Theodore* rivals the *Penitential of Cummean* in the amplitude of its treatment of homosexuality. In regard to male homosexual offences Theodore makes no significant additions to what has been said before him. He provides for the whipping of boys who fornicate among themselves (*Canons of Theodore* U 1.2.11; Finst 291) and in one canon complements the *Penitential of Cummean*, which provides for boys not over twenty, while Theodore says, 'Whoever is over twenty and has sexual relations with a male shall do penance for fifteen years.'[132] We have already examined the question of oral sex in Theodore and suggested that *Canons of Theodore* U 1.2.15 probably refers to homosexual practices.[133]

A significant feature of this penitential is the separate mention of female homosexual behaviour. 'If a woman commits fornication with a woman, she shall do penance for three years.'[134] Although this canon is not widely adopted by subsequent penitentials, it will have a long history in later collections. There is another text in Theodore which, in the edition of Finsterwalder, seems to apply to adultery and in the edition of Wasserschleben applies to a lesbian relation. The text is not taken up by any of the other early penitentials we have examined but is found in Hrabanus Maurus in the ninth century with the lesbian connotation.[135] The two possible readings are 'A woman who joins herself in adultery after the manner of fornication shall do penance for three years like a fornicator' and 'A woman who joins herself to another woman after the manner of fornication shall do penance for three years like a fornicator.'

There is a reference in Bede to a lesbian relationship between nuns using an instrument of some kind (*machina* – artificial phallus'?).[136] This text will also be found in later collections.

The *Excarpsus of Cummean* has a canon against sodomy with a graded set of penances for the clergy and laity which is found in Egbert and the *Merseburg Penitential*.[137] Finally, Bede has three brief canons on homosexuality which are peculiar to this penitential.[138]

While it is too much to say with Taylor that the penitentials 'devoted a disproportionately large amount of their space to prescribing penalties for homosexuality,'[139] it is certainly true that they show considerable interest in the subject. This is in sharp contrast, for instance, to the relative lack of interest shown in the heterosexual relations of unmarried

lay people. Different forms of homosexual relations are carefully distinguished, and the age of the participants is important, as is ecclesiastical
status, in the apportioning of penances. The numerous canons mention-
ing clerical homosexual activity do not suggest that it was rampant, but
they confirm the perfectly natural expectation that, in institutions whose
populations are all of the same sex, homosexuality will probably occur
and this will be reflected in works dealing with the pastoral care of such
people.

What is surprising, however, is the absence of explicit appeal either to
the Bible or to the Council of Ancyra.[140] There is an allusion to Leviticus
in the *Penitential of Columbanus*, and it is possible that canons which use
the age of twenty as a discriminating point of reference were influenced
by the provisions of Ancyra. As Bailey points out, no rationale is provided for the sinfulness of homosexuality at this time, nor is there any
explanation of why sodomy should be treated differently from femoral
intercourse or mutual masturbation. But the penances applied to these
different practices suggest that they were considered to vary in gravity.

BESTIALITY

The earliest Welsh documents mention bestiality, sometimes alone, sometimes along with other sexual offences,[141] and all of the penitentials have
at least one provision covering this activity. The *Penitential of Vinnian*
deals only with boys who engage in such behaviour, but it is not clear
whether the focus of the canon is on the bestiality or on the fact that the
boy has received communion in spite of the fact that he sinned with an
animal.[142]

Columbanus has two canons on bestiality, one for clerics or monks,
the other for laymen. In the first case the offence is mentioned along with
masturbation and both receive the same penance, which is graded according to whether the person is a cleric or not.[143] In the case of a layman a
distinction is made between whether he is married or not. The married
man receives double the penance of a single man, and the latter's penance
is said to be similar to that of a married man who commits masturbation.[144]

The *Canons of Theodore* has two canons on the act of bestiality and one
stipulating what is to be done with the animals so used. The first canon
deals with those who practise bestiality frequently and provides a ten-
year penance.[145] The second, which is said to come from another source,
imposes a penance of fifteen years.[146] Finsterwalder suggests that the

source referred to is Basil's canonical letters, but the penance also reflects the heavy penances of the Council of Ancyra:

[Rubric] Those who fornicate irrationally, that is, who mix with cattle or who are polluted with males.
[Text] Of those who have acted or who act irrationally: as often as they have committed such a crime before the age of twenty, after fifteen years of penance they should merit the community of prayers; then, after spending five years in this community, they can have the Eucharist. However, the quality of their lives is to be discussed during the time of penance, and so they might obtain mercy. And if they are given insatiably to these heretical crimes, they are to undertake to do penance for a longer time. However, if this is done after age twenty by those who are married, after twenty-five years of penance they will be received into the community of prayers in which they remain for five years and then they can receive the Eucharist. If they are married and over fifty and fall into this sin, they can receive the grace of communion at the end of their lives.[147]

In the *Excarpsus of Cummean* the penances of Theodore stand alongside the shorter penances of Columbanus.[148]
  In a much-used canon of the *Burgundian Penitential* the basic penance for a cleric is two years, and it is increased according to the ecclesiastical rank of the offender.[149] While Egbert reflects the provision of the *Burgundian Penitential*, he seems puzzled by the range of penances in other works, and so he enumerates them.[150] Bede's only reference to bestiality applies a basic penance of one year, with an additional year if the offender is a monk.[151] By contrast, the *Merseburg Penitential* (51; S 2.363), no doubt influenced by the Council of Ancyra, imposes a penance of twenty-five years for those over the age of twenty.
  Theodore, echoing Lev 20:15, directs that animals polluted by intercourse with men are to be killed and their flesh thrown to dogs:

Animals polluted by coitus with men are to be killed and the flesh thrown to dogs. But what they give birth to may be used and the hides taken. However, where a doubt exists, they are not to be killed.[152]

Finally, Egbert counsels that the confessor ought to discriminate between the quality of the animals and the quality of the men.[153] While he himself discriminates in regard to the various ecclesiastical ranks, he does not indicate what he means by discriminating in regard to the quality of the animals. Aside from the explicit mention of a dog in the Synod of the Grove of Victory (7; Bieler 68), none of the penitentials seems to intend to censure bestiality with particular species of animals.[154] There is no indication that the terms *animal, iumentum, pecus, pecoris, pecus, pecudis,* and *quadrupedes* are meant to make significant discriminations among various species of animals.[155]

What can one conclude from this ample treatment of bestiality in the penitentials? It might be expected that such activity would not be uncommon in a predominately rural society. What is not expected are the number of times relatively short penances are imposed for this act – a sign perhaps that the penitentials had not yet come under the influence of canons 16 and 17 of the Council of Ancyra. At the end of the eighth century Theodulf of Orleans proposed a ranking which is not reflected in the tradition of the penitentials:

Just as it is more abominable to mix with a mule than with a male, so it is a more irrational crime [to mix] with a male than with a female. To sin with a blood relative and with a nun are equal crimes. Therefore, the law of Moses lays down the death sentence for those having sexual relations with a mule and with a male and with a blood relative.[156]

MASTURBATION

There is no Latin word in the penitentials corresponding to the English term *masturbation*, nor do many Latin expressions unambiguously connote our meaning.[157] Some expressions are unproblematic, such as 'per se ipsum fornicaverit' ('fornicate by himself') in the *Penitential of Columbanus* (B.10; Bieler 100) or 'propriis membris se ipsum violaverit' ('has violated himself with his own members') in the same manual (B.17; Bieler 102). As it stands, a text in Theodore probably suggests female masturbation, and one might suspect that some instrument is in question.[158] There are canons with the expression 'touch with the hand,' which I would be inclined to interpret as referring to masturbation but which may simply refer to touching one's own genitals.[159] There is, finally, a group of canons using variants of an expression first encountered in a canon of the Synod of North Britain, 'Qui se ipsum quoinquinaverit' ('whoever defiles himself').[160] The penitentials allow for many ways one may be defiled, and they are not all through masturbation as we know it. However, I believe that the above expression from the Synod of North Britain in that reflexive form with its derivative expressions does in fact connote masturbation.

If these interpretations are correct, then all the penitentials deal with masturbation except the penitentials of Vinnian and Bede. The penances are not of long duration; frequently there is in the same penitential the same penance given for masturbation as for bestiality, and it is usually short. The three-year penance meted out by Theodore for female masturbation, which is the same as the penance provided for a lesbian relationship by the preceding canon, does not fit the usual pattern of penances for this offence.

Several penitentials are not content simply to censure masturbation in a general way but describe circumstances in which the act may sometimes occur. Theodore uses an expression usually associated with homosexuality but which seems in the context to refer to a person acting alone: 'If in the thighs, one year or the three Lents.'[161] Several Frankish penitentials speak of the cause of the act (concupiscence or lust), and the *Paris Penitential* singles out the time of awakening for particular mention:

If anyone has a sexual experience [*furnicare*] on arising by arousing his body, he shall do penance for forty nights; if he was polluted through this arousal, seventy days and an additional fast of seven days.[162]

I suspect that this type of prescription was written with a view to clerics and monks.

SAFEGUARDS OF CHASTITY

The institutions of clerical celibacy and monastic chastity naturally gave rise to prohibitions of overt sexual behaviour for persons who had taken on such commitments. These prohibitions have been encountered already. Concern was also expressed about what might be called the outer defences of the asexual way of life characteristic of monks and the clergy. In this regard women were often seen to be sources of temptation, and this would explain the long tradition of conciliar legislation dealing with the question of undue familiarity with women and with other measures meant to safeguard clerical continence.[163] These same concerns are also reflected in the penitential literature which was written during the period when much of this conciliar legislation was enacted.[164] One of the surprising omissions from the penitentials, however, is the third canon of the Council of Nicaea (325 AD) against clerical cohabitation. This canon was originally directed against an Eastern practice of clerics cohabiting with what might be called live-in virgins (*virgines subintroductae*), which was severely attacked by John Chrysostom.[165] I say it is a surprising omission because the text is quoted by numerous councils prior to the ninth century and for centuries afterwards:

In every way the great synod forbids a bishop, priest, deacon, and any other of clerical rank from having live-in women except perhaps a mother, or sister, or paternal aunt, or only those female persons who are above suspicion.[166]

In the penitentials I examined, this canon, in summary form, is found only in the *Merseburg Penitential* (137; S 2.367 = *Vallicellian Pentitential* I, 44; S 1.288–9).

The penitentials contain numerous canons dealing with embraces and kissing, thoughts, and desires which come to naught either because of lack of opportunity or because the woman refuses.[167] Frequently, penances are determined on the basis of whether seminal emission resulted or not, but this matter will be taken up in the next section. These penitential censures are addressed primarily to clerics and seem designed to remove the occasions for more serious overt sexual acts. The concern with thoughts and desires witnesses to an ethic which locates sinfulness not simply in overt acts but in the mind and will from which the acts proceed. Often the subject of these canons is a person with a desire to engage in illicit sexual relations with a woman but who is unable to do so. In a sense he is still guilty because of his willingness and so has to submit to some penance, although it is usually light. The position is perhaps best expressed by the *Penitential of Vinnian*:

But if he continually lusts and is unable to indulge his desire, since the woman does not admit him or since he is ashamed to speak, still he has committed adultery with her in his heart – yet it is in his heart, and not in his body; it is the same sin whether in the heart or in the body, yet the penance is not the same. This is his penance: let him do penance for forty days with bread and water.[168]

The substance of this canon is found in many of the later penitentials down to the *Capitula iudiciorum*, which lays down severe penances for members of the clergy.[169]

SEMINAL EMISSION

There is a sexually related theme encountered in numerous canons which is probably quite foreign to contemporary thinking. One of the most thoroughly handled subjects in the penitentials is that of seminal emission in contexts other than masturbation. We have already seen that penances for the kissing of small boys were differentiated according to whether emission occurred or not, and the same is prescribed for priests who kiss women.[170] What I understand to be seminal emission is usually connoted by the passive forms of such verbs as *polluere, coinquinare, inquinare,* or *maculare,* but sometimes the straightforward expression *semen fu(n)dere* ('emit a flow of semen') is used.

Peter Browe, in a chapter entitled 'Die Pollutionen,' claims that while the questions of the uncleanliness of married couples after intercourse and of pregnant and menstruating women are frequently dealt with in the Middle Ages, the attention devoted to those issues is minor compared to that accorded the question of whether a man should be allowed to approach the altar after a seminal emission.[171] Although Browe demonstrates this particular claim through a detailed analysis of monastic rules, his treatment of the penitential literature is sketchy and does not reflect the complex handling of the subject by these manuals. I suspect this is because Browe is primarily interested in the question of whether a man can receive communion or celebrate mass after a seminal emission, and this issue does not seem to have concerned the penitential writers.[172]

The majority of the canons deal with the occurrence of pollution, to use their term, in contexts in which the will is more or less involved. They can be divided into three classes for purposes of analysis. There is a group of early canons whose formulations for each of the various cases tend to be used by later penitentials, with minor modifications. There is another group saying much the same as the first but in different terms. There is a third group which add something to the main body of regulations but which stand in isolation, neither borrowing from the past nor influencing future works.[173] It is likely that concern with seminal emission arose originally in a monastic context and that the penitential canons dealing with the subject were addressed to monks and clerics.

Some canons pose problems of interpretation which are virtually impossible to resolve. What seems to underly the penitential concern with seminal emission is a belief that such an occurrence is of itself *spiritually* polluting – that is, it places the man in a state of ritualistic impurity which must be cleansed by some sort of spiritual activity.[174]

The first canon to gain a degree of subsequent popularity is found in the early Welsh *Excerpts from a Book of David*: 'He who willfully has become polluted in sleep shall get up and sing seven psalms and live on bread and water for that day; but if he does not do this he shall sing thirty psalms.'[175] This text apparently refers to a person who goes to bed wishing that a nocturnal pollution will occur, and perhaps he is considered to be responsible for bringing it on. Bieler's translation, which speaks of *intentionally* becoming polluted *in sleep*, does not dispel the ambiguity.[176] The canon has a long history with very few modifications.[177]

The canon following covers three situations, the first and second of which seem problematic: 'If he desired to sin in sleep but could not, fifteen psalms. If, however, he sinned but was not polluted, twenty-four. If he was unintentionally polluted, sixteen.'[178] The author introduces four variables: to desire, to sin, to be unable to sin, to become polluted. I do not know what 'to sin in sleep' means in this context, and the literal renditions of the translators are of little help.[179] If 'to sin' has the same meaning throughout, then it does not mean 'to be polluted,' since both verbs are used together in the second sentence. Perhaps 'to sin' refers to being aroused sexually or to having a type of dream; if so, the sentences would make sense, but there is nothing in the canon nor in any of the other canons of this document to support such an interpretation. Whatever the meaning, none of the other penitentials which repeat the canon in the form in which it is found in Cummean seems to have had trouble with the idea of sinning without being polluted.[180]

There are two canons in Cummean which are found in later penitentials, the first of which poses some problem of interpretation. It speaks of being polluted or defiled ('coinquinatus est') through foul language or a look ('per turpiloquium vel aspectu').[181] It is not clear whether this means that the language or looks defile of themselves or that through them one has a seminal emission; I suspect the latter is the case.[182] Another text deals with the violent onslaught of a thought from which pollution results.[183]

The early canons mentioned so far had a long history in the penitentials, but none of them is in the *Canons of Theodore*. Just as for other topics, a new set of canons which are also taken up by later manuals is introduced by this work. The first in Theodore's series refers to a priest being polluted through touching or kissing.[184] A second canon to gain some popularity seems to refer to bringing on a seminal emission through mental activity.[185] A canon in Theodore resembles Cummean's reference to the violent onslaught of a thought, and finally, Theodore mentions seminal pollution while sleeping in a church.[186]

There are several canons with no clear relation to preceding canons which are not found in subsequent penitentials. The *Bobbio Penitential* sheds some light on the problem of how one might sin in sleep: 'If he sinned in sleep as though with a woman he shall sing twenty-five psalms.'[187] This suggests a dream in which the sleeper is having sexual relations with a woman. A similar idea is found in the *Capitula iudiciorum* but is developed more fully there in a canon addressed to bishops, priests, and monks. If the pollution is accompanied by an impure fantasy, the bishop, priest, or monk is to wash and is not to receive communion the following day. However, if the pollution is not accompanied by a thought, the priest can offer the mass in case of necessity.[188] The language of this canon is reminiscent of the ninth response of Gregory to Augustine, which we shall see below. Another canon in the *Bobbio Penitential* refers to a spontaneous emission resulting from the natural buildup of semen (*ex corpore repleto*).[189] The notion of a buildup of semen resulting in spontaneous emission is also discussed by Gregory. Egbert covers the case of voluntary seminal emission resulting from bad thoughts ('mala cogitatione'),[190] and Bede provides a penance for pollution resulting from embracing and touching a woman.[191]

In his ninth response to Augustine, Gregory the Great replies to the question of whether one can receive communion or offer the mass after a nocturnal emission.[192] While some of the penitentials show signs that their authors may have been familiar with Gregory's remarks, only one of those we are examining clearly uses his reply. After paraphrasing the question, the *Merseburg Penitential* summarizes the section in which Gregory distinguishes various causes of seminal emission.[193] The penitential reproduces the text fairly faithfully but departs from it in one item. According to Gregory, seminal emission in sleep could result from previous overeating. In this case he allows a priest to receive communion when another priest is present to offer the mass. The *Merseburg Penitential* omits this indulgence.

It is clear from the preceding that although the penitenials share with the monastic rules examined by Browe a concern with seminal emission, few of them forbid communion following such emission. Perhaps this is because such a prohibition was understood or already provided for by monastic rules; it is difficult to say. What is clear is that the canons which deal with this question reflect a belief that the fact of seminal emission is spiritually polluting, demanding spiritual redress through psalm-singing, fasting, or other forms of penance. While the degree of wilfulness has some bearing on the severity of the penance, the absence of will or of consciously entertained thought seems not to imply total lack of sinfulness or guilt. Unfortunately, the penitentials do not offer any rationale for their positions. Gregory's reply to Augustine is the only sophisticated discussion of the matter, but very little of the reply is incorporated into the early penitential literature.

The penitentials we have examined represent a consistent and comprehensive treatment of sexual behaviour over two and a half centuries. In them one encounters the uncompromising implications of a sexual ethic which began from the premise that permissible sexual activity is restricted to men and women who are legitimately married to one another. Even in the case of marital sex the penitentials regulate both the times and the methods of sexual intercourse. Few sexual acts are omitted, and given the wide range of other subjects dealt with, there is no reason to assume that the treatment of sex is the result of a desire to concoct canons to cover all conceivable possibilities. The penitentials have the marks of practical manuals compiled to deal with the acknowledged offences of actual human beings. In many of the penitentials the canons dealing with sexual subjects comprise over 20 per cent of the total number of canons: it is difficult to believe that religious compilers would have continued to prepare manuals containing such a great deal of sexual material unless it was relevant to their needs.

In a representative sampling of penitentials up to the eleventh century, the following percentages emerge. The total number of canons represents the figure after counting as individual canons those which the editors grouped together under one number, such as was done in the *Capitula iudiciorum*.

Penitential of Vinnian (Bieler 74–95)
Total number of canons 57
Sexually related canons 21 = 37%
Penitential of Egbert (W 231–47)
Total number of canons 113
Sexually related canons 51 = 45%

Burgundian Penitential (S 2.320–2)
Total number of canons 41
Sexually related canons 11 = 27%
Capitula iudiciorum (S 2.218–51)
Total number of canons 301
Sexually related canons 76 = 25%
Merseburg Penitential (S 2.359–68)
Total number of canons 168
Sexually related canons 41 = 24%
Monte Cassino Penitential (S 1.401–31)
Total number of canons 124
Sexually related canons 34 = 27%
Arundel Penitential (S 1.437–64)
Total number of canons 97
Sexually related canons 39 = 40%

The terse style of the penitential canons served their practical purpose
very well. However, the price paid for brevity and conciseness is an
almost total lack of authoritative support for their prescriptions and an
absence of discursive comment. Explicit citation of biblical, patristic, or
conciliar authorities is not frequent. Allusions and oblique references are
made to the Bible, and some sentences or phrases are encountered which
suggest specific biblical passages. Vinnian's canon on periods of sexual
abstinence is a good example of this,[194] as is Theodore's mention of the
holy bread.[195] Throughout his edition, Finsterwalder suggests numerous
parallels between Theodore and St Basil, but aside from this possibility I
have been unable to identify other patristic sources in the penitential
canons dealing with sexual topics.[196] The *Excarpsus of Cummean* (3.21;
S 2.615) explicitly cites the Council of Ancyra in a canon dealing with
incest. It cites canon 20 of the same council on adultery, without naming
its source (*Excarpsus of Cummean* 3.22; S 2.615). The *Burgundian Penitential*
(30; S 2.321) seems to be based on the Council of Agde (506 AD), canon 9.
Except for the use of Gregory's replies to Augustine in the *Merseburg
Penitential* (89 and 90; S 2.365) I have been unable to detect the use of
decretal sources.[197]

The lack of any discernible effort to support their prescriptions with
traditional sources would count heavily against the penitentials in the
ninth century. The lack of discursive comment is probably an unavoidable
characteristic of this kind of pastorally oriented penitential literature,

from which theological and philosophical comment should not be expected. Nevertheless, the penitentials demonstrate relative unanimity in the sexual subjects which they treat and in their manner of treatment, so that a fairly homogeneous sexual code was mediated to the ninth century through these works. We now turn to the question of whether this body of regulations continued to influence the treatment of sexual behaviour.

2

The Ninth Century

The ninth century, particularly during the reigns of Charlemagne
(d 814 AD) and Louis the Pious (d 840 AD), was a period of intense
ecclesiastical and canonical reform in which numerous councils were
held, collections of imperial edicts and ecclesiastical laws were either
popularized or created, diocesan statutes were enacted for the better-
ment of the clergy, and new forms of penitential literature were compiled. This chapter does not pretend to be a detailed account of the
ecclesiastical literary history of the period.[1] Its purpose is simply to
examine some of the main lines of this history for signs of the influence
of the penitentials on the Church's handling of sexual behaviour. I
shall deal with the reception of the penitentials at the beginning of the
century, say a word about ninth-century penitentials written in the
traditional style, and finally touch on the works of Halitgar of Cambrai
and Hrabanus Maurus, who wrote penitentials in a new key.

THE RECEPTION OF THE PENITENTIALS

There is every indication that, prior to 813, within the lands controlled
by Charlemagne the penitentials were considered to be valuable tools
in the pastoral ministry. A number of documents of the period
recommend that priests have a penitential and that they be familiar
with it. Editors and commentators have some difficulty in accurately
dating these documents but agree, no doubt because of the condemnations of penitentials in that year, that they date from before 813. Three
texts edited by Boretius in his collection of capitularies suggest that the
possession of a penitential was expected of a priest and that he was to
be acquainted with its contents.[2]
    The ninth century also saw the beginnings of a form of pastoral

literature, diocesan statutes, which were issued by bishops and archbishops for the priests in their jurisdictions.[3] A number of these works dating from the early part of the century, probably from before the reform councils of 813, are quite explicit in recommending that priests possess a penitential and be familiar with it.[4] During this period there are no voices raised in opposition to the penitentials, and although Theodulf of Orleans (d 821 AD) does not cite earlier penitentials, his Second Diocesan Statute includes a penitential-like section.[5] In his instructions for confessors Theodulf recommends the use of a penitential for interrogatory purposes in order to jog the memory of penitents. But he issues a warning about their use:

Nonetheless, he [the priest] ought not to make known to him [the penitent] all the crimes since there are many vices recorded in the penitential which it is not proper for a person to know. Therefore, the priest ought not question him about everything, lest, perhaps, when he goes away he be persuaded by the devil to fall into one of the crimes of which he had previously been ignorant.[6]

An examination of Gaudemet's charts reveals the extensive treatment by Theodulf of numerous ecclesiastical subjects.[7] There is no evidence of direct literary dependence on previous penitentials for the sexual content of his statutes, but Theodulf seems to be writing in that tradition. Several of his provisions are original and will find their way into subsequent diocesan statutes and canonical collections.[8] Although it lacks the detail of some of the previous penitentials, Theodulf's Second Diocesan Statute avoids the confusion and inconsistencies sometimes found in those manuals. His work represents a well-planned and serviceable practical manual for use by the priests of his diocese and would probably satisfy the critics of the traditional penitentials.

In terms of the categories that I used in the first chapter to differentiate the various types of sexual behaviour, Theodulf's Second Diocesan Statute deals with almost all of the subjects mentioned in the penitentials. While it is true, as Gaudemet says, that the work has the allure of a traditional penitential with its tariffed penances, it is much more than that. One is struck by the discursive character of much of the work and the obvious intention of its author to instruct priests in the pastoral care of penitents and in the proper way of dealing with them. Theodulf constantly reminds his priests to *admonish* the people about how to conduct their lives and frequently points out topics for public *instruction*. But priests must set their own lives in order before they can hope to reform the people:

Priests are to be admonished and instructed that first of all they be far removed from every form of carnal fornication. Then they may preach in words to the people subject to them and show by example that they should abstain from every form of fornication and irrational lust and pollution, such as with animals, and prepare themselves for God, pure in body and mind.[9]

The subject of irrational lust is taken up again in a long discussion under the title 'De inrationali fornicatione' ('Concerning irrational fornication').[10] The title reflects a use of the Council of Ancyra in the version called by Turner *Isidori antiqua*, which interprets *inrationabiliter* ('irrationally') in a three-fold sense as referring to homosexuality, bestiality, and incest.[11] The final chapter is a summary of much of the contents of this seventh section and includes a censure of contraception:

If, would that it would never be, someone admits to [having committed] such a crime in holy places, his penance will be doubled. In the Scriptures the crime with a mule as well as with a male and a blood relative are called the worst of crimes. Not to have relations with a woman in a natural way is called uncleanness or a detestable sin, whence we read that Onan, the son of Juda, was struck by God after entering into his wife and spilling his seed on the ground. Likewise, masturbation is called uncleanness either on account of the touch or sight or memory of a woman, or because of some pleasure occurring to him when awake, or if he exercises impurity between his own thighs, alone or with another.[12]

Theodulf recommends to his priests that they admonish the people about the required periods of sexual abstinence.[13] In the section in which he treats of adultery, Theodulf is usually careful to use the language of *adulterium* and its derivatives when a married person is involved in the illicit sexual behaviour, the verb *fornicari* when no married person is involved.[14]

The only sign that perhaps the use of the penitentials was being questioned at the time Theodulf was writing occurs in a document found only in the collection of Ansegisus. It is dated 810–13 by Boretius, 800–13 by De Clercq. Apparently, questions were being asked as to how penitents were to be dealt with and according to which penitential, but an answer was deferred.[15]

In 813 councils were held at Arles, Reims, Mainz, Châlons, and Tours in preparation for a general assembly of the empire.[16] None of the councils recommends the use of penitentials, and the Council of Châlons directly condemns them. Penance is to be administered according to the ancient canons, the authority of Scripture, or ecclesiastical custom. Châlons goes on to say that the booklets called penitentials are to be repudiated and eliminated; they are marked by certain errors and uncertain authorship, imposing light and uncustomary penances for grave sins.[17] The Council of Tours, however, defers the question as to which penitential is to be used until the general assembly, which was planned for the fall of that same year at Aachen.[18] No mention is made of the penitentials in any of the documents emanating from the general assembly of September 813.[19]

Several years later the Council of Paris (829 AD) also explicitly condemned the penitentials, admonishing bishops to search them out and to burn those they found:

That the small codices that they call penitentials be completely abolished because they are opposed to canonical authority. Many priests, partly from carelessness, partly from ignorance, impose on those confessing their guilt a mode of penance at variance with what the canon laws determine, using certain small codices which they call penitentials written against canonical authority, and for this reason they do not cure the wounds of sin but rather foster them through flattery. For this reason, it has seemed right to us all that each bishop seek out with diligence these same erroneous codices in his diocese and throw those they find into the fire lest unskilled priests deceive men further through them.[20]

The Council of Mainz (847 AD) employs the language of Châlons in regard to the administration of penance, but it omits the explicit prohibition of that earlier council.[21]

In all, there are two condemnations of the penitentials by conciliar decree, no doubt motivated by a genuine concern for the proper administration of penance. That the prohibitions had some effect is evidenced by the fact that one no longer finds councils or capitulary decrees recommending the use of penitentials. Diocesan statutes too are generally silent about the possession of a penitential among the books to be owned, but the diocesan statute of Rodulph of Bourges (circa 850 AD) is the only ninth-century diocesan statute to condemn the

penitentials outright.[22] However, it will be more than a century after
Châlons before the explicit recommendation of a penitential is again
encountered in a diocesan statute.[23]

The diocesan statutes share with the penitentials a concern with the
everyday practices of the people. Although they omit to recommend the
penitentials, one might expect to find in the statutes some signs that
the penitentials had been used in the compilation of their censures of
illicit sexual behaviour.These statutes frequently condemn such behaviour, reiterating the third canon of Nicaea against clerical cohabitation, inveighing against marital incest, and continuing to propose
certain times of sexual abstinence for married people.[24] Isaac of Langres
(circa 860 AD) includes numerous sexual provisions in his lengthy and
systematically arranged collection of canons.[25] The statutes of Hincmar
of Reims, although restricted in scope, provide texts on illicit relations
between the clergy and women.[26] However, what Devisse says about
Hincmar's use of the penitentials can be said about all of the episcopal
writers of diocesan statutes: 'Hincmar a respecté la proscription qui
frappait ces textes depuis 829 [Council of Paris condemnation].'[27] An
inspection of the tables of sources compiled by C. De Clercq for
Rodulph of Bourges, Herard of Tours, and Isaac of Langres leads one
to the same conclusion.[28] These works depend almost exclusively on
the contemporary collections of Ansegisus and Benedictus Levita, two
collections which show no influence from the penitentials.

Ninth-century councils, capitular collections, the Pseudo-Isidorian
decretals, and the diocesan statutes all point to what must be called an
official ecclesiastical proscription in regard to the penitentials. Although
only two councils and one diocesan statute of the period explicitly
condemn the use of penitentials, it seems clear that in practice they
were eliminated from official ecclesiastical legislative documents.

NINTH-CENTURY PENITENTIALS IN THE TRADITIONAL STYLE

It would be incorrect to conclude from the preceding remarks that
penitentials written in the style of those examined in the first chapter
disappeared from the scene in the ninth century. First of all, there is
considerable evidence that the older penitentials continued to be
copied in the ninth century, an indication of their continued use. In
fact, as Kottje points out, the oldest manuscripts we have of the Irish
penitentials of Columbanus and Cummean date from the second half of

the ninth century.[29] The *Penitential of Vinnian* and the *Capitula iudiciorum* are found in a St Gall manuscript from the second quarter of the ninth century, and the oldest manuscript containing the penitentials of Bede and Egbert dates from the first third of the century.[30] Furthermore, several new penitentials written in the traditional style date from the ninth century. It is clear that the conciliar censures succeeded neither in eliminating the older penitentials nor in hindering the creation of new ones written on the model of the former. The following penitentials dating from this period are worthy of note: *St Hubert Penitential* (S 2.331–9), *Penitential of Pseudo-Gregory* (W 535–47), *Penitential of Pseudo-Theodore* (W 566–622), and the important *Bede-Egbert Double Penitential* (S 2.675–701).[31] The *St Hubert Penitential* and the *Penitential of Pseudo-Theodore* will be examined below. The *Bede-Egbert Double Penitential* will receive some consideration in the discussion in chapter 3 of the penitential sources of Regino of Prüm, and the *Penitential of Pseudo-Gregory* will be dealt with there in the discussion of the sources of the Collection in Nine Books (Vat lat 1349).

Against Wasserschleben, the dating by Schmitz of the *St Hubert Penitential* to the mid-ninth century seems more acceptable because of elements in the work which are derived from early ninth-century councils.[32] The first forty-one chapters closely parallel the canons of the *Burgundian Penitential*, but some new elements have been added to those already found in the penitentials hitherto examined. There is a canon on prostitution, entitled 'De meretricibus' ('Concerning prostitutes'), dealing with a subject which had not been encountered in any of the previous Irish, Anglo-Saxon, or Frankish penitentials. It is addressed to those who frequent prostitutes, not to the women themselves:

If anyone has committed fornication with women who have fornicated with others and have lost their virginity, or with widows, he shall do penance for three years; but if a monk, seven.[33]

In ruling against bestiality, the work distinguishes between those who have sexual relations with unclean animals and those having relations with clean animals. The former receive fifteen years' penance, while the latter receive twelve.[34] In the canon 'De raptu' further support is provided for the claim that sexual relations were not primarily connoted by the term *raptus*. It is clear from this canon that what is at stake is the forcing of a virgin or widow to live with her abductor or with another.[35] The penitential includes a canon against touching the breasts and genitals of girls and women[36] and seems to adapt a canon from the Council of Laodicaea against those who presume to bathe with women.[37] The feasts of the martyrs are added to the times for sexual abstinence of married people,[38] and the penitential takes a strong stand against those who enter a church after intercourse. Even after washing they are to stand in the vestibule of the church, except on Sundays; if they do otherwise, they are to do penance on bread and water for three forty-day periods.[39]

The *Penitential of Pseudo-Theodore* is 'a compendious and orderly ninth-century'[40] penitential which includes a comprehensive treatment of sexual questions. The principal chapters in this regard are:

16 De fornicatione laicorum/Concerning fornication committed by the laity
   (35 canons)
17 De observatione coniugatorum/Concerning the observance of spouses
   (11 canons)
18 De fornicatione clericorum sive sanctimonialium/Concerning fornication committed by clerics or by nuns (20 canons)
19 De adulterio/Concerning adultery (33 canons)
20 De incestuosis/Concerning the incestuous (26 canons)
28 De sodomitis et mollibus et immundis pollutionibus/Concerning sodomists, the effeminate, and unclean pollutions (33 canons)

There is little that is original in this work, but some items are not encountered in the penitentials previously surveyed. The use of an instrument (*machina*) by nuns for sexual activity has already been encountered in the *Penitential of Bede* (3.24; W 223). Using another term, the *Penitential of Pseudo-Theodore* censures the use of an instrument (*molimen*) by a woman acting either alone or with another woman.[41] A layman having sexual relations with a prostitute is to do penance for four years, and the woman is to do the same penance 'because the Christian religion condemns fornication in both sexes for the same reason.'[42] A confessional problem is solved in regard to a layman who has sexual relations with so many women that he loses count – he is to perform a ten-year penance, with four of these years on bread and water.[43] (It should, perhaps, be noted that years of penance on bread and water meant that during those years, on certain days of the week, usually Wednesdays and Fridays, the person was to have only bread and water.) A girl who has sexual relations in her parents' house is to do penance for three years.[44] Finally, several additions are made to the times when sexual abstinence is required of married people. They are to abstain for one day *after* communion, for forty days after Pentecost, and during the feasts of the saints. The feast days are not further specified.[45]

The eighteenth chapter is a more developed treatment of the sexual offences of the clergy than we have seen and is marked by the highly stylized graded penances according to rank characteristic of the canonical parts of the *Capitula iudiciorum*. The following chapter on adultery draws on various sources but depends primarily on the *Canons of Theodore*. The chapter on incest includes canons both on sexual incest and on marital incest from various penitential and non-penitential sources. It has already been noted that the *Penitential of Pseudo-Theodore* uses the term *mollis* in the context of masturbation.[46]

The *St Hubert Penitential* and the *Penitential of Pseudo-Theodore* are only two of the penitentials from the ninth century which were written in the style of the older penitentials. Not only were they written in that style, but they obtained most of their contents from those earlier manuals. Certainly, most of the canons which deal with sexual matters in these two works are drawn freely from previous penitentials, an indication that the older handbooks were accessible and were per- ceived to be sufficiently serviceable to be incorporated into the contemporary penitentials. In fact, the ninth-century works add very little to the fund of canons dealing with sexual offences. However, although the *St Hubert Penitential* and the *Penitential of Pseudo-Theodore* indeed witness to the persistence of the older penitential tradition, they were not the only kind of penitential compiled at the time. A new form of penitential literature also appeared which attempted to make up for the weaknesses condemned in the earlier penitentials, particularly for the lack of authoritative support for their prescriptions.

PENITENTIALS IN A NEW KEY

If the regulative efforts of the ninth century have anything in common, it is their desire to support rules and regulations with traditional conciliar and papal authority. Evidence for this is available at every turn, from the popularity of the *Dionysio-Hadriana* and *Hispana* collections, the structure of the ninth-century councils, and the work of Ansegisus, to the Pseudo-Isidorian falsifications.[47]

Particular mention should be made of the extremely influential collection of canons called the *Dacheriana* (circa 800 AD). It was one of the central instruments of the Carolingian reform of the early ninth century, and its influence continued to be felt down to the Gregorian reform at the end of the eleventh century.[48] The first book, which is consecrated to penance and confession, deals with the traditional categories of sin, including several kinds of sexual offence. While the elegant preface says nothing explicit against the penitentials, the sources for the proscriptions of sexual sins are all papal decretals and conciliar enactments as found in the *Dionysio-Hadriana* or *Hispana* collections.[49] The rubric of the fifteenth canon of the Council of Ancyra which is included in the *Dacheriana* (1.53) follows the rubric of the *Isidori antiqua* used by Theodulf of Orleans to cover offences of homosexuality, bestiality, and incest.

A manuscript of the Vatican Library (Vat lat 1347) contains a peculiar form of a collection in four books sometimes called the *Quadripartitus* or *Collectio vaticana*, dating from about the middle of the ninth century.[50] The *Dacheriana* constitutes the first three books; the fourth purports to be written in response to a request for a brief and succinct collection of authorities to be used for moral instruction (fol 144r). The material is claimed to be taken 'from the books and institutions of the sacred canons and orthodox fathers.'[51] In fact, the fourth book does rely predominantly on traditional decretal, conciliar, and patristic sources. However, it does not entirely eliminate the penitentials from its authorities. In its treatment of homicide it appeals to a Roman penitential several times (fols 158r–9v). The section dealing with sexual offences does not explicitly cite a penitential source, but chapter 84 seems to be from the *Bede-Egbert Double Penitential*.[52] Chapter 373 uses Gregory's response to Augustine on nocturnal emission, and the two preceding chapters deal with the same matter in a manner reminiscent of the penitentials, but the texts do not correspond to any of the printed manuals.[53]

Traditional patristic sources were also in vogue at this time, as is evident in the work of Jonas of Orleans, who was perhaps responsible for drafting the canons of the Council of Paris (829 AD), which so severely condemned the penitentials. In the second book of his *De institutione laicali* Jonas discusses the life of the married. The first eighteen chapters provide a virtual manual on marital sexual life, drawn from a rich store of patristic sources and covering the same ground as the traditional penitentials but without any reference or allusion to them.[54] In fact, Jonas seems to want to re-establish the penitential practice of the ancient Church.[55]

The explicit use of authoritative sources by councils, canonical collections, and monographs such as that of Jonas of Orleans indicates a method which is not a prominent feature of the earlier penitentials. The scarcity of such sources in the penitential canons has already been noted. However, this should not suggest that these older penitentials were written in disregard of tradition. The intention of their authors or compilers was certainly to be faithful to the ancient statutes of the Fathers. The following from the prologue of the *Penitential of Egbert* is representative:

The holy apostles, then the holy Fathers and saint Punifius [Paphnutius?], then the canons of the holy Fathers, then various others such as Jerome, Augustine, Gregory, and Theodore make up this arrangement of sayings.[56]

Many of the early penitentials make some such claim to reflect traditional teaching and ancient authority.[57]

Anyone wanting to write a practical penitential manual in the new spirit of the ninth century would be faced with the task of finding acknowledged authorities to support the treatment of such diverse sexual activities as masturbation and sexual incest. Frequently, there simply are no conciliar or papal authorities to support provisions on such matters. Consequently, authors who wanted to write penitentials in a new key had a number of options available to them. They could borrow from previous penitential materials (with or without attribution); they could omit matters not supported by recognized authorities; they could falsely attribute traditional penitential material to more authoritative sources; they could create their own penitential prescriptions; or they could attempt to authorize specific traditional penitentials by singling them out for special mention. Most of the authors and canonical collectors of the next few hundred years availed themselves of one or more of these options.

Halitgar of Cambrai and Hrabanus Maurus wrote penitential works in the new key, each claiming to have written his work in response to requests for a compendious collection of authoritative sources. Each demonstrates a different approach to previous penitential materials on sexual questions.

Halitgar of Cambrai

Sometime between 817 and 830, in response to a request made to him
by Ebbo of Reims, Halitgar of Cambrai composed a work in five books
entitled *De vitiis et virtutibus et de ordine poenitentium,* to which he added
a sixth book.[58] The whole work is prefaced by a discussion of the utility
of penance. The first two books are an anthology of statements on the
vices, on their remedies, and on the virtues, drawn largely from
Gregory the Great and Julianus Pomerius (cited as Prosper of Aqui-
taine). The third book is a general discussion of penance, and the next
two deal with the penances of the laity and the clergy respectively.

The fourth book has a section entitled 'De luxuria' (chapters 7–24;
S 2.280–4) which deals with sexual questions pertaining to the laity. With
one exception, all of the provisions in this section are based either on
previous conciliar enactments or on papal decretals.The result is a
rather impoverished treatment of sexual matters, touching on such
subjects as adultery, concubinage, homosexuality, and bestiality. The
exception is an excerpt from the *Canons of Theodore* on the times for
sexual abstinence.[59]

The fifth book deals with clerical offences, primarily by reiterating
the traditional rules of celibacy and continence. None of the chapters
borrows material from the penitentials, and none touches on the broad
areas of clerical sexual behaviour which were treated in the penitentials. The only departure in this book from the authoritative treatment
of clerical celibacy is a text which reproduces Gregory's ninth reply to
Augustine of Canterbury on the question of seminal pollution.[60]

In books 3 to 5 Halitgar provides little material on sexual matters
which would be of much assistance in dissipating the confusion and
inconsistencies of which Ebbo had spoken in his request.[61] What is
there is well supported by authority, but what is not there would
occasion even more uncertainty. Halitgar remedies this lack in his sixth
book, which contains at least some provision for most of the categories
encountered in the penitentials. He himself seems to be aware of the
inadequacies of the first five books when he says, 'if perchance those
decisions presented seem to anyone superfluous, or if he is entirely
unable to find there what he requires respecting the offences of
individuals, he may perhaps find explained, in this final summary, at
least the misdeeds of all.' These words are introduced by the remark,
'We add to our collection of excerpts another Roman penitential which

we took from a bookcase of the Roman Church, but we do not know who compiled it.'[62] The purpose of the sixth book is even more clearly stated at the end of the general preface: 'A sixth book on penance is placed here which is not the result of making excerpts but was taken from a bookcase of the Roman Church. It contains many different items which are not found in the canons.'[63] With these remarks Halitgar was able to distance himself from the composition of what is in truth a traditional type of penitential depending on older penitential sources and to give to his sixth book the authority which would come from its association with the Roman Church. In reality the prescriptions on sexual matters are taken from previous penitentials, many from the *Penitential of Columbanus*.

The heterosexual life of the married was previously discussed under the following rubrics: adultery, times of sexual abstinence, proper form of sexual intercourse, incest, aphrodisiacs, sterility and impotence, and contraception. Halitgar's penitential has canons concerning only two aspects of heterosexual married life, against a cleric's committing adultery with another's wife or fiancée and against those who practise magic 'pro amore.'[64] Several cases of illicit heterosexual intercourse are also mentioned: relations with widows or young girls[65]; relations between male and female virgins, who must do penance for a year before being allowed to marry[66]; and bishops, priests, and deacons committing natural fornication.[67]

Homosexuality is dealt with in two canons.[68] No reference is made to the Council of Ancyra in this regard, but such a reference is included in a previous book.[69] The first mention of bestiality is in a canon borrowed from Columbanus, where it appears together with a reference to masturbation. The base penance for both in Halitgar is three years and is the same for those with orders or a vow.[70] Another canon to treat of bestiality is also from Columbanus and seems to be directed to the laity (in Columbanus it is explicitly addressed to the laity); it provides for a year's penance for a married man, half a year for an unmarried man.[71] The final mention incorporates a version of the Council of Ancyra, with its severe penances.[72]

One might assume that the long excerpt from Gregory's replies to Augustine in the fifth book explains the absence in the penitential of any mention of seminal pollution.[73] By citing the complete reply of Gregory and not just the short excerpt we find in the *Merseburg Penitential* (90; S 2.365), Halitgar provides principles for judging cases of pollution and so avoids the need of cataloguing the numerous variations found in previous penitentials.[74] However, another explanation for the omission of canons dealing with pollution might be the absence of such material from the *Penitential of Columbanus*.

The complete work of Halitgar achieves a fine balance between the desire to ground prescriptions in authoritative sources and the exigencies of having to deal with the details of sexual behaviour not covered by such authorities. In the latter case Halitgar had recourse to the older penitentials, which offered an ample treatment of sexual questions. But it must also be recognized that his penitential borrowed the older materials from traditional sources without acknowledgment. In fact, Halitgar's claim that he had found the penitential in a bookcase of the Roman Church would have conferred an authority on it which it would not otherwise have had. While avoiding the risk of issuing a work similar to the type already condemned at Châlons (813 AD), Halitgar published the same type of material under the implicit blessing of Roman sanction.

Hrabanus Maurus

Hrabanus Maurus, abbot of Fulda (822–42 AD) and archbishop of Mainz (847–56 AD), wrote several works with sexual components bearing on penitential discipline.[75] He compiled two penitentials in response to requests similar to the request made of Halitgar by Ebbo for a compendious handbook of authoritative sources to aid in the administration of penance.[76] The *Paenitentiale ad Otgarium* is a collection in forty chapters which bears on some areas of sexual morality but which lacks the detail of the earlier penitentials. The second chapter on incest is restricted to the relationships forbidden for marriage; the third chapter, entitled 'Of those who commit adultery,' is primarily concerned with the question of remarriage after separation. Other chapters deal with the unfaithfulness of vowed virgins (chapters 4–5), homosexuality and bestiality (chapter 6 = Council of Ancyra, canons 16–17), concubinage (chapters 8 and 10), and clerical continence (chapter 29). In each case the chapter includes one or more conciliar or decretal source. None of the canons from earlier penitentials is incorporated into the work.

While surprise at the absence of penitential material in a work whose avowed aim was to provide a compendium of canonical sources is

perhaps unjustified, it is difficult to see how a work such as the
Paenitentiale ad Otgarium could be a practical tool to give to someone,
'that you might have ready at hand material from the opinions of the
fathers to enable you to judge the simple and uninstructed souls of the
new peoples of whom you just spoke.'[77] The work might have some
value in helping to demonstrate to the people and clergy alike that the
condemnations of certain sexual offences were not based on the whims
of ecclesiastics but on ancient traditions. It would have little use
beyond this.[78]

The *Paenitentiale ad Heribaldum* (853 AD), which was written some
years after the work sent to Otgar, has a different character from its
predecessor, and the circumstances of its composition were different.
Heribald of Auxerre had apparently written to Hrabanus requesting
answers to specific questions regarding homicide, fornication and
adultery, and the implications for ecclesiastics of illicit sexual relations
engaged in before they became ecclesiastics or afterwards. The main
body of the work largely reproduces the materials from the earlier
penitential, with some modifications. However, there are a few
significant differences. The first is in the preface, which counsels
Heribald to consult the Bible, where he will find answers to many of
his questions in both the Old and New Testaments. To illustrate his
point Hrabanus first gives a long quotation from Leviticus which covers
a wide range of sexual offences.[79] This is followed by a selection from
St Paul to the Galatians.[80]

Although the remainder of the work is virtually identical with the
Paenitentiale ad Otgarium, there is some indication that Hrabanus was
not unfamiliar with the penitential literature, since on a few occasions
he has recourse to it for replies to specific questions. Hrabanus takes
up the question of women who mix their menstrual blood in food or
drink and give it to their husbands to consume and the question of a
woman who drinks her husband's semen. He does not reply to the
particular questions but quotes 'the constitutions of Theodore, archbishop of the English people.'[81] This is the only explicit citation of
Theodore by Hrabanus in this work, but note that he refers to
'constitutions' and not to a penitential.[82] He quotes Theodore without
acknowledgment on two other occasions in this penitential. Chapter
25, entitled 'Of women who fornicate with each other or of those who
mix the semen of their husbands in food or drink,' provides penances
for lesbianism, for using semen as an aphrodisiac, and for female

masturbation. The chapter is a compilation of three canons from the *Canons of Theodore* but is attributed to the Council of Ancyra. The attribution seems to originate with Hrabanus himself.[83] In another chapter Hrabanus deals with the question of whether the woman or man may marry again if, after marriage, they discover they are unable to have sexual intercourse. After claiming no authority on the matter, he says, 'but we reply according to the statutes of certain persons,' and then reproduces Theodore's canon on impotence.[84]

On one occasion as abbot of Fulda (842 AD) and on another shortly before being made archbishop of Mainz (847 AD), Hrabanus Maurus was asked by Regimbald, a suffragan bishop of Mainz, to answer several questions dealing with moral cases and Church discipline. In his replies Hrabanus handles sexual questions in much the same way as in his *Paenitentiale ad Heribaldum*, which was written some years after the second response to Regimbald. In his first request Regimbald asked what was to be done with a father and son, or two brothers, or an uncle and nephew who had had sexual relations with the same woman. In reply Hrabanus first appeals to the Bible with an extended quotation from Leviticus.[85] After a brief discussion of the need for discretion in giving penance, Hrabanus responds to the specific question asked of him by referring to the second canon of the Council of Neocaesaraea. He again counsels moderation in the imposition of penance, adding, 'Therefore, Theodore judged that he who commits incest must do penance for twelve years.'[86] In none of his canons which deal either with relations of consanguinity or with sexual relations between blood relatives does Theodore impose a penance of twelve years, nor does he have a canon which condemns incest in general. However, in the section taken from Theodore, the *Tripartite of St Gall* does impose a penance of twelve years for sexual relations with one's mother.[87] Finally, Hrabanus refers to the diversity of penances found in other penitentials, without, however, censuring them.[88]

In another set of responses addressed to Regimbald, Hrabanus deals with the problem of bestiality and of what to do with the animals involved.[89] After quoting the Levitical condemnation of bestiality,[90] he cites the sixteenth canon of the Council of Ancyra. While he seems to be satisfied with the prescription of Leviticus which demands that the animals be killed, he does not insist that calves born of cows which had been used in this manner be denied to human use. It is interesting that in this context Hrabanus does not cite the clear regulation of Theodore, which provides for the killing of the animal sexually used by men but not for the killing of the offspring.[91]

The four works of Hrabanus Maurus which we have examined all deal with various questions of sexual morality. Each shows a marked preference for biblical and traditional authorities, which are used to censure different forms of illicit sexual behaviour, and each seems designedly to avoid the use of traditional penitential material. Although familiar with Theodore, Hrabanus chose to use him very sparingly, acknowledging authorship once, quoting him anonymously, bringing him in under an attribution to the Council of Ancyra, and finally naming Theodore in regard to a general reference to incest.[92] It would seem that in regard to the practice of penance and the censure of sexual misdeeds, the work of Halitgar, which culminates in a practically oriented penitential in the traditional style, would be more serviceable than the two penitentials of Hrabanus Maurus, which are no more than anthologies of conciliar and decretal sources.

This brief survey of the ninth century indicates a radical change from the previous centuries in the status of the penitentials. The positive attitude reflected in the recommendations that were common early in the century to possess and to be familiar with a penitential gave way to the condemnations of 813 and 829. An official ecclesiastical silence seems to have descended on the penitentials, evidenced by their absence from most canonical collections, conciliar canons, and diocesan statutes written after 829. A huge body of literature was built up with little influence from the penitential tradition. However, there were parallel undertakings that apparently thrived as well, evidenced in the surviving manuscripts of old penitentials copied in the ninth century, in the creation of contemporary penitentials in the traditional style, and in the works of Halitgar of Cambrai and Hrabanus Maurus, who compiled new forms of penitential literature.

In terms of the specific sexual issues that would inevitably arise in the context of private penance, however, no real substitute was created to meet these needs. Theodulf of Orleans clearly wrote his Second Diocesan Statute on the model of the traditional penitentials. Halitgar of Cambrai, recognizing that the traditional authoritative sources were inadequate, added a traditional penitential to his five-book anthology of such sources, and even Hrabanus Maurus had recourse to the penitential materials of Theodore for topics such as lesbianism, masturbation, incest, and bestiality.

It seems to me that, taken as a whole, the ninth century illustrates the continued role of the penitentials in transmitting a comprehensive code of sexual morality. However, a tension existed between the tendency of official literature quite consciously to steer away from these manuals and their unofficial use in the context of hearing confessions. The question now is how that tension was resolved and to what degree the penitentials could in succeeding centuries be assimilated into the types of literature which had eliminated them in the ninth century. Did the penitentials assume an acknowledged role in diocesan statutes, and did they find a place within the collections of canon law which would proliferate in the tenth and eleventh centuries? It is these questions which will be taken up in the next chapter.

3
Penitential Texts in Canonical Collections after 906

By the beginning of the tenth century the creative phase of penitential composition or compilation was drawing to a close. Developing the same time, however, were two trends which would open up a new phase in the history of the penitentials. First, there seems to have been a renewed willingness and perhaps a felt need to employ the penitentials in the pastoral ministry. Further, this century marked the beginnings of a long period, culminating in the *Decretum* of Gratian, during which numerous canonical collections were compiled. The earlier received collections such as those of Cresconius, the *Dionysio-Hadriana*, the *Hispana*, and the *Dacheriana* were largely restricted to the use of conciliar and papal decretal sources and had by the tenth century acquired a certain universal approbation in the Latin Church. The new collections had more local appeal and were frequently compiled to meet the need for conciseness, order, and system or the needs of particular reforming movements. Generally, they share the feature of being what could be termed 'mixed collections' – that is, they were open to the incorporation of texts which were not from councils or papal letters. Increasingly one encounters texts from the Fathers and other ecclesiastical writers, from Roman law, from the Carolingian capitularies, and from the Pseudo-Isidorian writings. Clearly, the compilers of these collections considered the sources of church order to spring from a more heterogeneous pool than had the compilers of the earlier pure collections.

The penitentials must be added to this pool of sources, and it is the purpose of this chapter to demonstrate the extent to which penitential canons furnished textual support to the collections for their regulations concerning sexual behaviour. The incorporation of these canons into canonical collections signals a new stage in the contribution made by these manuals to the life of the church. They would no longer simply be handbooks for priest-confessors, standing alongside but unrelated to other more authoritative sources. Mention has already been made of the existence of penitentials in manuscripts which also contain collections of ecclesiastical law, such as the *Dionysio-Hadriana* and the *Vetus Gallica*. The work of Halitgar of Cambrai marks a further stage, in which a penitential is one component of the whole composition. This particular approach to penitential literature will be repeated in more or less the same fashion by several of the collections examined below, but we do not find in them the sharp division between traditional canonical sources and penitential sources which is present in Halitgar. Penitential canons are found throughout these later collections and seem to assume a quasi-juridical status as sources of canonical regulations, incorporated into the collections along with more traditional sources.

The history of the contribution of penitentials to the developing canon law has not yet been written. The following analysis may throw some light on what will prove to be a most complex story. One of the complicating factors is the way in which the penitential canons were incorporated into the collections of canon law. Sometimes they are straightforwardly used and cited as coming from a penitential. In such cases no problem of identification arises. However, sometimes a penitential canon enters a collection under a false, non-penitential attribution, or what began in one collection as a penitential citation becomes changed in a later collection. An example of the latter is illustrative. Regino of Prüm has a chapter on fornication bearing the inscription 'Ex eodem' (2.135), which probably refers back to the inscription 'Ex poenitentiali' (2.133). Both texts seem to be from the *Bede-Egbert Double Penitential*.[1] The text on fornication (2.135) is taken up by Burchard of Worms but the inscription is changed to 'Ex concilio Meldensi,' and this inscription is retained by Ivo of Chartres and the *Polycarpus*.[2] I havè tried to identify such mis-attribution, but I have no doubt that many have been missed. The diocesan statutes of Theodulf of Orleans have been included among what will count as penitential sources, as have several much-quoted texts from the *Paenitentiale ad Heribaldum* of Hrabanus Maurus.

The canonical collections themselves contributed to the penitential tradition in at least three significant ways. Sometimes they modified the penitential canons, particularly in regard to the penances. In at least one case, that of Burchard of Worms (*Decretum* 19.5), a whole new penitential tradition is begun which had considerable influence in its own right.

Finally, there emerged in the tradition of the collections a number of apocryphal texts, some of which are structured along the lines of penitential canons and seem designed to serve a penitential purpose. These apocrypha have not been considered in the following analysis; they deserve separate treatment along the lines of L. Machielsen's discussion of the spurious texts attributed to Gregory the Great.[3]

The present chapter will trace out the transmission of penitential canons dealing with sexual subjects in a representative selection of canonical collections, from Regino of Prüm in the tenth century to Gratian in the twelfth. The collections have been chosen because they seem to have been important in their own right, or because of their influence on subsequent collections, or because they are representative of a significant penitential tradition. The following collections will be analysed in full: the *Libri duo de synodalibus causis et disciplinis ecclesiasticis* of Regino of Prüm; the Collection in Nine Books (Vat lat 1349); the *Decretum* of Burchard of Worms; the Collection in Five Books (Vat lat 1339); the *Collectio canonum* of Anselm of Lucca; and the *Decretum* of Ivo of Chartres. A concluding reference will be made to the *Decretum* of Gratian, without pretending to a complete analysis.

It is difficult to determine the most valuable and serviceable method of treatment. I have decided to deal with the collections in chronological order. For readers interested in a general account of the presence of penitential material in these collections, I have included a brief discussion of each work as a whole and a description of the use each makes of penitential canons dealing with sexual behaviour. These discussions will be followed by the catalogues of texts enumerated for each of the collections.

Needless to say, no attempt has been made to provide an exhaustive analysis of the edited collections or manuscripts which are used below. In recent years there has developed great interest in the study and editing of pre-Gratian collections. The examination of the use that these collections make of penitential canons dealing with sexual behaviour can at best represent a limited contribution to this ongoing study. Where appropriate, recent editions have been used and contemporary studies have been noted. However, the editorial state of the collections that are the object of our study makes detailed textual observations pointless.

Before beginning, a word should be said about some collections which have been examined but have been omitted from the following discussion.

The Collection in Two Books, Collection in Seventy-four Titles, and Collection of Deusdedit were compiled during the reform period of the last half of the eleventh century.[4] In none of these works is there any trace of penitential texts dealing with sexual matters. This may be an indication of the assumed opposition to the penitentials which is believed to characterize the Gregorian reformers and which is dramatically illustrated in Peter Damian's *Book of Gomorrah*.[5] However, aside from the remarks of Damian there seems to have been no general opposition to these manuals.[6] A careful examination of these three collections reveals that their scope does not embrace penance, confession, or the general pastoral care of the people. Consequently, there was little reason for the incorporation of penitential canons. Their purpose, which was to reinforce the centralizing tendencies of the Gregorian reform, led them to focus on different kinds of texts altogether.[7] As we shall see, in collections at this time whose scope did embrace penance, there is evidence of a willingness – in Anselm of Lucca and Ivo of Chartres, for example – to use some penitential material at least in a limited way.

The *Collectio Barberiniana* belongs to the group of collections which used Burchard and which is represented in our analysis by Ivo of Chartres.[8] Several chapters of the *Barberiniana* retain Burchard's penitential inscriptions:

[LIII]–XL Ex poenitentiali romano = Burchard 17.40 (PL 140.927A)
XLI Ex poenitentiali Theodori = Burchard 17.41 (PL 140.927C)
[LIV]–XLII Ex poenitentiali Bedae = Burchard 17.42 (PL 140.927D)
[LV]–XLIII Ex poenitentiali romano = Burchard 17.43 (PL 140.928A)

The *Liber de vita christiana* of Bonizo of Sutri has not been included among the collections chosen for detailed analysis.[9] However, there are in this work several penitential-like canons treating sexual matters. The difficulty is in identifying their sources, since the chapters do not correspond to any known penitential. The editor is usually satisfied to note, 'aus einem unbekannten Poenitentiale,' but it seems more likely that the chapters in question represent a reworking by Bonizo of generally available penitential canons.

The *Polycarpus* has been examined in the manuscript Paris BN lat 3881. There are in this work several of the apocryphal texts noted above.[10] Two consecutive chapters on spiritual incest (fol 105v) seem to be taken from Bonizo of Sutri (10.46, 47; Perels 321–2). There are very few explicit citations of penitential canons on sexual subjects, however:

Bk 6, tit 7 (fol 126v) 'Ex penitentiali Theodori' = cf Burch 19.141 (PL 140.1010C)
Bk 6, tit 8 (fol 134r) 'Ex penitentiali Romano' = cf Burch 17.38 (PL 140.926A)[11]

In the same manuscript (fols 191r–230r) there is the theological *Book of Sentences of Master A.* No explicit citations of penitential canons dealing with sexual behaviour were found therein.[12]

There is a canonical collection in the manuscript Milan Bibliotheca Ambrosiana, Cod I 145 inf, dated by its editor to about the middle of the twelfth century.[13] The compiler of this collection has incorporated virtually the whole of the penitential edited by Schmitz as *Poenitentiale Valicellanum* I (S 1.239–339). Given so straightforward a borrowing, I have not felt it necessary to devote space to the analysis of the penitential sources of this collection. However, it is important to note such a large-scale use of penitential material at a time when the era of the penitentials was practically at an end.[14] It should be recalled that this Vallicellian manual reflects an ancient penitential tradition that was first brought together in the late-eighth-century *Merseburg Penitential.* One cannot help wondering whether the Milan collection's ample employment of such a block of penitential canons is an aberration from the contemporary waning influence of penitential texts or a harbinger of a growing consciousness that something resembling the penitentials was needed – a need that would soon be filled by the more sophisticated *summae confessorum.*

The six canonical collections to be surveyed fall into two classes, each class representing different penitential traditions. The collections of Regino, Burchard, and Ivo of Chartres comprise one class; the Collection in Nine Books, the Collection in Five Books, and Anselm of Lucca comprise another class. Regino's collection depends almost entirely on the *Bede-Egbert Double Penitential,* and most of Regino is incorporated by Burchard into his *Decretum.* In addition, Burchard drew on the *Excarpsus of Cummean* and a version of the Bede-Egbert materials resembling the edition of Albers with the variants from Vat Pal lat 294. Ivo of Chartres (*Decretum*) drew all of the penitential canons dealing with sexual behaviour from Burchard, with the exception of a chapter comprised of canons from the *Penitential of Fulbert of Chartres.*

The other class of canonical collections depends on the *Capitula iudiciorum* and the *Penitential of Pseudo-Gregory.* Anselm of Lucca seems to depend directly on the former penitential. The Collection in Nine Books

Collections of Regino, Burchard, Ivo of Chartres

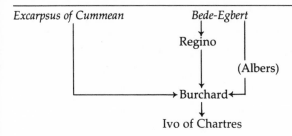

Collection in Nine Books, Collection in Five Books, Anselm of Lucca

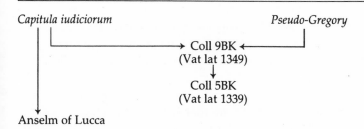

incorporates virtually all the canons dealing with sexual behaviour from both penitentials, and it is the primary source for the penitential canons of the Collection in Five Books.

The figures below outline the relationships of the two classes of canonical collection to the penitentials on which they predominantly depend. The canons dealing with sexual behaviour which were incorporated into each of these collections are listed in tabular form at the end of this chapter. What follows is a general description of the individual collections themselves and a brief account of their use of penitential sources.

Regino of Prüm

At the behest of Rathbod of Trier, Regino of Prüm compiled circa 906 AD the two books of his *De synodalibus causis et disciplinis ecclesiasticis*, the first dealing with matters clerical and ecclesiastical, the second dealing with seculars and the laity.[15] The work was written for bishops and their delegates as a handbook to guide them in making diocesan visitations.[16] In addition to using numerous penitential canons for his treatment of sexual behaviour, Regino is one of the first authors since the condemnations of the ninth century to recommend explicitly the use of penitential manuals. He rules that when the priest invites the people to confession on Ash Wednesday, he should not enjoin a penance on them arbitrarily but according to what is written in a penitential:

[Inquire] whether on the Wednesday before Lent he invites the people under his charge to confession, and whether he enjoins penance on them according to the nature of the fault, not arbitrarily but in accord with what is written in a penitential.[17]

Later in the same interrogatory Regino recommends that, when inquiring into the ministry of his priests, the bishop find out whether they have a penitential, and he stipulates that it be one of three, the Roman, the one compiled by Theodore, or the one compiled by Bede.

I believe that Regino is recommending one of three penitentials, although it is not at all certain that this is the import of his text: 'Si habeat poenitentialem Romanum vel a Theodoro episcopo aut a venerabili Beda editum, ut secundum quod ibi scriptum est, aut interroget confitentem, aut confesso modum poenitentiae imponat.'[18] This could be translated, 'If he have a Roman penitential, either the one put forth by Bishop Theodore or that by the Venerable Bede, so that according to what is there written he may either question the confessant or when he has confessed lay upon him the measure of penance,' as McNeill and Gamer do,[19] or, 'If he have a Roman penitential, or one put forth by Bishop Theodore, or by the Venerable Bede ... ' In the course of his work Regino never suggests a Roman penitential as one of his sources. His usual inscription is 'Ex poenitentiali.'[20] On a few occasions he departs from this usage, in one case suggesting a penitential by Theodore or Bede ('Ex Theodori Archiepiscopi vel Bedae presbyteri poenitentiali'), in another case suggesting a Roman penitential by Theodore and Bede ('Ex poenitentiali Romano Theodori episcopi et Bedae presbyteri').[21]

Whatever the correct translation of Regino's interrogatory (question 96), there is no doubt that his principal source is a version of the *Bede-Egbert Double Penitential*. This is a large composite work made up of the prologues to the individual penitentials attributed to Bede and Egbert, a ritual for penitential services, an interrogatory of thirty-five questions, confessional prayers, table of chapters, and penitential canons largely drawn from Bede and Egbert.[22] Most of the penitential prescriptions dealing with sexual matters are taken from this penitential.

Although the *De synodalibus causis* is not a penitential, in several places in the work Regino groups together items of practical pastoral concern relating to confession and penitential practice. The first book opens with an interrogatory of ninety-five questions meant to aid the bishop or his delegates in ascertaining the condition of parochial units. It is among these questions that reference is made to the possession of a penitential. Later in the same book there is a long section on confession and penance, from chapter 292 ('De confessione et poenitentia') to chapter 328 ('Quales esse debeamus erga impoenitentes'), which is a virtual penitential. A ritual for giving penance (chapter 304, 'Ordo ad dandam poenitentiam') contains another interrogatory which is dependent on the interrogatory found at the beginning of the *Bede-Egbert Double Penitential*.[23] No reference is made to authorities in this interrogatory, but the rubric of the chapter refers to a preceding source ('Unde supra'), which probably is the penitential inscription to chapter 301 ('Item de suscipienda confessione. Ex Theodori archiepiscopi vel Bedae presbyteri poenitentiali').

The second book begins with an interrogatory of eighty-nine questions to be addressed to the laity.[24] This interrogatory is simply a list of questions, concluding with the remark, 'These chapters which we have noted in order ought to be corroborated by canonical decrees.'[25] It is worthy of note that acknowledged penitential sources are included among the corroborating decrees. The supporting canons on sexual matters begin at chapter 98 under the general heading 'Abhinc de adulteriis et fornicationibus' and run to chapter 265 (Wasserschleben 251–317). Chapter 247 is entitled 'De diversarum personarum fornicatione. Ex poenitentiali Romano Theodori episcopi et Bedae presbteri.' Regino's treatment of sexual questions is not restricted to his use of the penitentials, but a great many of his chapters, particularly in the sections noted above, depend almost exclusively on material borrowed from them.

Most of the penitential canons are from the *Bede-Egbert Double Penitential* and they cover the whole range of sexual offences. Interestingly, in the first confessional interrogatory (1.304) seven of the twelve questions are inquiries as to whether the proper times for sexual abstinence have been observed. The same subject is dealt with in five other chapters (1.338–41, 2.250). I include among these the citation from the *Hibernensis* (46.11). Regino (2.130–2) quotes from the Second Diocesan Statute of Theodulf of Orleans on adultery and fornication, but he attributes the texts not to Theodulf but to a Council of Nantes. Finally, three texts are taken from the *Paenitentiale ad Heribaldum* of Hrabanus Maurus, but only one of them is attributed to this penitential. A long canon on incest (Regino 2.200) retains the misattribution to a Mainz council given by Hrabanus, and Regino (2.370) perpetuates the misattribution to the

Council of Ancyra of Theodore's canon on lesbianism. However, aside from these chapters, Regino is a generally faithful and straightforward reporter, introducing few modifications into his penitential sources.

Collection in Nine Books (Cod Vat lat 1349)

The Collection in Nine Books is found in one copy, Vat lat 1349, dated by Fournier to about 920 AD and believed to be Italian in origin.[26] The eighth book ('On the utility of penance') provides texts dealing with penance and confession in general. This book (Vat lat 1349, fols 193rb–196ra) concludes with a series of penitential texts of a prefatory nature found in several penitential documents, such as the *Excarpsus of Cummean*, the *Reims Penitential*, Halitgar 6, and the *Bede-Egbert Double Penitential*. These concluding canons of the eighth book serve as an introduction to the ninth, which provides penances for different classes of offences. Most of the penances for sexual offences found in the ninth book are taken from the *Capitula iudiciorum* and the *Penitential of Pseudo-Gregory*. A great deal of the material from the ninth book is transcribed by Schmitz in the course of his edition of the *Capitula iudiciorum* (S 2.218–51).

The *Penitential of Pseudo-Gregory* (W 535–47) is a substantial work in thirty-three chapters written in the ninth century, sometime after 830. Wasserschleben (W 85) suggests that it may be part of the pseudo-Isidorian falsification enterprise which went on in the middle of the century, since the penitential bears a false attribution to Pope Gregory III (731–41 AD). To the works noted by Wasserschleben which used this penitential (either immediately or derivatively) must be added the Collection in Nine Books, which reproduces almost the whole of the *Pseudo-Gregory*. Unfortunately, little research has been done on this penitential.[27]

The section of the ninth book of the Collection in Nine Books which is of concern here is the material in chapters 13 to 56 (fols 198va–206rb). It seems to me that the framework for the first part of this book is provided by the *Capitula iudiciorum*, which the compiler progressively works through, adding passages from the *Penitential of Pseudo-Gregory* and from non-penitential sources.[28] The section dealing with sexual offences begins with four chapters from the *Pseudo-Gregory* and then at chapter 18 takes up the structure provided by the *Capitula iudiciorum*, chapters 7 to 10. Several very long chapters (18, 22, 36) deal with a wide range of types of sexual behaviour which have not been individually identified in the following list of passages; I have simply noted that 'various sexual offences' are mentioned.

The passages from the *Pseudo-Gregory* are readily identifiable from the inscription 'Gregorius,' but the passages from the *Capitula iudiciorum* bear no consistent inscription. The penitential passages in the collection usually correspond with the edited texts of the penitentials which I have used. However, sometimes there is considerable divergence, and on a few occasions there are what seem to be interpolations in the manuscript text that are not found in the edited text. These apparent interpolations have been quoted in my observations.

The article by Fournier referred to at the beginning of these remarks loses a great deal of its value because of the author's use of the chapter numbers assigned by Mai (reproduced in PL 138.397–442). For the material of the ninth book of the Collection in Nine Books, Mai's numeration is frequently inaccurate, and from chapter 6 his numbering corresponds neither to the list of *capitula* in the manuscript at the beginning of the book nor to the numbered chapters throughout the manuscript. In fact, the chapter numbers in the manuscript correspond to the *capitula* numbers, aside from the repetition of XLIII in the list of *capitula* for book 9 (fol 196rb).

Burchard of Worms

Burchard (circa 965–1025 AD) says that he wrote his *Decretum* in response to a request to compile a collection 'from the opinions of the holy Fathers as well as from the canonical writings or from proven examples of penitents' to put order into the confusion and discrepencies which existed in the practices of his diocese.[29] Although in the introductory letter Burchard does not mention the penitentials among his acknowledged sources, he does refer to them in the second book, in a chapter attributed to St Augustine which enjoins that a penitential be among a priest's possessions.[30] Later, in book 19, he expands on which penitentials are to have privileged status:

And for this [he is to use] his penitential which has been drawn up according to the authority of the canons and the just opinions of the three penitentials – those of Bishop Theodore, the Roman pontiffs, and Bede. But while many useful items are found in Bede's penitential, many items are found inserted there by others which square neither with the canons nor with the other penitentials.[31]

In practice, Burchard will cite only what he calls a Roman penitential and the penitentials of Theodore and Bede; that is, Burchard names these penitentials, which does not mean that the material necessarily corresponds to the penitential so named.

The last book of the *Decretum* does not concern us since it is a theological treatise having no bearing on our subject. The nineteenth book, called by Burchard 'Corrector et medicus,'[32] is a penitential in its own right whose long fifth chapter represents a rich and original interrogatory. The first thirty-three chapters of this book are designed to aid the priest in the administration of private penance or confession. The role of these chapters in the *Decretum* is similar to those of the penitential sections of Regino and the eighth and ninth books of the Collection in Nine Books. The long interrogatory of chapter 5, some of whose provisions take up questions unanswered from the interrogatory of the first book, is of primary interest. Questions 1 to 152 apply to men and women in general, and questions 153 to 194 are said to apply especially to women.[33] Although the composition of the questions is original with Burchard, there are a number of expressions which indicate frequently that a penitential text stands behind them.

Like Regino, Burchard usually provides support for the matters dealt with in the interrogatory, either in the previous books or in later chapters of book 19.[34] One of the characteristic features of many of the questions dealing with sexual matters in *Decretum* 19.5 is the detail employed to describe some of the censured sexual acts. One might speculate about the reasons for such detail, but it would be a matter of pure speculation unless one were prepared to investigate the social conditions of Burchard's immediate environment. I suspect that the descriptions resulted from a lack of accepted common nouns to cover different classes of sexual behaviour, such as homosexuality and masturbation, in conjunction with a degree of ignorance among the clergy which demanded that these matters be spelled out.

Of the other eighteen books, some are more relevant to our purposes than others, notably book 1.94 (interrogatory), book 8 ('De viris ac feminis deo dicatis'), book 9 ('De feminis non consecratis'), and book 17 ('De fornicatione').[35]

The penitential sources in Burchard are frequently misnamed, and it would be fair to say that *a priori* none of his inscriptions should be accepted at face value.[36] Many of the penitential texts have been taken by Burchard from Regino; in such cases the penitential sources will not be given in the catalogue of the penitential texts used by Burchard. The reader is asked to refer back to the corresponding passage in Regino.

However, Burchard also seems to have had direct recourse to the *Ex-carpsus of Cummean* and to a form of the double penitential composed of materials from Bede and Egbert as represented in the manuscript Vat Pal lat 294.[37]

Burchard's collection marked a significant stage in the influence that penitential canons dealing with sexual matters had on collections of canon law. The *Decretum* was not simply one collection among many; it tended to dominate the canonical tradition of the eleventh century. Traditional penitential sources received widespread circulation, particularly through the seventeenth book, which deals with virtually every form of sexual offence. Furthermore, Burchard himself added to the penitential treatment of sexual behaviour in the fifth chapter of the nineteenth book, which represents an original composition and which deals with all types of sexual sin.

Aside from the long interrogatory of *Decretum* 19.5, the Migne edition of Burchard's *Decretum* will be used here. Gerard Fransen, who is preparing a new edition of Burchard, claims that the Migne edition is sufficient for work not demanding a minute comparison of texts. However, he does suggest that when attempting to establish a literary dependence of Burchard on previous collections or to establish an influence of Burchard on later collections, one should consult manuscripts.[38] I am not concerned with a minute comparison of texts in this catalogue. My proposals regarding immediate sources and penitential sources for the penitential texts of Burchard are not so much attempts to establish a strict literary dependence of Burchard on these sources as suggestions of highly probable sources. I do not believe that having recourse to manuscripts of Burchard would make a substantial difference in my suggestions. The reader should, however, take Fransen's remarks as precautionary when examining the catalogue of penitential texts used by Burchard.

Collection in Five Books

The Collection in Five Books is found in three manuscripts and is dated to between 1014 and 1023 AD by M. Fornasari, who has edited the first three books.[39] The collection makes a limited use of penitential canons in its second book and a more ample use in the fifth. Contrary to Fornasari, it seems that Fournier's claim that Vat lat 1339 made use of the Collection in Nine Books is the more probable view, as will become apparent in the catalogue.[40] The work is representative of an early eleventh-century Italian collection, showing no influence of Burchard's *Decretum*. In fact, Fournier has shown that some additions to Burchard's *Corrector* were probably taken from the Collection in Five Books, which seems also to have influenced several other canonical collections.[41]

The edition of Fornasari has been used for books 1 to 3 and the manuscript Vat lat 1339 for books 4 and 5. One of the interesting features of this manuscript is the miniatures of the writers used in the collection – for example, Theodorus episcopus (fol 11v), Commeanus (fol 12r), and Beda (fol 12v).[42]

The collection makes an ample use of penitential canons dealing with sexual behaviour. As in the case of earlier collections, the penitential canons stand alone as authorities for the proscription of types of sexual offence not otherwise censured by traditional papal and conciliar authorities. The Collection in Five Books is the last we shall examine which contains penitential canons dealing with virtually every sexual offence.

Anselm of Lucca

Anselm of Lucca (d 1086) was an important figure in the Gregorian reform whose *Collectio canonum* reflects the reforming tendencies of the end of the eleventh century, principally the use of what were considered authentic legal sources and the reinforcement of papal authority.[43] Collections from this period which make no use of penitential texts have been noted already.[44] Fournier points out that Anselm of Lucca is the only author of the Gregorian era who composed a complete canonical collection comprising a separate treatment of penance, the eleventh book of the *Collectio canonum*.[45] Apparently there was some resistance to this treatment of penance, because Anselm's collection circulated in two forms, one containing the eleventh book and one without it.

It is the view of Fournier that Anselm of Lucca is circumspect in his choice of texts for the treatment of penance, staying close to perceived authentic sources.[46] However, Anselm does use penitential texts, and his inclusion in this survey is meant to provide an example of at least a very limited use of texts dealing with sexual behaviour by one closely connected with the Gregorian reform. Fournier is probably correct in suggesting that Anselm used the *Capitula iudiciorum* directly for the penitential prescriptions he incorporated into his collection. If this is so, perhaps a hint of the spirit of the reform is seen in the scrupulous avoidance of texts attributed to 'Iudicium Commeani.'[47] Cummean would not be among the received authorities of the Gregorians.

I have used the manuscript Paris BN lat 12519, which contains the eleventh book, on penance.

Ivo of Chartres

Of the three canonical collections compiled by Ivo of Chartres (circa 1040–1115 AD), the *Decretum* alone will be used to illustrate the incorporation of penitential texts on sexual matters.[48] The *Decretum* is a huge collection of more than three thousand chapters dealing with all facets of ecclesiastical life and moral behaviour. The penitentials make an insignificant contribution to the treatment of sexual mores; nevertheless, one does not encounter an attack on the penitentials in the *Decretum*. In fact, there are indications in the work of Ivo of a positive attitude towards them. He cites a passage which speaks glowingly of Theodore:

Archbishop Theodore and abbot Adrian, a man equally learned, were sent by Pope Vitalian to Britain and nourished many churches of the English with the fruit of ecclesiastical teaching. From this teaching Theodore wrote wonderful judgments for sinners, that is, for how many years anyone would have to do penance for each sin.[49]

He has no trouble using a text which recommends that priests are to have a penitential among their official books.[50] He repeats a rubric of Burchard which directs that penances are to be given according to the statutes of the canons and the penitentials, even though no mention is made of penitentials in the text quoted.[51]

Aside from the short *Penitential of Fulbert of Chartres* which is incorporated into the *Decretum* (15.187; PL 161.897), virtually all of the penitential texts dealing with sexual topics entered the *Decretum* of Ivo through Burchard. Seven chapters are attributed to councils, with all of the inscriptions coming from Burchard except 9.70, where Ivo changed a Mainz reference to a Council of Orleans. One text is attributed to the letters of Gregory the Great (8.178), one to the Capitularies (8.80). The remaining chapters are attributed to the *Penitential of Theodore* by Burchard, whose inscription is retained by Ivo.

Gratian

For purposes of completeness Gratian's incorporation of several penitential canons has been noted. These seem to be the sum of his use of such
sources for sexual matters, but it is possible that I have overlooked some.
If so, they are surely few in number. Gratian's *Decretum* marks the end of
the long period of diverse collections of canon law and the beginning of
a more sophisticated, scientific, and 'authorized' approach. There is
nothing in Gratian which approaches the explicit use of the penitentials
such as is found even in Anselm of Lucca or Ivo of Chartres, to say
nothing of Burchard. As far as I can determine, there are just seven
canons in Gratian which include sexual material from the penitentials.[52]
Because the editor's notes give ample reference to previous canonical
collections in which each canon is found, there is no need to repeat that
information. Unfortunately, the edition fails to indicate Gratian's immediate source. The passages in which Gratian uses penitential texts for
sexual matters are found at the end of this chapter.

From the descriptions that follow of individual texts dealing with sexual
behaviour, it is clear that there was no widespread opposition to the use
of the penitentials in representative canonical collections of the tenth to
the twelfth century.[53] There seems to have been a tendency after the
Collection in Five Books to move away from the older, traditional type of
penitential and to use Burchard (*Decretum* 17 and 19),[54] but we can also
see Anselm of Lucca employing the *Capitula iudiciorum* at the end of the
eleventh century and a collection from Milan incorporating almost the
entire *Vallicellian Penitential* I (S 1.239–342) in the twelfth. On the other
hand, in Ivo of Chartres, the *Polycarpus*, and Gratian, the waning
influence of the penitentials is apparent. It is probable that the exigencies of legal development and the availability of more discursive, rea-
soned texts from the Fathers contributed to this trend. The desire for a
consistent, concordant body of ecclesiastical law would of itself per-
suade authors and compilers away from the frequent inconsistencies of
the penitentials. At the same time, this desire would divert attention
from the practical interests of tracts on penance such as the ninth book of
the Collection in Nine Books and Burchard's *Corrector* and focus on the
more juridical problems of penance and confession. This tendency is
evident in Gratian's tract on penance, which includes no penitential
canons on sexual matters – a striking contrast to previous collections of
canon law that have sections on penance.

What seems to have occurred in the early twelfth century is that the development of a science of canon law inevitably led to the abandonment of the penitential literature as an unsuitable source of legislation.[55] Furthermore, there is no evidence that new penitentials were created to meet the needs of the practical ministry of priest-confessors. The concerns of priests with the sexual behaviour of their penitents did not disappear, however. While elements of Gratian, particularly for the juridical aspects of matrimony, could be of considerable help, the *Decretum* was not a handbook of penance. By the middle of the twelfth century there was a need for a type of literature which would reflect the achievements of the new canon law and at the same time serve a guiding role similar to the older penitential literature – that is, specify offences and indicate appropriate penances for such offences.

This vacuum was not long in being filled by what are referred to under the generic name of *summae confessorum*.[56] From the work of Bartholomew of Exeter (circa 1050–70 AD) onwards these manuals would take a substantially different form from the early penitentials. However, when it came to dealing with sexual offences and providing penances for them, the general approach of the penitentials continued to prove useful. For example, the *Decretum* of Ivo of Chartres furnished many of the sexual proscriptions for Bartholomew, and frequently these texts are penitential texts which entered the collections under incorrect inscriptions.[57] Later, the fifth book of Robert of Flamborough continued to show the strong influence of both the contents and spirit of the penitentials.[58]

The continuation of penitential influence through the *summae confessorum* is a subject for another study.[59] However, I would suggest that a careful study of the sexual prescriptions of the *summae confessorum* written before 1215 will reveal a continuing influence of the penitentials in these *summae*, as there was in the pre-Gratian collections. Certainly the literature of penance and confession is enriched by Gratian and by the ongoing developments of law and theology in the twelfth century. Furthermore, the penitential texts themselves are usually used in a form bearing quite other inscriptions than penitential. But misattribution is an endemic trait of the penitential tradition, which in many cases began with the very attribution of authorship to such personages as Theodore of Canterbury, the Venerable Bede, or Pope Gregory III. What is of interest in this long and varied history is that there seemed always to be a need for practical guidelines in the treatment of sexual offences (and others, I am sure) at the level of casuistry, and this need was frequently met by penitential canons under varied inscriptional guises.

PENITENTIAL TEXTS IN SOME CANONICAL COLLECTIONS

Each text will be analysed according to six features:

Ru Rubric: the original Latin summary of the subject-matter
In Inscription: the attribution to a source by the compiler of the collection
ImS Probable immediate source: if not a penitential
PnS Penitential source: a penitential text taken from a penitential and not from a previous canonical collection. If the ImS is a canonical collection, no entry will be made under the PnS.
Subj Subject-matter: for texts in which the rubric does not sufficiently specify the subject-matter
Ob Observations: noteworthy features

Penitential Canons in Regino of Prüm

Page references to the Wasserschleben edition appear in parentheses.

1.304 (143)
   'Fecisti adulterium ... poenitere debes'
PnS *Bede-Egbert* interrogatory 4 (S 2.681)
Subj Adultery and fornication
Ob Expanded
1.304 (143)
   'Nupsisti ... retro?'
PnS *Bede-Egbert* interrogatory 5 (S 2.681)
Subj Proper form of sexual intercourse
1.304 (143)
   'Nupsisti ... ante partum?'
PnS *Bede-Egbert* interrogatory 12 (S 2.681)
Subj Sexual abstinence during pregnancy
1.304 (143)
   'Nupsisti dominica die?'
PnS *Bede-Egbert* interrogatory 15 (S 2.681)
Subj Sexual abstinence on Sunday
1.304 (143)
   'Fecisti raptum ...'
PnS *Bede-Egbert* interrogatory 19 (S 2.682)
Subj Raptus

1.304 (143)
  'Fecisti fornicationem sicut Sodomitae ...'
PnS Bede-Egbert interrogatory 6 (S 2.681)
· Subj Homosexuality and incest
Ob Omits reference to brother and adds sister.
1.304 (143)
  'Coinquinatus es ... dies poeniteas.'
PnS Cf Bede-Egbert 5.2d (S 2.688).
Subj Sexual abstinence during Lent
1.304 (144)
  'Hoc etiam caveri ...'
PnS Cf Bede-Egbert 5.1 (S 2.687).
Subj Sexual abstinence: various times
1.304 (145)
  'Bibisti ullum maleficium ...'
PnS Bede-Egbert interrogatory 30 (S 2.682)
Subj Contraception and aphrodisiac
1.304 (145)
  'Iunxisti te mulieri ...'
PnS Cf Bede-Egbert 6.1 (S 2.688).
Subj Sexual abstinence during menstrual period
1.304 (145)
  'Nupsisti cum uxore ... adimplerentur?'
PnS Cf Bede-Egbert 5.2 (S 2.687).
Subj Sexual abstinence after childbirth
1.304 (146)
  'Communicasti de sacrificio ...'
Subj Sexual abstinence before communion
Ob Details seem to be original with Regino.
1.338 (159)
Ru De temporibus quibus se continere debent coniugati ab uxoribus
In Ex concilio Eliberitano
PnS Hibernensis 46.11 (Wasserschleben 187)
Subj Sexual abstinence: various times
1.339 (159)
Ru De eadem re
In Ex poenitentiali
PnS Bede-Egbert 5.1–2 (S 2.687–8)
Subj Sexual abstinence: various times
1.340 (160)
Ru De quadragesima
PnS Bede-Egbert 5.2 (S 2.688)
Subj Sexual abstinence during Lent

1.341 (160)
Ru   Quod ante communionem abstinere debent coniuges
Subj Sexual abstinence before Communion
Ob   Seems to be original, but see *Canons of Theodore U* 2.12.1 (Finst 326).

2.5
Ru   Post haec ita per ordinem interroget (Wasserschleben 208)
     Deinde interrogandum de adulteriis et fornicationibus (210)

15 Adultery	29 Fornication
16 Adulterous concubinage	32 Impotence
22 Adultery	33 Incest
23 Adultery	34 Incest
24 Fornication	35 Homosexuality
25 Fornication	Bestiality
27 Raptus	36 Prostitution
28 Raptus	37 Adultery

Ob   Original interrogatory. Some of the matters raised in these questions will
     be supported with conciliar or decretal sources without the use of
     penitential canons.

2.130 (264)
Ru   Si cuius uxor adulterium perpetraverit
In   Ex concilio Nannetensi, cap. xxi
ImS Theodulf of Orleans 2.28 (De Clercq 1.333)
Subj Adultery
Ob   For the so-called Council of Nantes see Fournier 'Etudes critiques sur le
     Décret de Burchard de Worms' 325–7; Gaudement 'Le pseudo-concile de
     Nantes.'

2.131 (265)
Ru   Si non sociati coniugio fornicati fuerint
In   Ex eodem, cap. xxii
ImS Theodulf of Orleans 2.29 (De Clercq 1.334)
Subj Fornication
Ob   Penance reduced from 5 to 3 years

2.132 (265)
Ru   Quodsi unus absolutus et alter copulatus adulterati fuerint
In   Ex eodem
ImS Theodulf of Orleans 2.30 (De Clercq 1.334)
Subj Adultery
Ob   Where Theodulf had claimed that both the married partners and the
     unmarried partners are guilty of adultery and so deserve the same penance,
     Regino reserves a lighter penance for the single person, since the married
     person already has in his wife a legitimate outlet for his sexual desires.

2.133 (265)
Ru   De eadem re
In   Ex poenitentiali
PnS *Bede-Egbert* 1.1h (S 2.685)
Subj Adultery
Ob   Regino adds that the canon also refers to women.
2.134 (266)
Ru   Si uxoratus ancillam propriam tenuerit
PnS *Bede-Egbert* 1.1k (S 2.685)
Subj Adultery with female slave
2.135 (266)
Ru   Si laicus cum laica femina fornicatus fuerit
In   Ex eodem
PnS *Bede-Egbert* 1.1L (S 2.685)
Subj Fornication
Ob   Clarification added that both partners are unmarried.
2.200 (291)
Ru   Item de incestis et eorum poenitentia
In   Ex concilio Moguntiacensi
PnS Hrabanus Maurus *Paenitentiale ad Heribaldum* c 20 (PL 110.487)
Subj Incest
Ob   Attribution to a Mainz council is made by Hrabanus Maurus. See Kottje
     Die Bussbücher Halitgars 202–3.
2.243 (308)
Ru   De his qui matrimonio iuncti sunt et nubere non possunt
In   Ex epistola Rabani ad Heribaldum episcopum, cap. xxix
PnS Hrabanus Maurus *Paenitentiale ad Heribaldum* c 29 (PL 110.491)
Subj Impotence
Ob   See above, page 69.
2.247 (310)
Ru   De diversarum personarum fornicatione
In   Ex poenitentiali Romano Theodori episcopi et Bedae presbyteri
PnS *Bede-Egbert* 1.1–5 (S 2.685–6)
Subj Various heterosexual offences
Ob   The rubric corresponds to the title of *Bede-Egbert* 1 (S 2.685).
2.248 (311)
Ru   Item de incestis
PnS *Bede-Egbert* 2.1 (S 2.686)
Subj Incest with sister
2.248 (311)
In   Item alii
PnS *Bede-Egbert* 2.2–3 (S 2.686–7)

Subj Incest among members of nuclear family, and cases of marital incest
Ob Regino omits the counsel at the end, 'But all this rests with the free discretion of the priest ...'

2.249 (311)
Ru De sordidatione puerorum
PnS *Bede-Egbert* 3 (S 2.687)
Subj Boys: homosexuality, abuse, masturbation
Ob Rubric corresponds to the title of *Bede-Egbert* 3.

2.250 (312)
Ru De menstruis abstinendis
PnS *Bede-Egbert* 6 and 8.1–2 (S 2.688)
Subj Sexual abstinence, proper form of sexual intercourse, homosexuality
Ob *Bede-Egbert* 6 is summarized. Rubric corresponds to *Bede-Egbert* 6 (title).

2.251 (312)
Ru De mulieribus
PnS *Bede-Egbert* 9 (S 2.688)
Subj Lesbianism and female masturbation

2.252 (312)
Ru De illecebroso amplexu
PnS *Bede-Egbert* 4.1–2 (S 2.687), 11.1–2a (S 2.689)
Subj Kissing, pollution
Ob Selections. Rubric corresponds to title of *Bede-Egbert* 4 (S 2.687).

2.253 (313)
Ru De clericis
PnS *Bede-Egbert* 11.2 (S 2.689)
Subj Pollution
Ob Selections

2.254 (313)
Ru De quadrupedum fornicatione
PnS *Bede-Egbert* 12.1–2 (S 2.689)
Subj Bestiality
Ob Rubric corresponds to title of *Bede-Egbert* 12, variants (S 2.689)

2.254 (313)
Ru Item
PnS *Bede-Egbert* 12.3 (S 2.689)
Subj Bestiality (clerics)

2.255 (313)
Ru De sodomitis
PnS *Bede-Egbert* 10.1 (S 2.688)
Subj Homosexuality

2.255 (313)
Ru Item
PnS *Bede-Egbert* 10.3 (S 2.688)

Subj Homosexuality
2.369 (354)
Ru De menstruo sanguine
In Rabanus ad Heribaldum
PnS Hrabanus Maurus *Paenitentiale ad Heribaldum* c 30 (PL 110.491B)
Subj Aphrodisiac
Ob See above, page 68.
2.370 (354)
Ru De eadem re
In Ex concilio Anquirensi
PnS Hrabanus Maurus *Paenitentiale ad Heribaldum* c 25 (PL 110.490A)
Subj Lesbianism, aphrodisiac
Ob See above, page 68.

Penitential Canons in the Collection in Nine Books

Reference numbers are to book and chapter: for example, 9.21 = bk 9, chap 21. Longer chapters containing several provisions are indicated by numbers in brackets following the chapter numbers: for example, 9.21(1–7). The folio reference follows the first citation from the manuscript, which is usually either the rubric or inscription. The Latin is very irregular but has been transcribed as it is in the manuscript; e-cedilla has been expanded to ae.

7.110(2)
In Sinodus romana (160va)
PnS *Hibernensis* 46.11 (ed Wasserschleben 187)
Subj Sexual abstinence: various times
9.13
Ru De adulterio (198va)
In Gregorius
PnS *Ps-Gregory* 4 (W 538–9)
Subj Adultery
9.14
Ru De fornicatione (198vb)
In Gregorius
PnS *Ps-Gregory* 5 (W 539)
Subj Fornication
9.15
Ru De sodomitis (198vb)
In Gregorius
PnS *Ps-Gregory* 21 (W 543)
Subj Homosexuality

9.16
Ru   De his qui sine animalibus commiscuerunt (199ra)
In   Gregorius
PnS   Cf *Ps-Gregory* 22 (W 543).
Subj   Bestiality
Ob   The rubric clearly ought to read 'cum' for 'sine.'
9.17
Ru   De his qui cum quadrupedia peccaverunt (199ra)
In   Iudicium sinodale
Subj   Bestiality
Ob   Fournier, 'Un groupe de recueils canoniques italiens' 149–50, suggests this text is apocryphal. See Halitgar 6.104 (S 2.300) for similar expressions.
9.18(1–31)
Ru   De luxuriis et adulterii et ingenii fornicandi (199ra)
In   Iudicium Theodori
PnS   *Cap iudiciorum* 7.1–15 (S 2.222–4)
Subj   Various sexual offences
9.19
Ru   De concupiscentia consumata (199vb)
In   Gregorius
PnS   *Ps-Gregory* 6 (W 539)
Subj   Sexual desires
Ob   The rubric should probably read 'non consumata.' See above, page 48.
9.21(1–7)
Ru   De incestis coniunctionibus (200ra)
In   Gregorius
PnS   *Ps-Gregory* 11 (W 540–1)
Subj   Marital and sexual incest
Ob   There are glosses to *privigne* in 9.21(2).
9.21(8)
In   Synodus
     'Si quis cum sorore disponsata sua dormierit ...' (200rb)
PnS   ?
Subj   Incest
9.22(1)
Ru   De raptis et de incestis nuptiis (200rb)
In   Iudicium Commeani
PnS   *Cap iudiciorum* 8.1 (S 2.224)
Subj   Raptus
9.22(4)
In   Synodus romana
     'Clericus qui semel fornicans ...' (200va)
Subj   Fornication

Ob   Fournier, 'Un groupe de recueils' 150, suggest this is apocryphal. Cf
      Excarpsus of Cummean 3.29 (S 2.616); *Reims P* 5.18 (Asbach *Das Poenitentiale*
      Remense appendix, 33).

9.22(5)
      'Si quis vir non habens uxorem ...' (200va)
Subj Fornication
Ob   Although unlikely as a source, it has close parallels with Regino 2.131, 133
      (Wasserschleben 265).

9.22(6)
In   Gregorius
      'Si quis masculum cum masculo ...' (200va)
PnS   Cf *Cap iudiciorum* 7.10a (S 2.223).
Subj Homosexuality

9.22(7)
      'Mollis .1. an. peniteat' (200va).
PnS   Cf *Ps-Gregory* 30 (W 546).
Subj Homosexuality

9.22(8)
      'Si qua mulier cum altera ...' (200va)
PnS   Cf *Ps-Gregory* 30 (W 546).
Subj Lesbianism

9.22(9)
      'Si cum seipsa ...' (200va)
PnS   Cf *Cap iudiciorum* 10.1c (S 2.227).
Subj Female masturbation

9.23
      'Si quis virginem corrupserit ...' (200va)
PnS   *Ps-Gregory* 18 (W 542)
Subj Fornication establishing marriage impediment

9.30(6)
In   Iudicium canonicum (201ra)
      'Mulier tribus mensibus ...'
PnS   *Cap iudiciorum* 9.1h–i (S 2.226)
Subj Sexual abstinence during pregnancy and after childbirth

9.30(8)
      'Cuius uxor sterilis est ...' (201rb)
PnS   *Cap iudiciorum* 9.2b (S 2.226)
Subj Sterility
Ob   The sterile to remain continent in marriage

9.30(9)
      'Omnis itaque christianos abstinere ...' (201rb)
In   Iudicium canonicum

Ob   A long dissertation on periods of sexual abstinence, this seems to be original to the compiler; partially transcribed by Schmitz (2.227).

9.30(10)
'Qui nupserit die dominico .III. ebd. peniteat. Gregorius. Petat a deo indulgentiam et ille. .III. dies peniteat' (201rb).
PnS   Cf *Cap iudiciorum* 9.1j (S 2.226) and *Ps-Gregory* 30 (W 546).
Subj   Sexual abstinence on Sunday

9.30(11)
'Si quis menstruo tempore ...' (201rb–va)
PnS   Cf *Cap iudiciorum* 9.2 (S 2.226).
Subj   Sexual abstinence during menstrual period

9.30(12)
'In quadragesima vero publica ...' (201va)
PnS   Cf *P of Egbert* 7.4–5 (W 238–9)
Subj   Sexual abstinence in Lent
Ob   The *Penitential of Egbert* is an unlikely source given the practice of this compiler, but the parallel is close.

9.34
Ru   De viros et mulieres turpitudinem facientibus (201vb)
In   Gregorius
PnS   *Ps-Gregory* 30 (W 546)
Subj   Proper form of sexual intercourse

9.35(1–2)
Ru   De his qui in publica quadragesima peccaverit cum sua uxore (201vb)
In   Iudicium synodale
Subj   Sexual abstinence in Lent
Ob   See above, Coll 9Bk 9.30(12).

9.36(1–30, 32–3)
Ru   De vitiis luxuriandi et de ludis puerilibus inmundis pollutionibus (202ra)
PnS   *Cap iudiciorum* 10.1–4 (S 2.227–8)
Subj   Various sexual offences
Ob   'Qui semen dormiens in lecto fuderit .III. dies paeniteat' (n 31) seems to be an addition of the compiler.

9.37(1–8)
Ru   De pollutione (202rb)
In   Gregorius
PnS   *Ps-Gregory* 24 (W 543–4)
Subj   Various causes of seminal emission

9.38(1–3)
Ru   De menstruo (202vb)
In   Gregorius
PnS   *Ps-Gregory* 25 (W 544)

Subj Sexual abstinence and regulations regarding menstruation and church
    entry
9.38(4)
In Unde supra (203ra)
PnS Ps-Gregory 30 (W 546)
Subj Sexual abstinence and church entry
9.40
Ru De filia spiritale (203rb)
In Iudicium synodale
PnS Cf Penitential of Monte Cassino 25 (S 1.406).
Subj Spiritual incest, ie, sexual relations between confessor and penitent
Ob See another version of this chapter at Coll 9Bk 9.42(4) (203vb).
9.41
Ru De his qui in ecclesia fornicatur (203va)
In Iudicium quo supra
PnS ?
Subj Sexual relations in a church
9.49(2)
In Gregorius (205vb)
    'Qui cum suam commatre'
PnS Cf Ps-Gregory 11 (W 541).
Subj Spiritual incest, with godmother
Ob Seems to employ the wording of Ps-Gregory 11. The first section of this
    chapter bears the inscription, 'Epistola Gurdiani episcopi ad sanctum
    Desiderem episcopum urbis romae.' See Fournier 'Un groupe de recueils'
    150.
9.50
Ru De incestis fornicationibus (205vb)
In Gregorius
PnS Cf Ps-Gregory 11 (W 540–1).
Subj Sexual and marital incest
Ob Seems to employ the wording of Ps-Gregory 11.
9.51
Ru De his qui cum filia sua vel sorore fornicaverint (206ra)
In Gregorius
PnS Cf Ps-Gregory 11 (W 540–1).
Subj Incest with daughter or sister
9.52
Ru De his qui cum sua matre fornicaverint (206ra)
In Gregorius
PnS Cf Ps-Gregory 11 (W 541).
Subj Incest with mother
Ob 'cibum' added after 'non mutet'

9.53
Ru De fornicatione cum matre sua (206ra)
In Synodus romana
PnS Cf *Ps-Gregory* 11 (W 541) and *Cap iudiciorum* 7.10e (S 2.223–4).
Subj Incest with mother

9.56(1)
Ru De eo qui postquam se deo voverit ad saeculum revertitur vel stultis votis frangendis (206rb)
PnS *Cap iudiciorum* 11.1 (S 2.231)
Subj Clerical celibacy

9.74(2)
In Iudicium canonicum
'Si quis per amorem ...'
PnS *Cap iudiciorum* 16.1b (S 2.236)
Subj Aphrodisiac

9.92(5)
Ru De discretione ciborum et de his qui inmunda comedunt (210rb)
In Eiusdem [= 9.91: Iudicium synodale (fol 210rb)]
PnS Cf *Cap iudiciorum* 23.1, variant b, 'Animalia coitu ...' (S 2.240).
Subj Bestiality (how to dispose of animals so used)

9.92(16)
'Et illa que semen viri sui ...' (210vb)
PnS *Cap iudiciorum* 23.2b (S 2.241)
Subj Aphrodisiac

9.124(22)
'Et qui acciperit sacrificium pollutus ...' (215va)
PnS *Cap iudiciorum* 34.1p (S 2.249)
Subj Communion after seminal emission

9.124(36)
'Greci et romani abstinent se ...' (215vb)
PnS *Cap iudiciorum* 34.1y (S 2.250)
Subj Sexual abstinence before communion

Penitential Canons in the Decretum *of Burchard*

For the texts of the interrogatory of the fifth chapter of book 19 I have used the numbered edition of Schmitz for ease of reference.[60] The texts do not differ significantly from the edition in Migne. Reference in the form 19.5(52) = bk 19, chap 5, q 52, of the Schmitz numbering.

1.94 (PL 140.573–9)
Ru Prima interrogatio episcopi aut eius missi
In Ex eodem [see 1.91: ex decr. Eutychian. papae] cap. 9
ImS Regino 2.5

Subj Various sexual offences
Ob   Burchard has eighty-eight questions because Regino's questions 42 and
      43 = Burchard's question 42.

5.22 (PL 140.757)
Ru   Quandiu unusquisque ante sacram communionem ab uxore se abstinere
      debeat
In   Ex concil. Elibertan., cap. 3
ImS   Regino 1.341
Subj Sexual abstinence before Communion

9.40 (PL 140.821)
Ru   De his qui in matrimonio iuncti sunt, et concumbere non possunt
In   Ex epist. Greg. ad Ioannem Ravennatem episcopum
ImS   Regino 2.243
Subj Impotence
Ob   See Machielsen 'Les spurii de St. Grégoire le Grand' 254–5.

9.68 (PL 140.826)
Ru   Si laicus absolutus cum laica absoluta peccaverit
In   Ex concilio Meldensi, capite 7
ImS   Regino 2.135
Subj Fornication

9.70 (PL 140.827)
Ru   De viro uxorem non habente si cum alterius uxore adulterium perpetraverit
In   Ex concilio Nanneten., capite 6
ImS   Regino 2.132
Subj Adultery

13.14 (PL 40.887)
Ru   Ut in illis sacratis diebus ieiuniorum coniugati a coniugibus se abstinere
      debeant
In   Item eiusdem [Ex dictis Liber. papae], capite 5
ImS   Theodulf of Orleans *Capitula* chap 43 (PL 105.205)
Subj Sexual abstinence in Lent

17.8 (PL 140.920)
Ru   De illo qui cum duabus sororibus …
In   Ex concilio Mogunt., capite 3
ImS   Regino 2.200
Subj Various forms of incestuous relations

17.27 (PL 140.924)
Ru   De mulieribus quae aliquo molimine inter se fornicantur
In   Ex poenitentiali Theodori
ImS   Regino 2.251
Subj Lesbianism, female masturbation

17.28 (PL 140.924)
Ru   De sanctimonialibus si inter se fornicantur

In   Ex eodem
ImS   Regino 2.251
Subj   Lesbianism
17.29 (PL 140.924)
Ru   De muliere si cum altera fornicata fuerit
In   Ex concilio Anquiren., capite 8
ImS   Regino 2.370
Subj   Lesbianism, aphrodisiac
17.32 (PL 140.925)
Ru   De illis qui cum pecudibus peccant
In   Ex poenitentiali Theod.
ImS   Regino 2.254
Subj   Bestiality
17.34 (PL 140.925)
Ru   De illis qui fornicantur sicut sodomitae
In   Ex poenitentiali Theod.
Subj   Homosexuality, incest between natural brothers
Ob   The general homosexuality provision seems to be original with Burchard.
       The reference to sexual relations between natural brothers is found in
       numerous penitentials. See the two penitentials apparently used by
       Burchard, *Excarpsus of Cummean* 2.3 (S 2.608); *Bede-Egbert* (Albers) 6.5
       (Albers 406).
17.39 (PL 140.926–7)
Ru   De episcopo qui secundum naturam fornicatus fuerit
In   Ex poenitentiali Theod.
PnS   Cf *Excarpsus of Egbert* 5.1–22 (S 2.665) or *Bede-Egbert* (Albers) 7.1–22
       (Albers 407–9).
Subj   Various sexual offences
Ob   It is difficult to determine which penitential is the source. In either case,
       Burchard follows the tradition of Cod Vat Pal lat 294, which both editors
       use for variants.
17.40 (PL 140.927)
Ru   De sacerdote qui per turpiloquium aut per conspectum libidinosum
       pollutus fuerit
In   Ex poenitentiali Romano
PnS   Cf *Excarpsus of Egbert* 9.2–8 (S 2.668) or *Bede-Egbert* (Albers) 11.2–8
       (Albers 411–12).
Subj   Kissing and seminal emission
17.41 (PL 140.927)
Ru   De eadem re
In   Ex poenitentiali Theod.
PnS   Cf *Excarpsus of Egbert* 9.10, 9, 11, 12 (S 2.669) or *Bede-Egbert* (Albers)
       11.10, 9, 11, 12 (Albers 412).

Subj Pollution
Ob The changed order is characteristic of Cod Vat Pal lat 294
17.42 (PL 140.927–8)
Ru De illis qui per illecebrosos amplexus foeminarum polluuntur
In Ex poenitentiali Bedae pr.
ImS Regino 2.252
Subj Kissing and pollution
17.43 (PL 140.928)
Ru De clericis qui per malas cogitationes semen effuderint
In Ex poenitentiali romano
ImS Regino 2.253
Subj Pollution
17.56 (PL 140.931–3)
Ru De sodomitico peccato
In Ex poenitentiali romano
PnS *Excarpsus of Cummean* 2.1–25 (S 2.608–11)
Subj Various sexual offences
Ob Some modifications introduced

The fifth chapter of book 19 covers most sexual questions. What is of principal interest here is that most of these questions seem to be based on texts in Burchard himself. Consequently, I believe that the best way to present this section is in columnar fashion.

Burchard 19.5 (S 2)	Burchard (PL 140)	Comments
41	1.94(23) 9.70	Adultery
42	1.94(15) 9.70	Adultery
43	1.94(24) 9.68	Fornication. Note light penance of ten days.
46		Fornication with a nun
47	9.14	Fornication
49	9.39	Wife acquired by raptus
50	1.94(22) 9.69	Adultery at urging of husband[61]
52		Cf Regino 1.304 ('Nupsisti ... retro'). Proper form of intercourse
53	19.141	Cf Regino 1.304 ('Iunxisti ... menstruo'). Sexual abstinence

Burchard 19.5 (S 2)	Burchard (PL 140)	Comments
54	19.155	Cf Regino 1.304 ('Nupsisti ... partum'). Sexual abstinence
55		Cf Regino 1.304 ('Post conceptionem') and Regino 1.339. Sexual abstinence
56	19.157	Sexual abstinence
57		Cf Regino 1.304 ('Coinquinatus'). Sexual abstinence
105	17.3	Incest with wife's sister[62]
106	17.4	Incest (wife's sister enters your bed and you believe she is your wife)
107	17.5	Fornication with two sisters
108	17.13	Sexual relations with a woman whom brother later marries
109	17.10	Incest with stepdaughter
110	17.11	Incest with stepmother
112	17.18	Incest with son's fiancée
113		Cf Regino 2.248. Incest with mother
114	1.94(33) 17.24	Incest with godmother
115	1.94(33) 17.24–5	Incest with goddaughter
117	9.44	Impotence
118		Cf Regino 2.248. Incest with sister
119	17.8	Incest with paternal and maternal aunts
120	17.34	Homosexuality
121		Homosexuality (femoral). See detailed description.
122		Mutual masturbation. See detailed description.
123		Masturbation. See detailed description.
124		Masturbation (with perforated piece of wood)
125	17.42	Kissing and pollution
126	17.34	Bestiality
133	19.137	Touching
134	19.138	Common baths with women
154	17.27	Female masturbation and lesbianism. See detailed description.
155	17.27	Use of phallus (?)
156		Lesbianism. See detailed description.
157		Cf Regino 2.248. Incest (mother with young son)
158		Women and bestiality
166		Cf Regino 1.304 ('Bibisti'). Aphrodisiac

Burchard 19.5 (S 2)	Burchard (PL 140)	Comments
172		Cf *Arundel P* 81 (S 1.459). Aphrodisiac (using a fish)[63]
173		Cf *Arundel P* 81. Aphrodisiac (through preparation of bread)
176		Cf *Arundel P* 81. Aphrodisiac (menstrual blood)
184	1.94(36)	Cf Regino 2.141. Prostitution

19.75 (PL 140.1000)
Ru   Quod coniugati in quadragesima abstinere debeant ab uxoribus
In   Ex concilio Elibertan., capite 5
ImS   Regino 1.340
Subj   Sexual abstinence during Lent
19.104 (PL 140.1004)
Ru   De illis qui per amorem venefici fiunt
In   Ex poenitentiali Theodori
PnS   *Excarpsus of Cummean* 7.2 (S 2.626)
Subj   Aphrodisiac
Ob   Subdeacon added, priest omitted from source
19.137 (PL 140.1010)
Ru   De illis qui libidinose obtrectaverint puellam aut mulierem
In   Ex eodem [Roman penitential]
PnS   Cf *St Hubert P* 44 (S 2.337).
Subj   Immodest touches
Ob   Considerably modified
19.138 (PL 140.1010)
Ru   De illis qui balneo cum mulieribus se laverint
In   Ex poenitentiali Theod.
PnS   Cf *St Hubert P* 47 (S 2.337).
Subj   Common baths, men and women
Ob   Modified; penance reduced from 1 year to 3 days
19.141 (PL 140.1010)
Ru   De illis feminis quae ante mundum sanguinem ecclesiam intrant et quae nupserint his diebus
In   Ex poenitentiali Theod.
PnS   Cf *Excarpsus of Cummean* 3.15–16 (S 2.614) (?)
Subj   Sexual abstinence after childbirth
19.155 (PL 140.1013)
Ru   De temporibus quibus se continere debeant coniugati ab uxoribus
In   Ex concilio Eliberta.

ImS Regino 1.338
Subj Sexual abstinence: various times
19.157 (PL 140.1014)
Ru De illis qui in dominico die nupserit
In Ex concilio Triburiensi, capite 5
PnS Cf *Canons of Theodore* U 1.14.20 (Finst 309).
Subj Sexual abstinence on Sunday

Penitential Canons in the Collection in Five Books

2.64 (CC.CM 6.217)
Ru De facile fornicatione
ImS Cf Coll 9Bk 9.14(1) and 9.18(2) (Vat lat 1349, fols 198vb, 199rb).
Subj Fornication
Ob Modified
2.65 (CC.CM 6.218)
Ru De gravi fornicatione
In Iudicium Commeani
ImS Cf Coll 9Bk 9.18(2–3) (Vat lat 1349, fol 199rb).
Subj Fornication and adultery
2.66(1) (CC.CM 6.218)
Ru De diversis fornicationibus vitiorum
In Iudicium Commeani
ImS Cf Coll 9Bk 9.36(22) (Vat lat 1349, fol 202rb).
Subj Kissing without pollution
Ob Expanded
2.66(2) (CC.CM 6.218)
Ru Item
In Sequitur
ImS Cf Coll 9Bk 9.36(23) (Vat lat 1349, fol 202rb).
Subj Kissing and pollution
Ob Modified; penances very lengthy in comparison with the traditional penances for this behaviour
2.66(3) (CC.CM 6.219)
Ru Item
In Sequitur
Subj Pleasure is satisfied.
Ob Seems to be original.
2.66(4) (CC.CM 6.219)
Ru Item
ImS Cf Coll 9Bk 9.36(22) (Vat lat 1349, fol 202rb).
Subj Kissing without pollution

2.66(5) (CC.CM 6.219)
Ru   Item
In   De quo supra
ImS   Cf Coll 9Bk 9.36(23) (Vat lat 1349, fol 202rb).
Subj   Kissing and pollution
2.66(6) (CC.CM 6.219)
Ru   Item
In   Sequitur
ImS   See above Coll 5Bk 2.66(3).
2.66(7) (CC.CM 6.219)
Ru   Item
In   Et aliter
Subj   Kiss at kiss of peace in the liturgy
Ob   Original. There is a quote from 'Osius episcopus,' which seems to be apocryphal.
2.67(1) (CC.CM 6.220)
Ru   De concupiscentia non consumata
In   Gregorius
ImS   Cf Coll 9Bk 9.19 (Vat lat 1349, fol 199vb).
Subj   Sexual desires
Ob   An addition at the end, 'Sed tamen pro tactu ... ita poeniteat.'
2.67(2) (CC.CM 6.220)
Ru   Item
In   Iudicium Theodori
ImS   Cf Coll 9Bk 9.18(22–4).
Subj   Sexual desire
2.77 (CC.CM 6.225)
Ru   Qui cum uxore pro deo relicta fornicaverit
In   Iudicium Commeani
ImS   Cf Coll 9Bk 9.18(6) (Vat lat 1349, fol 199va).
Subj   Adultery with a woman whose husband has left 'propter Deum'
2.78(1) (CC.CM 6.225)
Ru   De his qui infra ecclesiam fornicaverint γel adulteraverint
In   Iudicium synodale
Subj   Sexual relations in a church
Ob   In *Vallicellian P* III 7 (W 685)
2.78(2) (CC.CM 6.227)
Ru   Item inde
In   Concilium Agatensi
ImS   Cf Coll 9Bk 9.41 (Vat lat 1349, fol 203va).
Subj   Fornication, immodest touches, pollution
Ob   Expanded

2.78(3) (CC.CM 6.227)
Ru   Item inde
In   Gregorius
PnS   Cf *Paris P* 46 (S 2.330).
Subj Fornication
2.79(1) (CC.CM 6.227)
Ru   De his qui cum filia spirituali fornicaverit
ImS   Cf Coll 9Bk 9.40 (Vat lat 1349, fol 203rb).
Subj Spiritual incest, ie, sexual relations between confessor and penitent
2.79(2) (CC.CM 6.227)
Ru   Item
In   Iudicium Commeani
Subj Incest
Ob   In *Vallicellian P* III 8 (W 685)
2.134(1) (CC.CM 6.266)
Ru   De eo qui postquam se deo voverit ad saecularem habitum revertitur et de
      stultis votis
In   Iudicium Commeani
ImS   Coll 9Bk 9.56(1–2) (Vat lat 1349, fol 206rb)
Subj Clerical celibacy
5.20
Ru   De rapturam (257ra)
In   Iụdicium Commeani
ImS   Cf Coll 9Bk 9.22 (Vat lat 1349, fol 200rb).
Subj Raptus
5.25
Ru   De eo qui cum sponsa alterius fornicaverit (257va)
In   Gregorius
ImS   Cf Coll 9Bk 9.18(4) (Vat lat 1349, fol 199rb).
Subj Fornication with another's fiancée
Ob   See Burchard *Corrector* 245 (W 678).

From here on the chapter numbers correspond to the numeration of the individual chapters and do not necessarily correspond to the list of *capitula* or chapter headings at the beginning of book 5.

5.142
Ru   De adulterio (289ra)
In   Gregorius papa
ImS   Coll 9Bk 9.13(1–2) (Vat lat 1349, fol 198va)
Subj Definition of adultery
5.150
Ru   De laico qui non habens uxorem si maculaverit uxorem proximi sui (289va)

In   Iudicium Commeani
Subj Adultery and prostitution
Ob   Perhaps suggested by Coll 9Bk 9.18(21) (Vat lat 1349, fol 199vb), but greatly developed and expanded

5.151
Ru   De coniugibus si adulterati inventi sunt (290ra)
In   Iohannes Constantinopolitani episcopus. Similiter Theodorus et Commeanus
ImS Cf Coll 9Bk 9.18(15) (Vat lat 1349, fol 199va–vb).
Subj Adultery

5.173
Ru   Inprimis quali tempore christianus a propria uxore abstinere se debet (295va)
In   Ex decreto patrum
ImS Cf Coll 9Bk 9.30(9) (Vat lat 1349, fol 201rb).
Subj Sexual abstinence
Ob   This passage seems to be a development of the corresponding passage in the Coll 9Bk.

5.174(1)
Ru   De eo qui cum uxore sua fornicaverit et alia turpia fecerit (296ra)
In   Gregorius
ImS Coll 9Bk 9.34 (Vat lat 1349, fol 201vb)
Subj Proper form of sexual intercourse

5.179
Ru   De menstrua (297vb)
In   Gregorius
ImS Coll 9Bk 9.38(1–3) (Vat lat 1349, fol 202vb)
Subj Sexual abstinence during menstrual period

5.184
Ru   De fornicatione sodomitica (297vb)
In   Iudicium Commeani
ImS Coll 9Bk 9.18(1) (Vat lat 1349, fol 199ra)
Subj Homosexuality

5.185
Ru   Item. De sodomitis (298ra)
In   Gregorius
ImS Coll 9Bk 9.15(1–3) (Vat lat 1349, fol 198vb)
Subj Homosexuality

5.188
Ru   De fornicatione puerorum (298rb)
In   Iudicium Commeani
ImS Coll 9Bk 9.36(4–21) (Vat lat 1349, fol 202ra–rb)
Subj Homosexuality (boys) and fornication

5.189(1)
Ru   De innaturale turpis fornicationibus (298vb)
In   Iudicium Theodori
ImS   Coll 9Bk 9.18(9) (Vat lat 1349, fol 199va)
Subj   Masturbation
5.189(2)
Ru   Sequitur item (298vb)
ImS   Cf Coll 9Bk 9.18(25) (Vat lat 1349, fol 199vb).
Subj   Masturbation
5.190(1)
Ru   De turpitudine fornicationis. Masculum cum masculo et femina cum
     femina (298vb)
In   Iudicium Theodori episcopi
ImS   Cf Coll 9Bk 9.22(6) (Vat lat 1349, fol 200va).
Subj   Homosexuality and lesbianism
Ob   Expanded
5.190(2–3)
     'Si mulier cum se ipsa ...' (299ra)
ImS   Cf Coll 9Bk 9.22(8–9) (Vat lat 1349, fol 200va).
Subj   Female masturbation and lesbianism
5.190(4)
In   Gregorius (299ra)
     'Si qua mulier ...' (299ra)
ImS   Coll 9Bk 9.22(8) (Vat lat 1349, fol 200va)
Subj   Lesbianism
5.190(5)
Ru   De molles (299ra)
In   Iudicium Commeani
ImS   Cf Coll 9Bk 9.22(7) (Vat lat 1349, fol 200va).
Subj   Molles
Ob   Developed. There are two marginal glosses on the word *molles* at fol 299rb:
     'Molles dicuntur et feminati qui super se feminas imponuntur et ipsi more
     feminarum succumbunt usque quo libidinosum desiderium compleant. se
     autem facientes feminas, feminas vero super se ponentes faciunt masculos.
     et ideo molles dicuntur' (marg 299rb). 'Molles dicuntur carnales qui mollia
     verba cum mulieribus locuntur; qui cum eis libenter conversantur; qui
     cogitationes immundas et muliebres recipiunt; qui mollia verba libenter
     audiunt vel locuntur; qui uxorem nimis diligunt; qui in eas [?] appetitibus
     nimis delectantur; qui se ipsos inpudice iungunt vel propria membra et
     quam maxima inpudica inpudice respiciunt et qui mollibus rebus utuntur'
     (marg 299rb).

5.190(6)
'Qualiscumque vir si desideria sua ...' (299ra)
ImS   Cf Coll 9Bk 9.18(30–1) (Vat lat 1349, fol 199vb).
Subj   Homosexual (?) oral sex

5.192
Ru   De his qui se cum animalibus commiscuerunt (299rb)
In   Gregorius
ImS   Cf Coll 9Bk 9.16 (Vat lat 1349, fol 199ra).
Subj   Bestiality

5.194
Ru   De fornicatione cum quadrupediis (299va)
In   Iudicium Theodori et Commeani
Subj   Bestiality
Ob   Seems to be a comment on Coll 9Bk 9.16.

5.195
Ru   De penitentia his qui cum animalibus fornicaverint (299va)
In   Iudicium synodale
Subj   Bestiality
Ob   Reformulated

5.196(2)
Ru   Item (300ra)
In   Iudicium Theodori
ImS   Cf Coll 9Bk 9.92(5) (Vat lat 1349, fol 210va).
Subj   Bestiality (what to do with animals so used)

5.197
Ru   De minoribus et inmundis pollutionibus (300ra)
In   Iudicium Commeani
ImS   Cf Coll 9Bk 9.36(24–7, 33, 32) (Vat lat 1349, fol 202rb).
Subj   Pollution

5.199
Ru   De pollutione (300va)
In   Gregorius
ImS   Coll 9Bk 9.37(1–8) (Vat lat 1349, fol 202va)
Subj   Pollution

Penitential Canons in the Collectio canonum *of Anselm of Lucca*

11.83
Ru   De penitentia eius qui adulteram mulierem non vult dimittere (188vb)
In   Ex penitentiale Theodori

PnS   *Cap iudiciorum* 7.10f (S 2.224)
Subj Adultery
11.86
Ru   De his qui fornicati sunt ut sodomitae (189ra)
In   Ex penitentiale Theodori
PnS   *Cap iudiciorum* 7.1 (S 2.222)
Subj Homosexuality
11.87
Ru   De penitentia eius qui virginem rapuerit (189ra)
In   Iudicium canonicum
PnS   *Cap iudiciorum* 8.1 (S 2.224)
Subj Raptus
11.88
In   In eodem (189ra)
PnS   *Cap iudiciorum* 8.2 (S 2.224)
Subj Incest
11.105
Ru   De his qui cum semetipsis fornicantur (191ra)
In   Theodori
PnS   *Cap iudiciorum* 7.9 (S 2.223)
Subj Masturbation
11.106
Ru   De his qui cum matre vel sorore fornicantur (191ra)
In   [Indented space left for an inscription?]
PnS   *Cap iudiciorum* 7.10e (S 2.223)
Subj Incest
11.107
Ru   Quamdiu mulier se debet abstinere de viro cum concipit (191ra)
In   [Indented space left for an inscription?]
PnS   *Cap iudiciorum* 9.1h (S 2.226)
Subj Sexual abstinence during pregnancy
11.108
Ru   De diversis statuta fornicationibus patrum (191ra)
In   Statuta patrum
PnS   *Cap iudiciorum* 10.1 (S 2.227–8)
Subj Various sexual offences
Ob   There seems to be a mix-up in the copying at the end of this chapter.
11.109
Ru   De eo qui fornicari vult et non potest (191rb)
In   Theodori
PnS   *Cap iudiciorum* 7.8 (S 2.223)
Subj Sexual desires

11.110
Ru   De his qui maleficio suo aliquos perdiderint (191rb)
In   Ex penitentiali Romano
PnS *Cap iudiciorum* 16.1b (S 2.236)
Subj Aphrodisiac

Penitential Canons in the Decretum *of Ivo of Chartres*

2.32 (PL 161.168)
Ru   Quandiu unusquisque ante sacram communionem ab uxore abstinere
     debeat
In   Ex concilio Eliberitano
ImS Burchard 5.22 (PL 140.757)
Subj Sexual abstinence before Communion
4.47 (PL 161.274)
Ru   Ut in sacris quadragesimae diebus coniugati a coniugio se abstineant
In   Ex eodem [Ex concilio Liberii papae], cap. 5
ImS Burchard 13.14 (PL 140.887)
Subj Sexual abstinence in Lent
8.80 (PL 161.600)
Ru   De eadem re
In   Capitulorum lib. ·VI, cap. 91
ImS Benedictus Levita *Capitularium collectio* 2.91 (PL 97.760)
Subj Impotence
Ob   Remote source is *Canons of Theodore U* 2.12.33 (Finst 330); see above,
     page 33.
8.178 (PL 161.621)
Ru   De illis qui matrimonio iuncti sunt, et concumbere non possunt
In   Ex epistola Gregorii ad Ioannem Ravennatem episcopum
ImS Burchard 9.40 (PL 140.821)
Subj Impotence
8.205 (PL 161.626)
Ru   Si laicus absolutus cum laica absoluta peccaverit
In   Ex conc. Meldensi, cap. 7
ImS Burchard 9.68 (PL 140.826)
Subj Fornication
8.207 (PL 161.626)
Ru   De viro uxorem non habente, si cum alterius uxore adulterium
     perpetraverit
In   Ex concilio Nannetensi, cap. 6
ImS Burchard 9.70 (PL 140.827)
Subj Adultery

9.70 (PL 161.677)
Ru De illo qui cum duabus sororibus, cum noverca ...
In Ex eodem concilio [Ex concilio Aurelianensi]
ImS Burchard 17.8 (PL 140.920)
Subj Incest
Ob Different inscription from Burchard

9.85 (PL 161.681)
Ru De mulieribus quae aliquo molimine inter se fornicantur
In Ex poenitentiali Theodori
ImS Burchard 17.27 (PL 140.924)
Subj Lesbianism, female masturbation

9.86 (PL 161.681)
Ru De sanctimonialibus si inter se fornicantur
In De eodem
ImS Burchard 17.28 (PL 140.924)
Subj Lesbianism

9.87 (PL 161.681)
Ru De muliere quae cum altera fornicata fuerit
In Ex concilio Ancyrano, cap. 15
ImS Burchard 17.29 (PL 140.924)
Subj Lesbianism, aphrodisiac

9.90 (PL 161.682)
Ru De illis qui cum pecudibus fornicantur
In Ex poenitentiali Theodori
ImS Burchard 17.32 (PL 140.925)
Subj Bestiality

9.92 (PL 161.682)
Ru De illis qui fornicantur sicut Sodomitae
In Ex poenitentiali Theodori
ImS Burchard 17.34 (PL 140.925)
Subj Homosexuality

15.88 (PL 161.882)
Ru Quod coniugati in quadragesima abstinere debeant ab uxoribus
In Ex conc. Eliberitano, c. 5
ImS Burchard 19.75 (PL 140.1000)
Subj Sexual abstinence in Lent

15.116 (PL 161.886)
Ru De illis qui per amorem venefici fiunt
In Ex poenitentiali Theodori
ImS Burchard 19.104 (PL 140.1004)
Subj Aphrodisiac

15.147 (PL 161.891)
Ru De illis qui libidinose obtrectaverint puellam aut mulierem

In   Ex eodem [Roman penitential]
ImS   Burchard 19.137 (PL 140.1010)
Subj   Immodest touches
15.148 (PL 161.891)
Ru   De illis qui in balneo cum mulieribus se laverint
In   Ex poenitentiali Theodori
ImS   Burchard 19.138 (PL 140.1010)
Subj   Common baths with women
15.151 (PL 161.891)
Ru   De illis feminis quae ante mundum sanguinem ecclesiam intraverint et
    quae nupserint his diebus
In   Ex poenitentiali Theodori
ImS   Burchard 19.141 (PL 140.1010)
Subj   Church entry and sexual abstinence during menstruation
15.163 (PL 161.893)
Ru   De temporibus quibus se continere debeant coniugati ab uxoribus
In   Ex concilio Eliberitano
ImS   Burchard 19.155 (PL 140.1013)
Subj   Sexual abstinence
15.165 (PL 161.894)
Ru   De illis qui in dominico die nupserint
In   Ex conc. Triburiensi, cap. 51
ImS   Burchard 19.157 (PL 140.1014)
Subj   Sexual abstinence on Sunday
15.187 (PL 161.897)
Ru   Quanto tempore poenitere debeat qui hoc vel illud fecerit
In   Ex poenitentiali laicorum
PnS   Cf *Penitential of Fulbert of Chartres* (W 623–4).
Subj   Various sexual offences
Ob   Ivo's text corresponds more closely to the Wasserschleben edition of
    Fulbert than to the Schmitz edition (S 1.773–4).

Penitential Canons in the Decretum *of Gratian*

C 27, q 2, c 29 (Friedberg 1071)
In   Unde idem [Gregory] scribit Venerio, Caratilano episcopo ita dicens:
Ru   Si mulier probaverit quod a viro suo numquam cognita fuerit, separetur
Subj   Impotence
Ob   Original source: Hrabanus Maurus *Paenitentiale ad Heribaldum* c 29
    (PL 110.491). Gratian comments on this canon.
C 30, q 1, c 9 (Friedberg 1099)
Ru   De eodem
In   Item Celestinus

ImS Bonizo of Sutri *Liber de vita Christiana* (ed Perels 321)
Subj Incest with spiritual daughter
Ob The text is found in this form in Coll 9Bk 9.40 (Vat lat 1349, fol 203rb).
C 32, q 1, c 4 (Friedberg 1116)
Ru Qui uxorem suam dimittere noluerit adulteram, duobus annis peniteat, si ei debitum reddiderit
In Item Iohannes Crisostomos
Subj Intercourse with one's wife who had committed adultery
Ob Cf Coll 5Bk 5.151 (Vat lat 1339, fol 290ra).
C 32, q 1, c 6 (Friedberg 1117)
Ru Qui adulterae reddit debitum, tribus annis peniteat
In Item ex Penitenciali Theodori
ImS Cf Anselm of Lucca 11.83 (Paris BN lat 12519, fol 188vb).
Subj Intercourse with one's wife who had committed adultery
C 32, q 7, c 23 (Friedberg 1146)
Ru Neutram habeat qui sororem uxoris polluit
In Item ex decreto Zachariae papae
ImS Cf Burchard 19.5(105) (S 2.432).
Subj Incest with wife's sister
C 33, q 1, c 1 (Friedberg 1149)
In Unde Gregorius scribit Iohanni Ravennati Episc.
Ru Licet mulieri nubere quam ob frigiditatem vir cognoscere non potuit
Subj Impotence
Ob Original source: Hrabanus Maurus *Paenitentiale ad Heribaldum* c 29 (PL 110.491). Wording slightly different from C 27, q 2, c 29.
De consec D 2, c 21 (Friedberg 1320)
Ru Ante sanctam communionem a propria uxore quisque contineat
In Item ex concilio Elibertano
ImS Cf Regino 1.341 (Wasserschleben 160)
Subj Sexual abstinence
Ob The last part, beginning 'nec inter catholicos,' is from Burchard 5.23 (PL 140.757) = Council of Agde (506 AD) c 18 (CCSL 148.202). Gratian has a canon (C 33, q 4, c 2) on sexual abstinence which seems to be from Caesarius of Arles, sermon 188 (CCSL 104.768).

4

General Conclusion

Sexual behaviour in early medieval society was governed by a fundamental principle which had been elaborated much earlier: sexual
intercourse was permitted only between a man and a woman who were
legitimately married to one another, and then only if done for the sake of
procreation. Although the procreative intention was never separated
from the activity, as early as Caesarius of Arles the absence of the
intention was not considered to be a serious offence unless procreation
itself was interfered with through contraceptive methods. Given this
principle, the logical implication was quite clear – all other forms of
sexual contact must be considered to be forbidden. There would further
be some need to spell out this implication in terms of specific forms of
proscribed sexual behaviour.

Both the duty of pastoral instruction and the practice of private
penance demanded guidance concerning what was forbidden and some
indication of the gravity of different sexual offences. In short, a
comprehensive code of sexual behaviour was necessary to realize
abstract sexual principle as everyday practice. It should also be
remembered that the evangelization of western Europe involved the
implementation of the moral teachings of Christianity in addition to the
preaching of its credal positions, and sexual morality comprised a
significant dimension of this moral teaching.

The formation of a code of sexual behaviour went hand in hand with
the creation and diffusion of the penitentials. Certainly the codes of
Theodosius and Justinian as well as the law codes indigenous to the
tribal groups of western Europe dealt with sexual offences – adultery,
rape, abduction, homosexuality – that were believed to affect the public

domain. However, they did not cover many areas of individual sexual conduct, and they were far removed from the interpersonal relation of confession and penance. The penitentials were the context in which the most comprehensive code of sexual behaviour was elaborated. They served to specify the whole range of proscribed activities and to establish a certain ranking among the various offences, the latter being accomplished principally through the differentiated penances which were levied against each kind of offence. In saying that the penitentials were 'the context' I do not intend to suggest that concern with sexual behaviour was not found in other contexts. However, this concern usually focused on broader institutional problems, such as the canonical requirements of clerical celibacy or the degrees of disqualifying incest relations. These and similar questions receive ample consideration in papal letters and conciliar legislation. The penitentials, on the other hand, provided for the day-to-day failings of Christians, which, we have seen, could be most varied.

The creative elaboration of this material was accomplished by the middle of the eighth century. From that stage on, the penitentials show little creativity in their sexual content; most is derived from previous manuals. Up to the tenth century the penitentials themselves constituted the sole tradition of a comprehensive sexual code. There is no indication that the numerous councils, capitularies, diocesan statutes, and collections of the ninth century were substantially influenced by the sexual content of the penitentials, although there continued to be a parallel development of penitential literature. This penitential tradition in its Irish, Frankish, and Anglo-Saxon expression is relatively unanimous and consistent both in the range of sexual content and in the manner of treatment, a feature no doubt accounted for by the borrowing characteristic of the transmission of the canons.

With Regino of Prüm and Burchard of Worms the exclusivity of a parallel penitential tradition in sexual matters comes to an end. The penitentials are important sources of sexual regulations for these two compilers, who incorporate a substantial number of penitential canons into their collections. Again this advance was the product of a need for a broadly based, comprehensive code of sexual behaviour which, given the previous development, only the penitentials could furnish. Although Burchard (*Decretum* 19.5) makes a significant original contribution to the handling of sexual offences, the additions are made in a penitential context and clearly modelled on that tradition. The same needs which prompted Regino and Burchard to incorporate penitential texts into their collections also led to the incorporation of similar texts into collections of canon law from the tenth to the twelfth century.

The basic implications of the principle legitimating sexual intercourse within marriage are quite clear. Censures of such activities as adultery, simple fornication, homosexuality, bestiality, and masturbation should come as no surprise. However, there are some peculiarities in the penitentials which are worthy of note. The first is that there are a few activities omitted from the penitentials whose omission one might not anticipate. With the exception of a canon in the *Bede-Egbert Double Penitential*, there is no canon censuring prostitution in any of the penitentials we have examined until the *St Hubert Penitential* in the middle of the ninth century. There are no censures of non-procreative sexual intercourse in general or even of contraceptive methods in so far as they are contraceptive. Finally, I believe it has been adequately demonstrated that *raptus* does not connote sexual rape in the penitential and conciliar documents which employ the term. The closest suggestion of a censure of rape is a penitential canon which mentions the case of a female slave being forced to have sexual relations with her master.

Since the present study has concentrated on delineating the sexual content of the penitentials and its transmission and incorporation into later canonical collections, this is not the place to attempt to explain the infrequent mention of prostitution, contraception, and rape. I suspect that the presence of prostitution in a society is a function of a degree of social organization and sophistication which simply was not present in the contexts in which the penitentials were written. That is, institutional prostitution was not a widespread social phenomenon in these contexts. In the more developed societies of the twelfth and thirteenth centuries the canon lawyers would give ample treatment to this subject.[1] Rape, in the predominant sense of sexual relations forced on a woman, with some degree of violence against her person, is certainly not present as a subject in the penitential and non-penitential literature before Gratian. Violence against persons is censured; illicit sexual relations are censured. Why these two notions were not brought together before the time of Gratian would be worthy of further study. The absence of explicit condemnations of contraception as such may be accounted for by the presence of canons censuring various activities which happen to have contraceptive effects. Nonetheless, there is no evidence of a consciously held anti-contraceptive stance in the penitentials.

In addition to codifying unambiguous cases of sexual offences, the penitentials were responsible for the inclusion of other kinds of sexual behaviour not so obviously reprehensible. They were the principal agents to foster the ever-lengthening list of periods of sexual abstinence, a list which continued to expand up to the *Decretum* of Burchard. To be sure, the penitentials did not originate the requirement of sexual abstinence at specific times, but they seem to have been the creators of many of the specific periods and were the main carriers of the tradition. Extra-penitential allusions to different times of sexual abstinence are infrequent.

Concern with two other areas of marital sexuality emerges in the penitentials. Aphrodisiacs, principally the use of semen, do not of themselves seem to be morally objectionable, but they are consistently condemned by the penitentials. This attack on the use of aphrodisiacs is probably best seen as part of the broader attack the penitentials frequently make on magic and folk superstition. Burchard of Worms shows a great interest in combating such practices.[2] Finally, these manuals reflect some interest in the proper method of sexual intercourse. Heterosexual oral practices do not seem to be of concern to the penitential writers, but they do show an interest in proper positions. Intercourse both *retro* and *in terga* is often censured, and these condemnations are incorporated into many canonical collections from Regino on. While anal intercourse clearly has a contraceptive effect, the practice is never explicitly censured for that reason. Dorsal intercourse, which I interpret as intercourse from behind, would not be contraceptive, but perhaps Burchard's use of the expression 'dog-like' points to its perceived unseemliness. His relatively mild penance of ten days reinforces this suggestion. The penitentials, then, contributed to the assembling of a class of marital sexual offences in the areas of abstinence periods, aphrodisiacs, and proper method of intercourse.

The penitentials also played a major role in giving literary currency to an underlying belief in the uncleanliness of sexual intercourse and involuntary seminal emission. Particularly in regard to the latter, there were from very early on the clear, nuanced treatment by Gregory the Great in his letter to Augustine of Canterbury. However, this discussion had little effect on the penitentials, and even when it is incorporated by Burchard, we also find several accompanying penitential canons on seminal pollution that reflect a more primitive taboo-approach to the question. The requirements of washing after sexual intercourse and refraining from immediately entering a church, which were introduced by the *Canons of Theodore*, although not universally adopted are occasionally found in the later penitential tradition.

At the beginning of this study an assumption was made that the penitentials reflect sexual practices sufficiently common to warrant their inclusion in such manuals, and issue was taken with Bieler's apparently gratuitous claim that references to homosexuality, incest, and such like in the Irish penitentials have little to do with reality.[3] A few additional remarks on this question might be made here. It must be borne in mind that in the history of Christian pastoral literature the penitentials do not represent a meteoric phenomenon which disappeared as quickly as it had appeared. For four and a half centuries the penitentials were an important and widespread presence. They were practical handbooks which would have had no conceivable raison d'être aside from their functional utility in the administration of private penance. If they had not reflected the reality of human behaviour, this functional utility would have been lost. There is no indication that the penitentials were conceived to have any other independent literary value such as a treatise of Augustine or a Biblical commentary of Jerome might have. Besides, the transmission of penitential materials and their incorporation into the canonical tradition were conscious acts, conscious acts which we can reasonably assume demonstrate judicious selectivity, reformulation, and adaptation. The numerous sexual canons must have been viewed as desirable elements of these manuals and collections.

One sometimes encounters the argument that many of the penitential canons were simply the result of a desire for conceptual completeness and do not necessarily reflect practice. However, I have found this argument used only in regard to canons censuring sexual behaviour, not in regard to theft or superstitions, for example. Such an argument would seem to have more in common with an overly modest approach to this material than with rational plausibility. This approach is evident in the remarks of Charles Plummer,[4] in the generic translation into English of regulations more specifically described in Latin, in the decision to leave in Latin the sexual content of the *Old-Irish Penitential,* which is otherwise translated into English, and in the omission by McNeill and Gamer of many of the sexual canons from the penitential materials they translate (this is particularly true of their translation of selections from Burchard's *Corrector*).

This issue is not one of historical sociology but one of methodology. I know of no body of data that could be used to substantiate empirical claims about the actual incidence of particular forms of sexual behaviour, their distribution among particular classes, or their frequency among the population in the early Middle Ages. However, there remains the methodological question of the significance of a body of literature which for more than four centuries continued to transmit a relatively consistent and comprehensive code of sexual behaviour. The most rational methodological position would seem to be that the specific sexual content of the penitentials is a reflection of actual behaviour on a scale to warrant inclusion. The inclusion of canons against bestiality, for instance, does not need to mean that the activity was rampant; on the other hand, it would be gratuitous to suggest that their presence in the penitentials was simply the result of a legalistic desire to cover all the conceivable categories of sexual offence. It is worth recalling that one of the specific questions asked of Hrabanus Maurus concerned those who have sexual relations with female dogs and cows.[5] It is unlikely that such a question was prompted by abstract legal concern.

Given the long tradition of the penitential handling of sexual behaviour, the burden of proof is on those who wish to view this content as a reflection of abstract categories. The very existence of the tradition suggests otherwise.

Collections after Burchard's *Decretum*, such as those of Ivo of Chartres and Gratian, show a tendency not to use the sexual materials from the penitentials. It is not clear why this occurred. If Peter Damian's fierce attack on the sexual contents of the penitentials is symptomatic of a general attitude, then the reason may be a profound distrust of the authoritativeness of such material.[6] However, I suspect that the reason lies more in the developing sophistication of the canon law and in an emerging division of labour between strictly canonical works and pastoral or penitential manuals. Aside from Damian, there are no signs of widespread violent opposition to the penitentials in the first half of the eleventh century, although Cardinal Atto does demonstrate a critical approach to them at the end of the century.

The penitentials played a decisive role in the early medieval handling of sexual offences. They recorded the various kinds of offence, provided commensurate sanctions, and in so doing ranked them in terms of their comparative gravity. In addition, they ensured the transmission of this sexual code throughout the whole period we have examined. It is true that the penitential treatment of sexual behaviour tends to be authoritarian, apodictic, legalistic, and even negative. It is also true that Western attitudes may have suffered because of this particular approach to sexuality over such a long period of time. However, this is no reason to censure the penitentials. They did what they were designed to do within the limits of that design – as practical handbooks of penance. The fault, if there is one, perhaps lies in the failure of the society to provide parallel reflective critical discussion of human sexuality. In the age we have surveyed, there is a code of sexual behaviour provided by the penitentials; there are numerous laws, rules, and regulations which attempt to safeguard clerical celibacy and monastic continence or to enforce intricate incest regulations. But there is virtually no theological reflection aside from occasional borrowings from patristic literature, such as one finds in the work of Jonas of Orleans on the laity.

Perhaps after this journey through the penitentials one might be allowed a few words of speculation. The penitentials are characterized by a sameness and monotony which can be deadly for anyone who sets out to read all of them, as I did. Yet I had a feeling while reading these manuals that they were engaged in strenuous combat against urges and forces in human nature which were long in being brought to heel. The newly converted peoples of western Europe seem to have had a strong attachment to a more diversified, open, and freely expressed sexuality than could be countenanced by the Christian ethic. One has the same feeling in regard to the repeated efforts to enforce clerical celibacy[7] and to eradicate local superstitions and magic. Only further work in the details of social history will confirm the validity of such feelings. However, I suspect that confirmation will be forthcoming, as I also suspect that research into the post–twelfth-century treatment of sexuality will show that the sexual culture of our more recent past is a product of four central factors: 1/continued penitential development through the

summae confessorum and the subsequent moral theology; 2/the intellec-
tual rationalizing of the earlier tradition by the scholastic theologians,
who elaborated a sophisticated theory of natural law which provided an
intelligible explanation of the immorality of various classes of sexual
behaviour; 3/the work of the canon lawyers, who tended to take over
much of the discussion of the details of marital sexuality; and 4/the
extension of sexual moral regulations into the civil law.

The history of sexuality in the West has yet to be written, and a
comprehensive, synthetic study will be impossible until the detailed
analysis of the separate facets of the history is undertaken. I have
attempted to provide such an analysis of only one aspect of this story.
It is hoped that others will contribute to our understanding of a subject
which seems to be so central to contemporary interests but which is too
important to be left to those who have little respectable knowledge of
our past. A non-judgmental understanding of the past will illumine
how and why we got to the present. Without this understanding our
fragmented knowledge of the present will simply be a catalogue of
trends and beliefs uninformed by the intelligibility provided by
historical insight.[8]

Appendixes
Notes
Bibliography
Tables of Reference
General Index

General Areas of
Sexual Behaviour Covered
in the Penitentials

The following charts indicate the general sexual topics for which there is at least one canon in the pre-813 penitential literature that we have used. The abbreviations are self-evident, except perhaps:

Abst periods of sexual abstinence
Form proper form of sexual intercourse

	Gildas	Synod of N Brit	Grove of Victory	Book of David
Adultery			x	x
Abst				
Form				
Incest			x	x
Aphrod				
Fornic	x	x		x
Homo	x	x	x	x
Bestiality	x		x	x
Masturb	x	x	x	
Pollution	x			x

	Vinnian	Columbanus	Cummean
Adultery	x	x	x
Abst	x		x
Form			
Incest			x
Aphrod	x	x	
Fornic	x	x	x
Homo	x	x	x
Bestiality	x	x	x
Masturb		x	x
Pollution			x

	Theodore	Ex Cummean	Bede	Egbert
Adultery	x	x	x	x
Abst	x	x	x	x
Form	x	x	x	x
Incest	x	x	x	x
Aphrod	x	x		
Fornic	x	x	x	x
Homo	x	x	x	x
Bestiality	x	x	x	x
Masturb	x	x		x
Pollution	x	x	x	x

	Burgundian	Merseburg	Cap iudiciorum
Adultery	x	x	x
Abst		x	x
Form		x	x
Incest		x	x
Aphrod	x	x	x
Fornic	x	x	x
Homo	x	x	x
Bestiality	x	x	x
Masturb	x	x	x
Pollution		x	x

Periods of Sexual Abstinence

The following chart indicates the references to canons in the penitentials prior to 813 which provide for periods of sexual abstinence. The periods of time are listed in the order of appearance in the penitentials. The three Lents or the three forty-day periods are the forty days before Easter, before Christmas, and after Pentecost.

The Index may be consulted for additions made by later penitentials or canonical collections. See also Payer 'Early Medieval Regulations concerning Marital Sexual Relations.'

	Vinnian	Cummean	Theodore	Ex Cummean
3 Lents	46	2.30		3.18
Sunday	46	2.30	1.14.20	3.17, 18
Saturday	46	2.30		3.18
After conception	46	2.30	2.12.3	3.18
Wednesday		2.30		3.18
Friday		2.30		3.18
Menstruation		2.30	1.14.19	3.13, 16, 18
			1.14.23	
After birth		2.31	1.14.19	3.16
			2.12.3	3.18
Before Communion			1.12.3	3.18
			2.12.1	
Lent			2.12.2	
Easter octave			2.12.2	
Before Christmas				

	Bede	Egbert	Merseburg	Cap iudiciorum
3 Lents		7.3		9.3
Sunday	3.37	7.3	133	9.1, 3
Saturday		7.3		9.3
After conception	3.37	7.1		9.1, 3
Wednesday	3.37	7.3	135 (Lent)	
Friday	3.37	7.3	135 (Lent)	
Menstruation	3.37		96	9.3
			157	
After birth	3.37	7.1	134	9.1
			158	
Before Communion		7.3	135	9.3
				34.1
Lent	3.37	7.4		
Easter octave	3.37	7.4		
Before Christmas	3.37			

Penances as Measures of Gravity

On a few occasions I have mentioned or drawn particular attention to penances, with the implication that penances which are attached to sins suggest something about the gravity of those sins. However, I have avoided making a concentrated study of the gravity of sexual offences on the basis of their penances, and no attempt has been made to compare the gravity of these offences with the gravity of different offences in the same penitential or to compare the gravity of the same offence in different penitentials. The motive for avoiding such consideration of penances has been the methodological risks attendant on using penances in this way. This appendix will examine these methodological risks and provide an example of the task involved in a serious analysis of penances.

The penitentials seldom use evaluative terms such as *bad, horrendous, terrible, mortal, venial, worse,* or *worst* to characterize the sins which they censure. Nor do they provide an explicit ranking of various offences such as we have seen in a text of Theodulf of Orleans (above, page 46). However, the penitentials implicitly rank offences through the penances which they impose. One trait which the penances share is length of time in years, months, weeks, or days, so it would seem reasonable to use length as the primary feature for ranking the different sins. Using length of time, it is possible to construct a time-scale arranged in sequential order. The penitential canons usually add various modalities (for example, part of the time on bread and water) to the length of the penances, which should also be appended for clarification. In principle it is possible to make a continuum for each penitential and to range all the offences along it according to the duration of their penances.

On the basis of this ordered scale one could then reasonably argue to the *comparative gravity* of the various sins in the same penitential. In the absence of explicit weighting such as that in the text of Theodulf of Orleans, the concept of gravity must be understood to be a relative notion which gains intelligibility in comparative contexts. Sins higher on the time-scale will be considered more grave than sins lower down. This inference is justified from a purely rational consideration of the way human beings behave. If act x is considered more serious than act y, we tend to penalize x more severely than y. If the penalties were reversed, we would consider the imposition to be unreasonable. There is no reason to believe that the system of penances in the penitentials operated on different principles. Given this assumption, one can reasonably assume that for each individual penitential the length of penances is a function of the perceived gravity of the corresponding offences.

As a further influence on the position of sins on the time-scale, the descriptions of offenders and offences must be taken into account. The penitentials frequently distinguish among various classes of offenders according to marital, ecclesiastical, or monastic status, according to age, and sometimes according to the reasons and motives of the agents. They also show considerable ingenuity in specifying the circumstances surrounding the activities which they censure. Seldom do they simply proscribe generic acts such as adultery, murder, or homosexuality. The *Penitential of Vinnian* has five separate canons on adultery, each making distinctions in regard to the people involved or in regard to whether or not the act results in the birth of a child (above, pages 21, 22). Theodore's seven canons on killing introduce several variations (*Canons of Theodore U* 1.4.1–7; Finst 294–5), and we have already seen the many distinctions made in regard to homosexual behaviour. A scale for any given penitential must therefore record the complexities associated with penances, offences, and offenders if it is to be a serviceable indicator of comparative gravity. The construction of such scales is both possible and valuable but demands extreme care if it is to yield worthwhile results. To do otherwise would be a grave injustice to the sophisticated handling of sin by the penitentials.

A properly devised scale will reflect the comparative gravity of the various offences in a penitential on the basis of the ranking of these offences according to the length of their penances. Assuming that scales are devised for individual penitentials, one may then want to study the comparative gravity of the same offence in different penitentials through a comparison of lengths of time. Noonan, for example, in his study of contraception implies that this is a legitimate undertaking when he charts the penances from different penitentials (page 164). However, there is a fallacy here based on the belief that identical lengths of time in different penitentials mean the same in terms of gravity. Lengths of time gain their meaning from their relative positions on a scale. If, for example, the longest time of any penance in penitential A is five years and the shortest time in penitential B is the same, it is clear that the five-year length of time signifies two quite different degrees of censure for these two works. If act x has a five-year penance on the scale of A and a five-year penance on the scale of B, the reasonable conclusion prima facie is that the act is considered more grave by A than by B. Beyond benefiting from such logical considerations, however, little is to be gained by attempting to compare the same offence in different penitentials. Numbers on a scale indicating length of time according to which sins are ranked and from which comparative gravity is inferred are only meaningful for the penitential for which the scale is devised. They are unhelpful in making comparisons between penitentials simply because they are meaningless in that context. Unless a method can be devised for standardizing the scales of different penitentials, there are no grounds for comparing offences in different penitentials.

A word should be said here about the notion introduced earlier of a base penance. The base penance is understood to be the penance levied on a generic offence committed by an unspecified agent, or by the least specified agent if the former is not provided for in a particular penitential. The *Canons of Theodore* provides a good example of a base penance for perjury: 'Perjurors, a penance of three years' (1.6.5; Finst 298). None of the penitentials has such pure base penances for all of the acts it censures. In some cases one must find the least specified version of the offence committed by the least specified agent and use that as the base penance. The value of base penances is that they provide the point below which penances fall because of mitigating circumstances and above which they rise because of aggravating circumstances. Youth, necessity, and force, for example, are mitigating circumstances, while superior ecclesiastical rank and connection with the sacred are aggravating circumstances. In Theodore the penance for committing perjury in a church is eleven years (1.6.1; Finst 297).

It must also be remembered that the penitentials are usually not the pure products of their authors. They are the offspring both of the contemporaneous penitential practice of their authors and of the sources used by the authors or compilers. Frequently, the penances are simply taken over unchanged from the source; sometimes the penance of the source is altered by the compiler. Often the same offence is found several times in the same penitential with different penances. This complicates the effort to determine base penances but highlights the latitude allowed by the penitential towards the levying of penances. The *Canons of Theodore* has a classic censure of adultery between a married man and his neighbour's wife: 'Whoever stains the wife of his neighbour shall fast for three years, without his own wife, two days a week and on the three forty-day periods' (1.14.9; Finst 308). One is tempted to select the three-year penance in Theodore. However, a few lines later we read, 'A woman who has committed adultery shall do penance for seven years. And this matter is dealt with the same way in the canon' (1.14.14; Finst 308). Is this a case of a heavier penance being imposed on the woman than on the man, signalling some kind of discrimination, or is it more likely an example of the collector's penchant for completeness? On several occasions Egbert is content simply to list different penances for the same offence without further comment (*P of Egbert* 3.1; 5.17, 20; W 234, 237). This is probably a sign of the discretion allowed the confessor in assigning penances. A careful study of the penances in the penitentials would have to take these variations into account.

In the next section I give the ranking for five offences along with their specific forms in two penitentials and note the base penance for each offence in each work. It is apparent even from this limited analysis how complex the undertaking would be were one to rank all the offences in each penitential, and the enterprise would have limited value since the results would not allow for accurate inter-penitential comparison. They would, however, provide a rough idea of the comparative gravity of similar offences in different penitentials. Length of time, after all, has some absolute significance. Ten years is ten years – a long time to do a penance, no matter where it occurs on a numerical scale. Perhaps the greatest benefit to be gained from carefully constructed scales of penances for individual penitentials would be the foundation they would lay for insights into the attitudes of their authors and compilers towards the different sins. They would also provide a basis for comparison with contemporary non-penitential works, such as secular law codes.

The following analysis will illustrate the complexity of the handling of five offences (adultery, bestiality, killing, perjury, and theft) in two penitentials, those of Cummean and Theodore, which stand at the source of the penitential tradition. The penances are arranged in ascending order of length under each offence in order to demonstrate the effect that mitigating and aggravating circumstances have on the determination of the length of penances. I have listed the penances found in the texts as edited, realizing that the numerals may have been misread by copyists or editors. I have noted the base penance for each offence in each penitential where this seems reasonable. The *Penitential of Cummean* has a canon which provides a base penance for each of the offences. The *Canons of Theodore*, on the other hand, is problematic for adultery, bestiality, killing, and theft. For adultery the penance could be either three or four years, but there is the anomalous penance of seven years for an adulteress. The penances for bestiality are simply inconsistent; fifteen years is laid down for the least specified form of the offence, but then an aggravating circumstance – frequency – results in a ten-year penance. A layman who kills another layman with premeditation would seem to be the classic basic murderer. He is to receive a seven-year penance. But the more straightforward example of 'a person who commits homicide [*homicida*]' is penanced with ten or seven years. The base penance for theft would probably fall between three and seven years. No base penance has been noted for these offences in the *Canons of Theodore*.

It should be recalled that a complex system of commutations for penances recorded in the penitentials was introduced early in the penitential tradition; see Vogel 'Composition légale et commutations dans le système de la pénitence tarifée.'

PENITENTIAL OF CUMMEAN (Bieler 108–35)

Adultery
A layman with his neighbour's wife or virgin daughter: 1 year (2.23). *Base penance for adultery*

A layman with his female slave: 1 year, sell the slave (2.26); if he begets a child, set the slave free (2.27)
A layman with a vowed virgin: 1½ years (2.25)
A layman with a vowed virgin and he begets a child: 3 years (2.24)

Bestiality
A boy who receives communion also: 100 days (10.5)
Anyone: 1 year (2.6). *Base penance* for bestiality

Killing
By anyone, unintentionally, by accident: 1 year (4.8)
By anyone, in anger: 3 years (4.7)
By anyone, with premeditation: life, lay down weapons, live for God dead to the world (4.5). *Base penance* for killing
After taking vows: live dead to the world in perpetual exile (4.6)

Perjury
Anyone, led unknowingly and later recognizes it: 1 year (3.10)
Anyone, suspects he is being led into it but swears anyway: 2 years (3.11)
Anyone: 4 years (3.8). *Base penance* for perjury
A person leading another into perjury: 7 years (3.9)

Theft
Boy of ten years: 7 days (1.13)
One over twenty, a small theft: 20 or 40 days (1.14)
Anyone, food: 40 days (1.12)
Boy: 40 or 30 days according to age and state of knowledge (3.1)
Anyone, food for the second time: 3 × 40 days (1.12)
Anyone, once: 1 year (3.1). *Base penance* for theft
Anyone, food for the third time: 1 year (1.12)
Anyone, a second time: 2 years (3.1)

CANONS OF THEODORE U (Finst 285–334)

Adultery
Anyone, with female slave: 6 months, free slave (1.14.12)
Anyone, with neighbour's wife: 3 years (1.14.9)
Anyone, with vowed virgin: 3 years (1.14.11)
Anyone, with married woman: 4 years (1.2.1)
Adulteress: 7 years (1.14.14)

Bestiality
Anyone, often: 10 years (1.2.2)
Anyone: 15 years (1.2.3)

Killing
By anyone, on command of the secular lord: 40 days (1.4.6)
By anyone, in a public war: 40 days (1.4.6)
By anyone, by accident: 1 year (1.4.7)
By anyone, out of revenge: 3 years (1.4.2) or 10 years
By anyone, in anger: 3 years (1.4.7)
By layman, another layman with premeditation: 7 years (1.4.4)
Anyone killing a monk or a cleric: 7 years (1.4.5)
By anyone, through potions or trickery: 7 years (1.4.7)
A person who commits homicide: 10 years (1.4.3) or 7 years
By anyone, in a quarrel: 10 years (1.4.7)

Perjury
Forced out of necessity: 3 Lents (1.6.2)
On unconsecrated cross and lying: 1 year (1.6.4)
Solemn swearing and lying: 3 years (1.6.4)
Perjurors: 7 years (1.6.5). *Base penance* for perjury
In a church: 11 years (1.6.1)

Theft
Of consecrated objects: 3 years (1.3.5)
Frequent: 7 years, reduced if restitution made (1.3.3)

Homosexuality and the Penitentials

In his recent work entitled *Christianity, Social Tolerance, and Homosexuality* John Boswell deals briefly with the contribution of the penitential literature to the history of attitudes towards homosexuality and with the specific contributions of Regino of Prüm, the *Penitential of Silos*, and Burchard of Worms. Boswell believes that the penitentials are not 'an index of medieval morality' (page 182) and that their treatment of homosexuality suggests 'a relatively indulgent attitude adopted by prominent churchmen of the early Middle Ages toward homosexual behavior' (page 183). I hope that the present work has made a reasonable case that the penitentials are an index of medieval morality, at least an index to what was believed to be morally reprehensible. The attitude betrayed by their treatment of homosexuality can be argued endlessly, but the argument must be based on a more thorough analysis of the penitentials than Boswell offers. What might be helpful would be to have the information for such an argument. The following summary of penitential references to male homosexuality and lesbianism and of the treatment of these topics in Regino and Burchard is offered to this end.

MALE HOMOSEXUALITY

All of the penitentials have at least one canon censuring homosexuality and many have a relatively extensive treatment of the subject. A list of the edited penitentials which have canons censuring homosexual behaviour is given at the end of this section.

Two factors influence the penitential treatment of homosexuality: the specific kinds of offence and the agents involved. The various types of homosexual behaviour distinguished in these manuals may be grouped according to the following characteristic types of reference:
– general references to males relating sexually with males
– specific mention of *sodomites* or the use of a derivative linguistic form such as *fornicatio sodomita, sodomitico more, sodomitico ritu, in scelere sodomitico, sodomiti-*

cum peccatum: There is no doubt that such expressions connote homosexual behaviour. This study has suggested that the use of these terms probably refers to male anal intercourse.

- references to relations *in terga*: This appears to be an alternate expression for anal relations. However, this offence is usually penanced more mildly than 'sodomy.' I am not sure what to make of this. Two points might be made. The references to relations *in terga* are very few for adult males. Perhaps this reflects an older usage which survives in some of the later manuals. On the other hand, the expression seems to be used to identify a particular form of behaviour of youths. Only once is the sodomite expression used to refer to the homosexual relations of youths (*P of Egbert* 5.17).
- references to femoral relations (sometimes also referred to as relations *intra crura*)
- references to mutual masturbation
- references to oral sexual relations
- references to young boys (*minimi*) simulating sexual relations and stimulating each other
- references to a form of forced relations in which a younger boy is 'oppressed' by an older youth
- the singling out of the sexual relations of natural brothers.

The range of persons addressed has some effect on the focus of the canons:
- canons addressed to unspecified persons (introduced by 'si quis' or referring to *viri*): These canons censure all of the specific forms of homosexual behaviour.
- canons addressed to bishops, priests, deacons, subdeacons, clerics, monks: These canons do not mention the different types of homosexual acts but invariably speak of 'acting as the Sodomites did' and grade the penances according to the ecclesiastical rank of the offender, the higher position receiving the more severe penance. In these canons covering ecclesiastical persons the intention of the reference to 'what the Sodomites did' is probably a general reference to any form of homosexual relation.
- canons addressed to youths: These canons censure the whole range of homosexual behaviour but use variants for the reference to sodomites.

It would be pointless to attempt a detailed comparison of the gravity of the different kinds of homosexual acts based on a comparison of their relative penances. However, an examination of the tradition reveals a striking consistency in the apparent weighting of the different offences. Restricting ourselves to canons whose subjects are unspecified males, we might note the following:
- The general mention of male sexual relations which are not specified further usually carries a penance of ten to fifteen years: for examples, see *Canons of Theodore U* 1.2.4 (Finst 290); *Reims P* 4.40 (Asbach *Das Poenitentiale Remense* appendix, 29); *Arundel P* 52 (S 1.452).
- Censures using a linguistic variant of *sodomites* usually carry a penance of ten years but range from seven to twenty years.

- Censures of relations *in terga* invariably carry a penance of three years: for examples, see *P of Vinnian* (2) (Bieler 74); *Paris P* 58 (S 2.330).
- Femoral relations are censured with one to three years' penance.
- Mutual masturbation is mentioned only three times for adult males: Synod of the Grove of Victory 8 (2 years; Bieler 68); *Bigotianum P* 2.2.3 (100 days; Bieler 220); *Arundel P* 67 (30 days; S 1.455).
- The penance for oral sexual relations ranges from three to seven years but is most frequently three or four years: for examples, see *P of Vinnian* (3) (Bieler 74); *Reims P* 4.12 (Asbach *Das Poenitentiale Remense* appendix, 26); *Vallicellian Penitential* I 28 (S 1.281); *Vienna P* 55 (S 2.354).

These edited penitentials contain canons censuring homosexual behaviour:

Gildas 1 (Bieler 60)
Synod of North Britain 1 (Bieler 66)
Grove of Victory 8 (Bieler 68)
Excerpts from a Book of David 5 (Bieler 70)
Vinnian (2), (3) (Bieler 74)
Columbanus A.3; B.3, B.15 (Bieler 96, 100, 102)
Cummean 2.8–10; 10.4, 6, 8, 9, 14–16 (Bieler 114, 128)
Theodore 1.2.2, 4–8, 11, 15, 19 (Finst 290–2)
Bigotianum 2.2.1–5; 2.3.1 (Bieler 220)
Burgundian 4 (S 2.320)
Bobbio 3 (S 2.323)
Bede 3.19, 21, 22, 30, 31, 32 (W 222–3)
Egbert 2.2; 4.5; 5.4, 17–19 (W 234, 236–7)
Paris 37, 53, 55, 57 (S 2.329–30)
Excarpsus of Cummean 2.2–6, 11, 15–17 (S 2.608–10)
Reims 4.1, 12, 14, 24, 26, 28, 29, 31–3, 35–6, 38, 40, 42, 44, 53 (Asbach *Das Poenitentiale Remense* appendix, 25–30)
Capitula iudiciorum 7.1, 10, 15; 10.1 (S 2.222–4, 227)
Merseburg 4, 56, 76, 145, 152–5 (S 2.359, 363, 367–8)
Silos 9.1, 10, 11 (ed Gonzales Rivas 177–8)
Vigila 56, 75 (W 531–2)
St Gall 14 (S 2.347)
Fleury 4 (S 2.341)
Vallicellian I 13, 27, 28, 68 (S 1.265, 281, 299)
Halitgar 6.6, 13 (S 2.294–5)
Pseudo-Theodore 16.8, 9; 20.16; 28.4–6, 16–18 (W 574, 585, 599)
St Hubert 4 (S 2.333)
Pseudo-Gregory 21 (W 543)
Vienna 4, 55, 67, 68 (S 2.351, 355)
Bede-Egbert Double P interrogatory 6; c 3; 8.4; 10.1, 2 (S 2.681, 687–8)

Arundel 38, 52, 55, 67, 72, 73 (S 1.448, 452–3, 455–6)
Monte Cassino 11, 21, 31 (S 1.403–4, 408)

LESBIANISM

Lesbian relations do not receive the attention in the penitentials that is given to male relations. However, they are mentioned, and they provide an interesting confirmation of a text from Hincmar of Reims quoted by Boswell. Speaking of women, Hincmar says that 'they are reported to use certain instruments [*quasdam machinas*] of diabolical operation to excite desire' (Boswell 204, n 132). Several penitential censures of lesbian relations make reference to such instruments. The following comprise the references to lesbian relations in the penitentials:

Canons of Theodore U 1.2.12; 1.14.15 (Finst 291, 308)
Bede 3.23, 24 (W 223)
Excarpsus of Cummean 3.35 (S 2.616)
Reims 5.68 (Asbach *Das Poenitentiale Remense* appendix, 38)
Tripartite of St Gall (Theodore) 16 (S 2.183)
Merseburg 95 (S 2.365)
Fleury 49 (S 2.344)
Vallicellian I 25 (S 1.281)
Silos 9.50 (ed Gonzales Rivas 179)
Hrabanus Maurus *Paenitentiale ad Heribaldum* c 25 (PL 110.490)
Pseudo-Theodore 16.4; 18.20 (W 574, 581)
Bede-Egbert Double Penitential 9 (S 2.688)
Monte Cassino 62 (S 1.413)
Arundel 53 (S 1.453)

REGINO OF PRÜM AND BURCHARD OF WORMS

The references by these authors to homosexual relations have already been surveyed. It must be remembered that the works in question are collections of texts, which makes it difficult to ascertain the compilers' personal views. What Boswell takes to be the personal opinions of Regino of Prüm (page 183, n 49) are simply excerpts from the *Bede-Egbert Double Penitential* (see my references under Regino of Prüm).

Even in regard to the interrogatory of Burchard (*Decretum* 19.5, not *Decretals* as in Boswell, page 205), there is a strong influence of previous penitential sources. However, the rather explicit descriptions in Burchard of homosexual acts seem to reflect a personal view of the behaviour. Much of what Boswell says in this regard is accurate enough (205–6), but his comment about the censures applying to married men is incorrect. He refers to 'the immediately following section on bestiality' (206, n 140). Presumably this is to *Decretum* 19.5 (126; S 2.437), which deals with bestiality *and* homosexuality and which explicitly refers to unmarried men:

Have you fornicated against nature, that is, have you had intercourse with males or with animals, that is, with a mare or a cow or a donkey or with some other animal? If once or twice and if you had no wife to enable you to expend your lust, you must do penance for forty days on bread and water, which is called a *carina*, along with the following seven years, and never be without penance. If, however, you had a wife, you must do penance for ten years on the established days, and if you were in the habit of this crime, you must do penance for fifteen years on the established days. If, however, this happened to you as a youth, you must do penance on bread and water for a hundred days.

Fecisti fornicationem contra naturam, id est ut cum masculis vel cum animalibus coires, id est cum equa, cum vacca, vel cum asina, vel cum alio aliquo animali? Si semel vel bis fecisti: et si uxorem non habuisti, quod adimplere tuam libidinem potuisses, quadraginta dies in pane et aqua, quod carinam vocant, cum septem sequentibus annis poenitere debes, et nunquam sis sine poenitentia. Si autem uxorem habuisti, decem annos per legitimas ferias poenitere debes. Si autem in consuetudine habuisti illud scelus, xv annos per legitimas ferias poenitere debes. Si in pueritia tibi contigerat, c dies in pane et aqua debes poenitere.

This is not the place to engage Boswell in his thesis about the tolerant attitude towards homosexuality which he claims to have found in the early Middle Ages. However, it would seem that the penitentials, which gained wide geographical circulation for four hundred years or more, do not support this conclusion. And when it is recalled that these documents enjoyed even wider circulation through the canonical collections into which they were incorporated, it becomes difficult to maintain such a conclusion against the evidence of the penitential practice of the early Middle Ages.

Notes on the Language of the Penitentials

At several points in this study I have had occasion to remark on aspects of the language used by the penitentials to speak about sexual behaviour. This appendix is meant to supplement those remarks and to draw together a representative sample of the expressions found in the penitentials for sexual acts. The appendix is divided into four parts. In the first three parts, what are felt to be significant features of the language will be mentioned briefly. The fourth part is an alphabetical list of words which are used in canons dealing with sexual offences. It must be remembered that the penitentials are not morally neutral discussions of human sexual behaviour. Their purpose is to regulate, condemn, and penalize activities considered to be immoral, in addition to providing confessional instruction and direction. They are not treatises on human behaviour but manuals of instruction on how to deal with moral faults and failures, sexual faults and failures being one aspect of this concern. Consequently, one should not be surprised if much of the vocabulary is marked by strong negative connotations.

The penitential tradition from the early Irish manuals to the *Corrector* of Burchard is composed of several core components which can be relatively easily specified. The works making up this core introduce the fundamental terminology used to express their censures of sexual behaviour. In penitentials deriving from these sources, one will not find in the canons dealing with sexual matters many terms which are not found in the originating sources. Consequently, I have chosen to confine my remarks and the subsequent list of terms to the texts which represent original contributions to the penitential tradition. These are, first, the central penitentials comprising the basic elements of the tradition: the penitentials of Columbanus, Cummean, Theodore, Bede, and Egbert. Second, there is a significant core of Frankish components, which is adequately represented by the *Burgundian Penitential* and by the seventh chapter of the *Capitula iudiciorum*. Finally, three interrogatories make original terminological contributions to the tradition: the interrogatory introducing the *Bede-Egbert Double Penitenitial*, the interrogatory in Regino of Prüm, *De synodalibus causis* 2.5, and that of Burchard, *Decretum* 19.5.

A few exceptions to the generality of the above ought to be noted:
- While the Spanish penitentials show a strong influence from insular penitentials, they also have a core derived from Spanish councils, particularly from the
Council of Elvira. No study of the language of these manuals would be complete without a control study of the terminology of the Council of Elvira.
- Aside from the term *lenocinium* in Regino and Burchard, which is probably
derived from the Council of Elvira canon 12, and one mention of *meretrix* in
Burchard 19.5(34), there is nothing in our representative penitentials on prostitution. However, *meretrix* is found in Cod Vat Pal lat 294 and given in the
variants to the *Ex Egberti* 5.7, 5.13, by Schmitz (2.665). The term is also found in
the *St Hubert Penitential* 12, rubric (S 2.334).
- The *Pseudo-Theodore Penitential*, as noted already, has several canons (16.6, 7,
26; 18.2, 7, 10, 12, 13, 14) which use the verb *imitari* for sexual relations. I am
unable to find any dictionary entry for such usage, nor is the term used in
other penitentials before or after the *Pseudo-Theodore* in that sense.

An English-language writer discussing sex in the penitentials finds himself in the
curious position of employing a vocabulary which has virtually no counterpart in
the works being analysed. There are no Latin terms corresponding to our *fornication, homosexuality, lesbianism, masturbation, aphrodisiac, impotence*. (The adverb
bestialiter is used in Magister A, ms Paris BN lat 3881, fol 198v marg. 'Qui bestialiter utitur' is a marginal gloss on a text of Augustine on the procreative purpose
of sexual relations.) I have already remarked on the extension of the term *adulterium* in the penitential usage and on the proper interpretation of *raptus* and
rapere, which is not that of sexual rape as we understand it. Furthermore, the
discussion of sexual offences in the early penitentials was divided according
to relatively self-contained, logically discriminated categories which are not
reflected in the divisions of the penitentials.

Scholarship frequently has to impose concepts and categories foreign to its
subject-matter in order to achieve intelligibility. However, in doing so it often
blinds the reader to the context in which the subject-matter is found and runs the
risk of distorting the actual state of affairs. The following remarks on the language of the penitentials are offered in an attempt to offset possible distortions in
this regard. I shall not comment on every word found in the list of terms at the
end of the appendix but restrict my observations to three areas: the use in the
penitentials of *fornicatio* and its cognates, the penitential terms for heterosexual
intercourse, and the conceptualization in the penitentials of sexual behaviour.
References to specific passages may be found by referring to the alphabetical list
following these remarks. See L. Bieler, *The Irish Penitentials* 27–47 and indices to
that work, for valuable information about the Latinity of the Irish penitentials.
The only attempt at a serious study of the language of sexuality in an early work
is that of S. Laeuchli, *Power and Sexuality. The Emergence of Canon Law at the Synod
of Elvira*. This is not the place to discuss the validity of Laeuchli's conclusions. A

recent study by J.N. Adams, *The Latin Sexual Vocabulary*, provides a fascinating survey of classical Latin usage. However, little of this usage is reflected in the sexual language employed by the penitentials. The following are of some interest: *nuptiae* for sexual intercourse (159–61), *rapio* for dragging off into captivity (175), *stuprum* with the original meaning of 'disgrace' (200–1). Finally, there is evidence of a little-used verb, *masturbor*, for masturbation (208–11).

FORNICATIO AND ITS COGNATES

Five forms of the *fornicatio* vocabulary are found in the penitentials, although the adjective *fornicarius* and the noun *fornicator* are each found only once. The more classical deponent form of the verb (*fornicari*) is encountered at least once in several of the manuals, but the regular *fornicare* is the more usual form and is always used intransitively. The noun *fornicatio* frequently occurs as the object of a verb, often with *facere*.

Fornicatio and *fornicare* are used more often than other terms, no doubt because of the purpose of the penitential canons on sex. They are general-duty words used for virtually every sexual encounter, and this polymorphous diversity is signified in the title 'De fornicatione,' which usually covers all sexual offences. However, there is a central connotation which is usually respected. *Fornicatio* refers to sexual acts which are understood to be illicit under any circumstance. For example, one does not call sexual intercourse between a man and his wife, even if done during a prohibited time, *fornicatio*. In addition, an act of adultery as a rule is not called *fornicatio*, nor is the verb *fornicare* applied to those committing adultery. This last point, though, is not an invariable trait of this vocabulary.

The diversity of usage of *fornicatio*, *fornicare*, and *fornicari* raises the question of the translation of these terms. An examination of Bieler's translation of Columbanus and Cummean and McNeill's translation of Theodore shows that the most frequent translation of the verb is 'to commit fornication.' When these translators depart from this translation, they have some trouble, apparently out of a sense of modesty or shame. There seems to be some hesitation about translating the sexual provisions of the penitentials – an attitude very different from that suggested by the blunt language of the works themselves. Bieler does not translate the grades of homosexual relation in Grove of Victory 8 (page 69); Binchy translates into Latin the sexual parts of the *Old-Irish Penitential*, which he otherwise translates into English (*The Irish Penitentials* 263–5); McNeill leaves several Latin phrases untranslated in his translation of Theodore 1.2.8 and 15 (MHP 185, 186).

In Columbanus B.10 we read, 'Si quis per se ipsum fornicaverit aut cum iumento ... ' ('If anyone has committed masturbation or has had sexual relations with a beast of burden ... ') *Fornicaverit* is understood to govern the two activities coming after it. Bieler translates this, 'If anyone has defiled himself or sinned with a beast ... ' There are numerous expressions for defiling; *fornicare* is not one of them, and the verb *to sin* is not in the text. In the *Penitential of Cummean* Bieler correctly translates 'inter femora fornicans' as 'practises femoral intercourse.' However, he is not so precisely accurate when it comes to 'in terga vero fornicantes,' which he translates as 'those practising homosexuality' (10.15). The point is that various kinds of homosexuality are in question here. Femoral intercourse is one type, anal intercourse is another, and it is the latter which is meant by 'in terga vero fornicantes' ('those practising anal intercourse'). Finally, Theodore has a canon on lesbianism: 'Si mulier cum muliere fornicaverit' ('If a woman should have sexual relations with a woman'). McNeill translates this, 'If a woman practises vice with a woman.' But there are many non-sexual ways for women to practise vice together. I do not wish to belabour this point of translation, but regulations dealing with sexual behaviour deserve the same care as those dealing with homicide or perjury.

Fornicatio and its cognates are used by the penitentials for virtually every sexual act. Nothing is gained by a literal translation or transliteration. Each use of the term is determined by the context, and it is the latter which should determine the translation. Latin expressions usually have counterparts in English which do not employ the term *fornication*, and one would be well advised to use these parallels in translating the Latin. For example, it makes no sense to translate the title 'De fornicatione' by 'Of fornication,' since the English does not connote what the Latin does. One would be better off translating the title as 'Of sexual offences.'

TERMS FOR HETEROSEXUAL INTERCOURSE

There is no single Latin word which is regularly used to connote the act of heterosexual intercourse. There are many verbs which imply a sexual union but whose connotations are other than the union as such. *Adulterare, coinquinare, contaminare, corrumpere, maculare, moechari, peccare cum,* and *polluere* are all used in contexts implying heterosexual union. However, they are all either morally or emotively loaded terms whose connotations point to the illegitimacy or undesirability of the act more than to the act itself. There are a few verbs which are morally and emotively neutral and which connote the act of intercourse: *cognoscere, coire, concumbere, coniungere, dormire, intrare ad, iungere, miscere, nubere.* The noun *coitus* is not used in a heterosexual context, and the verb *coire* is usually reserved for non-heterosexual relations. The morally neutral verbs are as a general rule used for relations between a husband and his wife which are for one reason or another forbidden or not possible because of impotence.

THE CONCEPTUALIZATION OF SEXUAL BEHAVIOUR

Class nouns signify levels of abstraction and conceptualization. The penitentials, particularly those from Theodore on, make use of a wide range of class terms to designate categories of immoral behaviour, such as *homicidium* ('homicide'), *furtum* ('theft'), *periurium* ('perjury'), and the words for the capital sins. This usage has parallels in the English language and corresponds to our own ways of conceptualization. The penitentials designate categories of illicit sexual behaviour quite otherwise, however. The general tendency is to cover the field of sexual immorality under the broad category 'De fornicatione,' which, we have seen, includes virtually every sexual offence. Within that category, regulations are centred on particular kinds of acts which are descriptively identified but not brought under a class term such as we have in English – *fornication, homosexuality, masturbation, bestiality*, and so on. Of course, there are some general terms used by the penitentials, such as *adulterium, raptus, incestus*, and *pollutio* for seminal emission (see the chapter headings to *Capitula iudiciorum* [S 2.217] and *Excarpsus of Cummean* [S 2.597–8]). The *Bede-Egbert Double Penitential* (S 2.683–4) has more specific divisions for sexual offences, which indicates a further level of conceptualization and discrimination, as does the *Penitential of Pseudo-Theodore* (W 567), but the traditional vocabulary is not expanded or substantially generalized. The practice of using descriptive expressions for kinds of sexual activities continues throughout the period covered by this study, both in the penitential literature and in the canonical collections. A level of conceptualization sufficiently general and abstract to produce a vocabulary of class terms will not be reached until the thirteenth century.

THE SEXUAL VOCABULARY OF THE PENITENTIALS

The following list of expressions arranged in alphabetical order represents the vocabulary used by the major penitential traditions to speak about sexual offences. I have tried to be as thorough but also as brief as possible in the choice of phrases. Where there may be any misunderstanding, I have indicated in brackets after the quotations the offence referred to in the texts. The works selected are those believed to be representative of the major penitential traditions or of original contributions made by interrogatories. However, phrases under a particular term do not necessarily represent the first occurrence of the term in the penitential literature. This is particularly true of the texts from Burchard's interrogatory, which sometimes borrow from Regino of Prüm terms that have not been noted previously. Nonetheless, Burchard contributes a sufficient enough number of original terms to the tradition to justify his inclusion here.

Abstinere
De menstruis abstinendis (*Bede-Egbert* 6, title)

Abstinentia
De abstinentia viri ac femine (*Bede-Egbert* 5, title)

Adultera
molles sicut adultera (*Theodore* 1.2.6)
vir uxorem suam invenerit adulteram (*Theodore* 1.14.4)
mulier adultera (*Theodore* 1.14.14)
mulier si adultera est (*Theodore* 2.12.11)
reconciliari mulieri adulterae (*Theodore* 2.12.12)
promisisti meretrici vel adulterae [*Burchard* 19.5(34)]
tu autem et adultera [*Burchard* 19.5(105)]

Adulterare
adulterare voluerit (*Columbanus* B.23)
cum uxore alterius adulteraverit (*Cap iudiciorum* 7.3)
cum alterius uxore adulteratus fuerit [*Regino* 2.5(15)]
adulterasse accusatur [*Regino* 2.5(31)]
se renuente et reluctante adulterata sit [*Burchard* 19.5(50)]

Adulterium
sciat se adulterium perpetrasse (*Columbanus* B.8)
adulterium commiserit (*Columbanus* B.14)
adulterium perpetraverit (*Theodore* 1.9.5)
adulterium perpetraverit illa (*Theodore* 1.14.4)
mulier adulterium perpetravit (*Theodore* 2.12.12)
adulterium perpetraverit (*Egbert* 4.8)
adulterium commiserit (*Burgundian* 8)
sciat se adulterium commisisse (*Burgundian* 12)
De fornicationibus vel adulteriis (*Cap iudiciorum* 7, title)
fecisti adulterium (*Bede-Egbert* interrogatory 4)
adulteria perpetrari [*Regino* 2.5(37)]
ecce unum adulterium ... ecce aliud adulterium [*Burchard* 19.5(42)]
adulterium perpetraret [*Burchard* 19.5(50)]
adulterium perpetratum habuisti [*Burchard* 19.5(109)]

Cognoscere
suam cognoverit clientelam (*Columbanus* B.8)
non illis liceat suas cognoscere uxores (*Columbanus* B.18)
ante pascha cognoscet mulierem (*Egbert* 7.4)
iterum eam cognovit (*Burgundian* 12)
dicit quod non cognovisses eam [*Burchard* 19.5(117)]

Coinquinamentum
inlecebrosum osculum sine coinquinamento (*Cummean* 10.2)

Coinquinare (se)
se ipsum quoinquinaverit (*Columbanus* A.7)
se invicem manibus coinquinantes (*Cummean* 10.6)

vir semetipsum coinquinans (*Cummean* 10.13)
si se ipsum coinquinat (*Theodore* 1.2.9)
qui se ipsum coinquinant (*Theodore* 1.8.11)

Coinquinari
per turpiloquium vel aspectu coinquinatus est (*Cummean* 2.12)
inpugnatione cogitationis violenter coinquinatus est (*Cummean* 2.13)
sed coinquinati non sunt (*Cummean* 10.4)
tangendo mulierem aut osculando coinquinabitur (*Theodore* 1.8.1)
per turpiloquium seu aspectu coinquinatus (*Egbert* 9.2)
qui inpugnatione violenter quoinquinatus est (*Egbert* 9.6)
coinquinatus es ... quadragesima [*Burchard* 19.5(57)] (for sexual intercourse)

Coire
cum pecoribus coierit (*Theodore* 1.2.3)
coierit cum masculo (*Theodore* 1.2.4)
menstruo tempore coierit (*Theodore* 1.14.23)
non possit cum ea coire [*Regino* 2.5(32)]
ita ut non potuisses coire cum ea [*Burchard* 19.5(117)]
et sic secum coires more sodomitico [*Burchard* 19.5(120)]
cum masculis vel cum animalibus coires [*Burchard* 19.5(126)]
quasi coire debeant [*Burchard* 19.5(156)] (lesbian relation)
et sic coiret tecum [*Burchard* 19.5(158)] (bestiality)

Coitus
cum masculo coitu faemineo peccaverit (*Columbanus* B.15)
sola cum se ipsa coitum habet (*Theodore* 1.2.13)
animalia coitu hominum polluta (*Theodore* 2.11.9)
illud iumentum provocares ad coitum [*Burchard* 19.5(158)]

Commixtio
et negat aliquam commixtionem inter vos esse [*Burchard* 19.5(117)]

Complere
desideria labiis complentes (*Cummean* 10.16)

Concubina
si quis concubinam habet (*Theodore* 1.9.6)
concubinam simul habuerit [*Regino* 2.5(16)]

Concumbere
concubuisti ... retro [*Burchard* 19.5(52)]
(See Burchard 19.5, qq 53–6, 105, 106, 109.)

Coniugium
sine diliciis coniugioque (*Cummean* 2.32)

Coniungere
virgo virgini coniunctus est (*Columbanus* B.16)

Coniunctio
abstineant se a coniunctione (*Theodore* 2.12.1)

Contaminare
monachus laicam contaminat (*Bede* 3.7)
uxoratus virginem contaminat (*Bede* 3.12)

Corrumpere
vel virginitate corruperit (*Burgundian* 8)
vel virginem corrupisti (*Bede-Egbert* interrogatory 4)
si corrupisti virginem [*Burchard* 19.5(47)]

Dormire
qui cum uxore sua dormierit, lavet (*Theodore* 2.12.30)

Excitare
si excitat ipse (*Theodore* 1.8.9)

Femur, -oris
si vero in femoribus (*Cummean* 2.9)
si in femoribus (*Theodore* 1.2.8; 1.8.10)
si in femoribus (*Bede* 3.21)

Fornicare
si fornicaverit semel (*Columbanus* A.3)
fornicaverit sicut sodomitae fecerunt (*Columbanus* B.3)
fornicaverit quidem cum mulieribus (*Columbanus* B.4)
per se ipsum fornicaverit aut cum iumento (*Columbanus* B.10)
fornicaverit sodomitico ritu (*Columbanus* B.15)
fornicaverit de laicis cum mulieribus (*Columbanus* B.16)
laicus cum iumento fornicaverit (*Columbanus* B.17)
adulterare voluerit aut fornicare (*Columbanus* B.23)
clericus semel fornicans (*Cummean* 2.17)
inter foemora fornicans (*Cummean* 10.8)
inter femora fornicantes (*Cummean* 10.14)
in terga vero fornicantes (*Cummean* 10.15)
fornicaverit cum virgine (*Theodore* 1.2.1)
aut cum pecode fornicat (*Theodore* 1.2.2)
si masculus cum masculo fornicat (*Theodore* 1.2.5)
qui concupiscit fornicare (*Theodore* 1.2.10)
mulier cum muliere fornicaverit (*Theodore* 1.2.12)
quae virum habet si fornicaverit (*Theodore* 1.2.14)
cum matre quis fornicaverit (*Theodore* 1.2.16)

qui cum sorore fornicaverit (*Theodore* 1.2.17)
frater cum fratre naturali fornicaverit (*Theodore* 1.2.19)
mulier cum muliere fornicans (*Bede* 3.23)
sepe fornicat (*Bede* 3.27)
cum quadrupede fornicaverit (*Egbert* 4.2)
cum matre fornicaverit (*Egbert* 4.3)
mater cum filio suo parvulo fornicaverit (*Egbert* 4.6)
viri inter femora fornicantes (*Egbert* 5.18)
in terga fornicans (*Egbert* 5.19)
episcopus cum quadrupede fornicans (*Egbert* 5.22)
non tamen voluit fornicare (*Egbert* 9.2)
fornicaverit sicut sodomite fecerunt (*Burgundian* 4)
fornicaverit quidem cum mulieribus (*Burgundian* 11)
fornicaverit cum sanctimoniale (*Burgundian* 13)
propter concupiscentiam vel libidinem per ipsum fornicaverit (*Burgundian* 14)
fornicaverit ut sodomite fecerunt (*Cap iudiciorum* 7.1)
cum deo sacrata fornicaverit (*Cap iudiciorum* 7.3)
vidua vel sponsa alterius fornicaverit (*Cap iudiciorum* 7.4)
cum quadrupediis fornicaverit (*Cap iudiciorum* 7.7)
per semetipsum quocumque ingenio fornicaverit (*Cap iudiciorum* 7.9)

Fornicari
concupierit ... fornicari (*Columbanus* A.2)
cum aliqua puella fornicari nitens (*Cummean* 10.17)
pueri qui fornicantur inter ipsos (*Theodore* 1.2.11)
si cuius uxor fornicata fuerit (*Theodore* 2.12.5)
cum quadrupedia fornicatus fuerit (*Burgundian* 33)
vel cum matre sua fornicatus fuerit (*Cap iudiciorum* 7.5)
cum ea quam propter deum relinquit uxore fornicatus fuerit (*Cap iudiciorum* 7.6)
concupiscit fornicari (*Cap iudiciorum* 7.8)
mulier conscio viro suo fornicata fuerit [*Regino* 2.5(22)]
cum alterius coniuge fornicatus fuerit [*Regino* 2.5(23)]
cum femina quae virum non habet fornicatus fuerit [*Regino* 2.5(24)]
vel ipsis consentientibus cum eis fornicatus fuerit [*Regino* 2.5(30)]
aut cum ea fornicatus est [*Regino* 2.5(34)]

Fornicarius
inludetur fornicaria cogitatione (*Theodore* 1.2.21)

Fornicatio
De fornicatione (*Cummean* 2, title)
episcopus faciens fornicationem (*Cummean* 2.1)
presbiter aut diaconus faciens fornicationem (*Cummean* 2.2)
minimi vero fornicationem imitantes (*Cummean* 10.4)
De fornicatione (*Theodore* 1.2, title)

mater cum filio suo parvulo fornicationem imitatur (*Theodore* 1.2.20)
vel sacra virgo fornicationem faciens (*Theodore* 1.8.6)
episcopus ... fornicationem facientes (*Theodore* 1.9.1)
propter fornicationem (*Theodore* 2.12.5)
De fornicatione (*Bede* 3, title)
fornicationi ... servivit (*Bede* 3.28)
mater cum filio parvulo fornicationem imitatur (*Bede* 3.29)
fornicationem facit cum ancilla dei (*Egbert* 2.3)
pontifex fornicationem faciens naturalem (*Egbert* 5.2)
Teodorus dixit: Monachus faciens fornicationem (*Egbert* 5.11)
si monachus querens fornicationem (*Egbert* 5.12)
monachus fornicationem faciens (*Egbert* 5.13)
fecisti fornicationem sicut sodomitae (*Bede-Egbert* interrogatory 6)
Burchard uses the expression 'fornicationem facere' numerous times throughout
   Decretum 19.5 for most kinds of sexual offence. There is nothing to be gained
   by noting these formulaic expressions.

Fornicator
licet sit fornicator (*Theodore* 2.12.6)

Frigidus
dixisti te esse frigidae naturae [*Burchard* 19.5(117)] (male impotence)

Inquinare
se manibus inquinantes (*Bede* 3.30)

Intrare
ad suam intrat ancillam (*Cummean* 2.26)

Irritare
et inritantes se invicem (*Cummean* 10.4)

Iungere
iunxisti uxori tuae menstruo tempore [*Burchard* 19.5(53)]

Lenocinium
lenocinium fecerit [*Regino* 2.5(36)]
exercuisti lenocinium [*Burchard* 19.5(184)]

Libido, -idinis
propter concupiscentiam vel libidinem (*Burgundian* 14)
quomodo impleres tuam libidinem [*Burchard* 19.5(42)]
quod adimpleres tuam libidinem [*Burchard* 19.5(126)]
quando libidinem se vexantem extinguere [*Burchard* 19.5(156)]

Machina
si sanctaemoniales cum sanctaemoniale per machinam (dildo?) (*Bede* 3.24)
De machina mulierum ('The artifice of women') (*Egbert* 7, title)

Machinamentum
ut faceres quoddam molimen aut machinamentum (dildo?) [*Burchard* 19.5(154)]
supradicto molimine vel alio aliquo machinamento [*Burchard* 19.5(155)]

Maculare
laicus maculans uxorem (*Cummean* 2.23)
puellam dei maculaverit (*Cummean* 2.24)
qui maculat uxorem proximi sui (*Theodore* 1.14.9)
si puellam dei maculaverit (*Theodore* 1.14.11)
laicus maculans se cum ancilla dei (*Egbert* 5.15)

Matrimonium
abstineat se a matrimonio eius (*Theodore* 1.14.4)

Membrum virile
ut tuum virile membrum intra coxas [*Burchard* 19.5(121)]
tuum virile membrum in manum tuam [*Burchard* 19.5(123)]
tuum virile membrum in lignum perforatum [*Burchard* 19.5(124)]
in modum virilis membri [*Burchard* 19.5(154)]

Meretrix, -tricis
promisisti meretrici [*Burchard* 19.5(34)]

Miscere
nam qui tunc miscerit (marital intercourse) (*Bede* 3.37)
cum masculis et mutis misceatur animalibus [*Regino* 2.5(35)]

Moechari
moechantes in labiis (*Cummean* 2.8)
laica virgo moechata fuerit [*Regino* 2.5(25)]
cum aliqua christiana moechatus fuerit [*Regino* 2.5(29)]
cum commatre spirituali moechatus fuerit [*Regino* 2.5(33)]
moechatus es cum uxore alterius [*Burchard* 19.5(41)]
si moechatus es tu uxoratus [*Burchard* 19.5(42)]

Moechator
moechator matris (*Cummean* 2.7)

Molimen, -inis
ut faceres quoddam molimen (dildo?) [*Burchard* 19.5(154)]
supradicto molimine [*Burchard* 19.5(155)]

Mollis
molles sicut adultera (*Theodore* 1.2.6)

Natis
et discoopertis natibus, iubent ut supra nudas nates conficiatur panis [*Burchard* 19.5(173)]

Nubere (for sexual intercourse)
qui autem nuberit (*Theodore* 1.14.19)
qui nubet die dominico (*Theodore* 1.14.20)
retro nupserit (*Theodore* 1.14.21)
in tergo nupserit (*Theodore* 1.14.22)
de viro non posse nubere (*Theodore* 2.12.33)
retro nupserit (*Bede* 3.38)
qui autem nupserit his diebus (*Egbert* 7.2)
retro nupserit ... si vero terga nupserit (*Egbert* 7.10)
nupsisti ... retro (*Bede-Egbert* interrogatory 5)
nupsisti ... ante partum (*Bede-Egbert* interrogatory 12)
nupsisti die diminico (*Bede-Egbert* interrogatory 15)

Opprimere
puer parvulus oppressus a maiore (*Cummean* 10.9)
parvolus oppressus talia patitur (*Bede* 3.22)
parvulus a maiore puero oppressus (*Bede* 3.32)

Polluere
in somnis voluntate pullutus est (*Cummean* 2.15)
sive pullutus sine voluntate (*Cummean* 2.16)
si inpolluta revertitur (*Theodore* 1.14.13)
animalia coitu hominum polluta (*Theodore* 2.11.9)
vacans uxorem alterius polluit (*Bede* 3.13)
adulescens sororem suam polluit (*Bede* 3.17)
animalia ab hominibus polluta (*Bede* 3.26)
conplexu feminam [sic] illecebrose pollutus est (*Bede* 3.33)
se pollutus est volens (*Bede* 3.34)
turpiloquio pollutus negligens (*Bede* 3.35)
in somnis non voluntate pollutus est (*Egbert* 9.7)
qui pollutus sit sine voluntate (*Egbert* 9.8)
si ex cogitatione pollutus (*Egbert* 9.10)
et sic te polluisti [*Burchard* 19.5(125)]

Puerperium (= female genitals)
et coniungunt in invicem puerperia sua [*Burchard* 19.5(156)]
et mittunt eum [fish] in puerperium suum [*Burchard* 19.5(172)]

Rapere
quis virginem vel viduam raptus fuerit (*Burgundian* 37)
alterius sponsam rapuerit [*Regino* 2.5(27)]
vel viduam deo sacratam rapuerit [*Regino* 2.5(30)]
rapuisti uxorem tuam (= 'Did you obtain your wife through abduction?')
    [*Burchard* 19.5(49)]

Raptus
fecisti raptum (*Bede-Egbert* interrogatory 19)
aut viduam per raptum traxerit [*Regino* 2.5(28)]

Scelus, -eris
qui faciunt scelus virile ut sodomite (*Cummean* 2.9)
hoc virile scelus semel faciens (*Theodore* 1.2.7)
quia sodomiticum scelus est (*Bede* 3.39)
idem scelus perpetrasti [*Burchard* 19.5(120)]

Semen
qui semen in os miserit (*Theodore* 1.2.15)
per cogitationem semen fuderit (*Theodore* 1.8.3)
per violentiam cogitationis semen fuderit (*Theodore* 1.8.7)
semen dormiens in ecclesia fuderit (*Theodore* 1.8.8)
semen viri sui in cibo miscens (*Theodore* 1.14.15)
semen fuderit clericus (*Egbert* 9.4)
semen fundit in ecclesia (*Egbert* 9.11)
voluntarie semen in ecclesia fundit (*Egbert* 9.12)
semine mariti tui (*Bede-Egbert*, interrogatory 30)
sic agitando semen effunderes [*Burchard* 19.5(121)]
semen a te proiiceres [*Burchard* 19.5(122 and 123)]
gustasti de semine viri tui [*Burchard* 19.5(166)]

Sodomita = 'sodomist'; however, the expression 'sicut sodomitae fecerunt' should
    probably be translated, 'like the residents of Sodom did.'
sicut sodomitae fecerunt (*Columbanus* B.3)
qui faciunt scelus virile ut sodomite (*Cummean* 2.9)
sodomitae (*Theodore* 1.2.6)
sodomite (*Bede* 3.19)
item sodomitis (*Egbert* 2.2)
item sodomite (*Egbert* 5.17)
sicut sodomite fecerunt (*Burgundian* 4)
ut sodomite fecerunt (*Cap iudiciorum* 7.1)
sicut sodomitae fecerunt (*Bede-Egbert* interrogatory 6)
sicut sodomitae fecerunt [*Burchard* 19.5(120)]

Sodomiticus
aut sodomiticum fecerit peccatum (*Columbanus* A.3)
sodomitico ritu (*Columbanus* B.15)
quia sodomiticum scelus est (*Bede* 3.39)
sic secum coires more sodomitico [*Burchard* 19.5(120)]

Sordidare
se inter femora sordidantes (*Bede* 3.31)

Sterilis
cuius uxor est sterilis (*Cummean* 2.28)

Stupro
vidua et stuprata (*Bede* 3.5)
et soror sororem a te stupratam [*Burchard* 19.5(107)]

Stuprum
cum femina vacante stuprum perpetrasti [*Burchard* 19.5(43)]
For this term in Roman law: 'Illicit intercourse with an unmarried woman or a
widow of honorable social condition. *Stuprum* is distinguished from adultery
(*adulterium*) where a married woman is involved'(A. Berger *Encyclopedic Dictionary of Roman Law* Transactions of the American Philosophical Society, ns vol
43, pt 2 [Philadelphia 1953], sv).

Turpitudo (= female genitals)
si obtrectasti turpitudinem [*Burchard* 19.5(133)]
ut filium tuum supra tuam turpitudinem ponderes [*Burchard* 19.5(157)]

Verenda, -orum (= female genitals)
mamillas et eius verenda obtrectasti [*Burchard* 19.5(133)]
et illud loco verendorum tuorum [*Burchard* 19.5(154)]

Veretrum
in manum tuam veretrum alterius acciperes [*Burchard* 19.5(122)]

Violare
propriis menbris se ipsum violaverit (*Columbanus* b.17)

Virga
in masculi terga et in posteriora virgam tuam immitteres [*Burchard* 19.5(120)]

Notes

1 See McNeill *The Celtic Penitentials and Their Influence on Continental Christianity*; and see Oakley *English Penitential Discipline and Anglo-Saxon Law in Their Joint Influence* and 'The Penitentials as Sources for Medieval History.'

2 'Les tarifs augmentent considérablement pour les fautes sexuelles *dont la casuistique occupe une place prépondérante* dans tous les *Libri paenitentiales*' Vogel *Les 'Libri Paenitentiales'* 39 (my emphasis).

3 See, for example, May *Social Control of Sex Expression* 60–9; Taylor *Sex in History* 50–5; Bailey *Homosexuality and the Western Christian Tradition* 100–10; and Noonan *Contraception* 152–70. It is a weakness of John Boswell that he does not give adequate attention to the penitentials; see *Christianity, Social Tolerance, and Homosexuality* 180–3; for further remarks on Boswell, see Appendix D.

4 Perhaps the most extreme judgment on the penitentials, one that betrays a complete lack of appreciation of their role, is the notorious statement of Plummer: 'On the whole the arguments are against Bede's authorship, and we should be thankful to believe that Bede had nothing to do with such a matter. The penitential literature is in truth a deplorable feature of the medieval Church. Evil deeds, the imagination of which may perhaps have dimly floated through our minds in our darkest moments, are here tabulated and reduced to system. It is hard to see how anyone could busy himself with such literature and not be the worse for it' C. Plummer *Venerabilis Baedae opera historica* Tomus prior, prolegomena et textum continens (Oxford 1896) clvii–clviii. By contrast, in recent years several fine studies of the treatment of marriage in the penitentials have appeared; see Manselli 'Il matrimonio nei penitenziali' and 'Vie familiale et éthique sexuelle dans les pénitentiels'; and Kottje 'Ehe und Eheverständnis in den vorgratianischen Bussbüchern.'

5 See the documentation provided by D. Lindner in *Der usus matrimonii* 33–72. Discussion and comment on this doctrine and its sources may be found in Noonan *Contraception* 1–139; the most influential work of Augustine in this regard is *De bono coniugali* ed Zycha.

6 See Jerome, *Adversus Iovinianum*, and letter 22, 'Ad Eustochium,' in *Epistolae* ed Hilberg (CSEL 54.143–211); Camelot 'Les traités *De virginitate* au IVe siècle'; and Rosambert *La veuve en droit canonique jusqu'au XIVe* siècle. For the beginnings of celibacy, see Gryson *Les origines du célibat ecclésiastique du premier au septième siècle*; Gryson's work is glossed by H. Crouzel in 'Le célibat et la continence ecclésiastique dans l'Eglise primitive'; see also Callam 'The Origins of Clerical Celibacy.'

7 Noonan *Contraception* 58

8 Caesarius of Arles *Sermones*, particularly sermons 41–4 (CCSL 103.180–200)

9 Particularly instructive in this regard are a number of papal decretals addressed to specific questions: Siricius to Himerius of Tarragona, 'Directa ad decessorem (385 AD), Jaffé-Wattenbach *Regesta pontificum romanorum* 255, PL 13.1131; Leo I to Rusticus of Narbonne, 'Epistolas fraternitatis' (458–9 AD), Jaffé-Wattenbach 544, PL 54.1197–1211; the responses of Gregory the Great to Augustine of Canterbury in *Bede's Ecclesiastical History of the English People* ed Colgrave and Mynors, bk 2, chap 27. Some eighth-century decretals: Gregory II to Boniface, 'Desiderabilem mihi' (726 AD), Jaffé-Wattenbach 2174, in *Die Briefe des heiligen Bonifatius und Lullus* ed Tangl, n 26, and Kelly *Pope Gregory II on Divorce and Remarriage*; Zachary to Boniface, 'Susceptis sanctissimae' (743 AD), Jaffé-Wattenbach 2264, in Tangl, n 51; Zachary to Pepin, 'Gaudio magno' (747 AD), in *Codex Carolinus* 1.479–87 and PL 89.930–8, Jaffé-Wattenbach 2277; Stephen II, 'In epistola Leonis' (754 AD), Jaffé-Wattenbach 2315, PL 98.1021–31. For an indication of the subsequent use made of the Council of Elvira (ca 306 AD), which includes a considerable number of canons dealing with sexual matters, see Gaudemet 'Elvire. II. Le concile d'Elvire,' particularly 339–47. For the council itself, see Laeuchli *Power and Sexuality*.

10 In the East there were the influential canonical letters of St Basil: see *The Letters*, trans Deferrari, 'To Amphilochius, on the Canons,' letter 188 (canons 1–16, pp 5–47), letter 199 (canons 17–50, pp 103–35), letter 217 (canons 51–84, pp 241–67). The first letter is dated to 374; the second and third are dated to 375.

11 'For these and other reasons the research necessary to produce the definitive history of sexual mores, without which no adequate interpretive history can be written, must take many years to prepare and is unlikely to be carried out in the near future' Taylor *Sex in History* 8.

12 English studies of the origin of private penance: Mortimer *The Origins of Private Penance in the Western Church*; Poschmann *Penance and the Anointing of the Sick*. Still the most comprehensive introduction to the subject of penance is Amann 'Pénitence': early history (749–845, *Tables générales* 3558–63), private penance (845–948, *Tables générales* 3563–9). For the liturgical rites of penance, see Jungmann *Die lateinischen Bussriten in ihren geschichtlichen Entwicklung*. For an excellent account of how private penance and the penitentials might have arisen out of indigenous Irish practices, see Frantzen *The Literature of Penance in Anglo-Saxon England* 19–60 ('Early Ireland and the Origins of Private Penance').

13 I deal with this question in a forthcoming article in *Mediaeval Studies* entitled

'The Humanism of the Penitentials and the Continuity of the Penitential Tradition.'

14 Vogel Les 'Libri Paenitentiales'; in particular see pp 59–93 for a generally reliable survey of editions and studies of the penitentials accompanied by a rough indication of the dates for each work. A revised edition of Vogel's book is in preparation. The following are particularly valuable: Fournier 'Etudes sur les pénitentiels'; Le Bras 'Pénitentiels'; McNeill and Gamer Medieval Handbooks of Penance; and Kottje 'Überlieferung und Rezeption der irischen Bussbücher auf dem Kontinent.'

15 Bieler Irish Penitentials 3

16 Ibid, 3–4 (Vinnian), 5 (Columbanus)

17 Ibid, 5–7. The Bigotian Penitential has not been included among the Irish penitentials since, in its present form, it includes non-Irish penitential sources; see Bieler Irish Penitentials 10.

18 The following works are associated with the name of Theodore: Iudicia Theodori Greci et episcopi saxonum (Finst 239–52; sometimes referred to as Capitula Dacheriana); Canones sancti Gregorii papae urbis Romae (Finst 253–70); Iudicium de penitentia Theodori episcopi (Finst 271–84; sometimes referred to as Canones Cottoniani); Canons of Theodore, Discipulus Umbrensium (Finst 285–334); Canones Basilienses (Asbach Das Poenitentiale Remense appendix, 80–9). See LeBras 'Notes pour servir à l'histoire des collections canoniques. v. Iudicia Theodori' 95–115; Kottje 'Paenitentiale Theodori.' I use the title Canons of Theodore U to indicate the work in two books attributed to an otherwise unknown Discipulus Umbrensium in the salutation of that work (Finst 287).

19 Much uncertainty and confusion surround the penitentials attributed to Bede and Egbert. Both of the works I use were written in the eighth century, but the further questions of authorship and dating cannot be broached here. Further remarks are made at the end of the introduction. See Frantzen Literature of Penance 69–75.

20 See Frantzen 'The Significance of the Frankish Penitentials.'

21 See R. Haggenmüller 'Eine weitere Überlieferung des Paenitentiale Burgundense'; Kottje 'Überlieferung und Rezeption' 520 (first half of the eighth century). The following works provide useful synoptic tables showing the relations among the contents of many of the Frankish penitentials: Wasserschleben Die Bussordnungen der abendländischen Kirche 438–40; Schmitz Die Bussbücher und die Bussdisciplin der Kirche 701–5; Asbach Das Poenitentiale Remense 132–3; R. Haggenmüller 'Eine weitere Überlieferung' 53–4.

22 See Schmitz Die Bussbücher und das kanonische Bussverfahren 159–74.

23 Fournier 'Etudes sur les pénitentiels' RHLR 6 (1901) 289–317. See the parallels between the Merseburg and Vallicellian penitentials in Schmitz Die Bussbücher und die Bussdisciplin 701–5.

24 Asbach Das Poenitentiale Remense 222–5; edition of the Reims Penitential in Asbach, appendix, 2–77; edition of Excarpsus of Cummean in Schmitz Die Bussbücher und das kanonische Bussverfahren 597–644

25 For Capitula iudiciorum see Kottje 'Überlieferung und Rezeption' 520; Fournier dates the Merseburg P 'towards the end of the eighth century' in 'Etudes sur les pénitentiels' RHLR 6 (1901) 315–16. The Capitula iudiciorum is entitled

Poenitentiale xxxv capitulorum in the edition of Wasserschleben, *Die Bussord-nungen* 505.

26 See LeBras 'Notes pour servir à l'histoire des collections canoniques. VI. Pénitentiels espagnols' 115–31; Gonzales Rivas *La penitencia en la primitiva iglesia española*; Díaz y Díaz 'Para un estudio de los penitenciales hispaños.'

27 The following are translated in their entirety: *Canons of Theodore U* (*MHP* 182–215); *Burgundian Penitential* (*MHP* 273–7); Halitgar 6 (*MHP* 297–314). Many non-penitential works cited throughout the following are available in English translation. Such translations are indicated in the bibliography following the reference to the original.

28 'De ce qui précède il ne faudrait pas conclure que le livre pénitentiel soit d'ordre purement juridique. Il n'est pas une œuvre didactique ou d'érudi-tion ou de documentation. Il est destiné à la pratique quotidienne de la discipline pénitentielle' Vogel *Les 'Libri Paenitentiales'* 31.

29 'Allen diesen *Libri Paenitentiales* war eigentümlich, dass sie aus der Praxis für die Praxis geschaffen waren ...' and '... aus praktischer Erfahrung und für eine konkrete Praxis verfasst worden sind' Kottje 'Ehe und Eheverständnis' 22, 24.

30 Chadwick *The Age of the Saints in the Early Celtic Church* 149 (emphasis mine). Likewise, Hughes's suggestion that the penitentials 'attempt to list every-thing' (*The Church in Early Irish Society* 84) is unsubstantiated.

31 Bieler 'Irish Penitentials' 339

32 Ibid

33 *Table of Commutations* c 8 (Bieler 279)

34 By 'base penance' I mean the penance applied to unspecified persons (eg, 'si quis') or to the laity for offences described in generic terms, which descrip-tions are unaffected by tendencies to inflate the penances in accord with the ecclesiastical rank of the offenders or other aggravating circumstances or to reduce the penances in accord with mitigating circumstances such as age or emotional state.

35 For some indication of actual penitential practice, see Vogel 'La discipline pénitentielle en Gaule.' Vogel avails himself of Hertling 'Hagiographische Texte zur frühmittelalterlichen Bussgeschichte' and 'Hagiographische Texte zur Bussgeschichte des frühesten Mittelalters.'

36 The system of commutations was introduced to allow prayers and alms-giving to substitute for the impossibly long and severe penances imposed by the penitential canons. The system seems to have had its origins in Irish practices. For lists of commutations, see *Canones Hibernenses II* (Bieler 162–6); *The Old-Irish Table of Commutations* (Bieler 278–82); *P of Bede* 10, 11 (W 229–30); *P of Egbert* 13.11, 15 (W 244–6). McNeill suggests that the sections in Bede are by a different author than the one who wrote the first nine chapters (*MHP* 235, n 14). See Vogel 'Composition légale et commutations dans le système de la pénitence tarifée.' In canons dealing with sexual offences, financial compositions are rarely stated in the penitentials; see *P of Egbert* 7.4 (W 238); *Merseburg P* 43, 148 (S 2.362, 368). For what seem to be two texts determining composition in the secular law, see *De compositione sacrilegiorum*

(S 1.737–8; translated in MHP 405–6) and *De compositione emunitatis et sacrilegii* (S 1.738–41).

37 Michel Foucault deals with some of these conceptual questions in reference to more modern times in *The History of Sexuality* vol 1.

38 The ninth-century *Penitential of Pseudo-Theodore* often subjects women to the same grades of penance as their ecclesiastical partners; see *P of Ps-Theodore* 18, passim (W 578–81).

39 *Poenitentiale Bedae* (W 220–30), *Poenitentiale Egberti* (W 231–47). See Kottje *Die Bussbücher Halitgars von Cambrai und des Hrabanus Maurus* 207, n 180.

40 *Poenitentiale Bedae* (S 1.556–64), *Poenitentiale Egberti* (S 1.573–587). See Kottje *Die Bussbücher Halitgars* 40–1.

41 *Excarpsus [Bedae]* (S 2.654–9). See *Codices Palatini Latini Bibliothecae Vaticanae* ed H. Stevenson (Rome 1886) 1.74; Frantzen *Literature of Penance* 71.

42 *Excarpsus [Egberti]* (S 2.661–74). See Kottje *Die Bussbücher Halitgars* 121; Kottje 'Überlieferung und Rezeption' 516, n 31 (after 860 and before 875); Frantzen *Literature of Penance* 107, n 45.

43 *Poenitentiale Pseudo-Bedae* (W 248–82), edited by Schmitz without giving a Latin title ('Das Doppel-Poenitential des Beda-Egbert'schen Excarpsus': S 2.679–701). See Kottje *Die Bussbücher Halitgars* 38–9.

44 Albers 'Wann sind die Beda-Egbert'schen Bussbücher verfasst worden, und wer ist ihr Verfasser?' See Kottje *Die Bussbücher Halitgars* 122, n 136. Professor Allen J. Frantzen has kindly allowed me to refer to an article he has written entitled 'The Penitentials Attributed to Bede,' which is soon to appear in *Speculum*. In this article twenty manuscripts containing different versions of the penitential attributed to Bede are arranged in five classes which Frantzen believes represent different stages of the evolution of the text. Frantzen makes the reasonable suggestion that the version of Bede that I have used (Vienna Österreichische Nationalbibliothek ms 2223) does not represent the most primitive state of the text in spite of the early date of the manuscript. He also points out that although this Vienna manuscript is the earliest manuscript containing a penitential attributed to Bede and the earliest containing penitentials attributed to both Bede and Egbert, there is an earlier manuscript containing the text of Egbert alone, Vatican Pal lat 554 (s viii–ix); and see Kottje *Die Bussbücher Halitgars* 101, n 36. Problems of authorship and provenance are also raised. Frantzen suggests that the initial penitential attributed to Bede is probably of continental origin and so not properly attributable to Bede.

45 The penitential itself is dated to the end of the eighth century or the beginning of the ninth by Fournier and Le Bras, *Histoire des collections canoniques* 1.87. See 'Censimento dei codici dei secoli x–xii' *Studi medievali* 3rd ser, 11 (1970) 1060–1, s xi (V. Jemolo). H. Mordek dates the manuscript to the second half of the tenth century; see [*Collectio Vetus Gallica*] *Kirchenrecht und Reform im Frankenreich* 131; and see 131, n 154, for additional manuscripts of this penitential. One of these additional manuscripts has been edited: Madoz 'Una nueva recension del Penitencial "Vallicellanum 1"'; see Kottje *Die Bussbücher Halitgars* 15–16 and the forthcoming study by G. Hägele, *Frühmittelalterliches Kirchenrecht in Oberitalien: Das Paenitentiale Vallicellianum Primum*.

46 See Fournier and Le Bras *Histoire des collections canoniques* 1.352 (probably of the tenth century); the manuscript is dated s xii, second quarter, 'Censimento' 1037 (V. Jemolo).

47 'Censimento' 1030–1 (M.C. Di Franco); Mordek *Kirchenrecht und Reform* 140 (s xi, Italien)

48 The collection is dated by Fournier and Le Bras (*Histoire des collections canoniques* 1.449) to the end of the eleventh century; the manuscript is dated to s xii in., 'Censimento' 1066 (M.C. Di Franco).

49 The collection is dated to the eleventh century by Fournier and Le Bras, *Histoire des collections canoniques* 1.446; the manuscript is dated to s xi ex, 'Censimento' 1072 (L. Avitabile).

50 See Bieler *Irish Penitentials* 22.

51 See Mordek *Kirchenrecht und Reform* 276–7; Asbach *Das Poenitentiale Remense* 19–20; Kottje *Die Bussbücher Halitgars* 167, n 74.

52 See Mordek *Kirchenrecht und Reform* 279–80; Asbach *Das Poenitentiale Remense* 23.

53 See Mordek *Kirchenrecht und Reform* 281–3; Asbach *Das Poenitentiale Remense* 30–1; Kottje *Die Bussbücher Halitgars* 167, n 72. See the descriptions of the following: Stuttgart Württembergische Landesbibliothek, Cod HB VI 112, s x, in J. Autenrieth *Die Handschriften der Württembergischen Landesbibliothek Stuttgart* 2: *Die Handschriften der ehemaligen königlichen Hofbibliothek* vol 3: *Codices iuridici et politici* (Wiesbaden 1963) 110–13; Stuttgart Württembergische Landesbibliothek, Cod HB VI 113, s x ex, in ibid, 113–16; Vienna Österreichische Nationalbibliothek, Cod lat 2171, s ix$^{3/4}$, in Mordek *Kirchenrecht und Reform* 299–300. Along with the *Collectio Vetus Gallica*, these manuscripts contain the *Excarpsus of Cummean* and penitentials attributed to Bede and Egbert.

CHAPTER 1: THE PENITENTIALS TO 813

1 A drawback of this approach is that one does not obtain an appreciation of the breadth of coverage by individual penitentials. Appendix A is designed to compensate for this weakness.

2 Treatment of some of these subjects in the early Middle Ages prior to the penitentials is to be found in the sermons of Caesarius of Arles, sermons 41–4 (CCSL 103.180–200). There is an admonition to observe conjugal chastity and to refrain from concubinage in a ninth-century manuscript of St Gall (Stiftsbibliothek, Cod 150, 173–180), which also contains a number of penitential texts. The admonition is, in reality, sermon 43 of Caesarius of Arles (CCSL 103.189–94). R. Kottje has kindly sent me reproductions of the pages of the St Gall manuscript. And see letter 1, 'Ad Optatum,' in Fulgentius of Ruspe *Opera* ed Fraipont (CCSL 91.189–97).

3 See *Excarpsus of Cummean* 3.4 (S 2.613), *Cap iudiciorum* 11.1 (S 2.231), *Merseburg P* 28 (S 2.361); Council of Agde, canon 9 (CCSL 148.196).

4 *P of Vinnian* 27 (Bieler 83)

5 See *Burgundian P* 12 (S 2.321), *Excarpsus of Cummean* 3.2 (S 2.612), *Merseburg P* 12 (S 2.360).

6 'Si quis adulterium fecerit, id est cum uxore aliena aut sponsa vel virgine corruperit, aut sanctimoniale aut deo dicata ...' *Excarpsus of Cummean* 3.1

(S 2.612). Five mss read 'sponsam ... virginem ... sanctimonialem' (S 2.612); the text in Migne reads 'sponsam ... virginem ... sanctimonialem ... deo sacratam feminam' (PL 87.985A).

7 *Burgundian P* 8: 'id est cum uxore aliena aut sponsa vel virginitate corruperit' (S 2.320); *Paris P* 7: 'id est cum uxore alterius, aut sponsam vel virginitatem corruperit' (S 2.327); *St Gall P* 6: 'Si quis adulterium commiserit cum muliere alterius aut sponsa vel deo sacrata vel virginem violaverit ...' (S 2.346). The above-mentioned *Paris Penitential* in the editions (S 2.326–330; W 412–18) is taken out of its liturgical context. See Lowe [Loew] 'The Vatican ms of the Gelasian Sacramentary and its Supplement at Paris'; Mohlberg, Eizenhöfer, and Siffrin *Liber sacramentorum romanae aecclesiae ordinis anni circuli* 254–9.

8 'Adulterium dicitur cum quis alterius violat uxorem vel sanctimonialem' *Penitential of Pseudo-Gregory* 4 (W 538–9). For the date, see Fournier 'Etudes sur les pénitentiels' RHLR 9 (1904) 101, and MHP 429.

9 'Si quis fornicaverit cum sanctimoniali vel deo dicata, cognoscat se adulterium perpetrasse, sicut in superiore sententia unusquisque iuxta ordinem suum poeniteat' *Paris P* 8 (S 2.327); see *Reims P* 5.3 (Asbach *Das Poenitentiale Remense* appendix, 31). Isidore's definitions of *adulter* and *adulterium* include the notion of befouling another's bed; see *Etymologiarum sive originum libri xx* ed W.M. Lindsay (Oxford 1911) 10.10 and 5.26.13.

10 *Cap iudiciorum* 35.1: 'Qui multa mala fecerit, id est adulterium cum pecude et cum muliere ...' (S 2.251). 'He who commits many evils, that is, adultery with an animal and with a woman ...' *Collection in Nine Books*: 'Si quis autem sacerdos cum filia sua spirituali fornicetur, sciat se grave adulterium commisisse' (ms Vat lat 1349, fol 203rb, and see fol 203vb). 'However, if a priest commits fornication with his spiritual daughter he should realize that he has committed a serious act of adultery.'

11 For Welsh material prior to Vinnian, see *Synod of the Grove of Victory* 3, *Book of David* 5 (Bieler 68, 70).

12 With another's wife or virgin daughter: *P of Vinnian* 36, *P of Cummean* 2.23 (Bieler 86, 116) = *Canons of Theodore* U 1.14.9–10 (Finst 308); cf *Cap iudiciorum* 7.13b (S 2.224), *Merseburg P* 11 (S 2.360); with a vowed virgin: *P of Vinnian* 38, *P of Cummean* 2.25 (Bieler 88, 116) = *Canons of Theodore* U 1.14.11 (Finst 308); *P of Egbert* 5.15 (W 237); 'vowed virgin' is Bieler's translation of *puella dei*. With his own female slave: for sexual relations with one's female slave the text of Vinnian is found in a short version (V: Vienna Österreichische Nationalbibliothek, Lat 2233 [Theol lat 725] s viii ex) and a longer version (S: St Gall, Stiftsbibliothek 150, s ix). *P of Vinnian* 39 (V), *P of Cummean* 2.26 (Bieler 88, 116) = *Excarpsus of Cummean* 3.32 (S 2.616); cf. *Canons of Theodore* U 1.14.12 (Finst 308). The longer version, *P of Vinnian* 39 (S) (Bieler 88), is reflected in *P of Bede* 3.15 (W 222), reformulated and expanded.

13 If the vowed virgin begets a child: *P of Vinnian* 37, *P of Cummean* 2.24 (Bieler 88, 116) = *Canons of Theodore* U 1.14.11 (Finst 308); cf *P of Egbert* 5.15 (W 237). If the female slave begets a child: this canon is also found in two versions in Vinnian. *P of Vinnian* 40 (V) is in *P of Cummean* 2.27 (Bieler 88, 116) = *Excarpsus of Cummean* 3.32 (S 2.616); cf *P of Bede* 3.16 (W 222), *Merseburg P* 60 (S 2.363).

14 'Si autem genuerit ex illa ancilla filium unum aut duos vel tres, oportet [per?]
   eum libera fieri ancilla, et si voluerit venundari eam, non permittatur ei, sed
   separentur ab invicem et peniteat annum integrum cum pane et aqua per
   mensuram; et non intret amplius ad concubinam suam, sed iungatur pro-
   priae uxori' *P of Vinnian* 40 (S) (Bieler 88). This canon is not found elsewhere.
15 'Sciendum est enim laicis quod tempore paenitentiae illis traditae a sacerdotibus non illis liceat suas cognoscere uxores nisi post paenitentiam trans-
   actam; demedia namque paenitentia non debet esse' *P of Columbanus* B.18
   (Bieler 102). The question of sexual abstinence during the time of a penance
   will be taken up later in the section dealing with periods of sexual abstinence.
16 See *P of Vinnian* 51 (Bieler 92).
17 *Canons of Theodore* U 1.14.4 (Finst 307) = *Reims P* 5.94 (Asbach *Das Poenitentiale Remense* appendix, 40), somewhat reformulated in *Cap iudiciorum* 7.10f
   (S 2.224)
18 '... dans insuper praetium pudititiae marito uxoris violatae' *P of Columbanus*
   B.14 (Bieler 102). '... giving in addition the price of chastity to the husband
   of the violated wife.'
19 '... reddito tamen humiliationis eius praetio parentibus eius' *P of Columbanus*
   B.16 (Bieler 102). '... provided that he pays her relatives the price of her
   disgrace.' If the man is single, however, and the couple wants to marry and
   the parents are willing, both must first do penance for a year. The compensation is reminiscent of Deut 22:28–9; see *MHP* 36.
20 *Canons of Theodore* U 1.14.14 (Finst 308)
21 Finsterwalder suggests Basil, letter 217, canon 76 (trans Deferrari 259); but
   see Council of Ancyra, canon 20 (*Dionysio-Hadriana Collection*; PL 67.155B).
   The *Bigotian Penitential* (2.5.2) says of the seven-year penance, 'Aliter quidam
   aiunt intollerabilius: paenitentia concoitus mulieris alicuius mariti vivi .vii.
   annis cum pane et aqua' (Bieler 220). 'Others say differently, and too severely: the penance for intercourse with a woman whose husband is still alive is
   seven years on bread and water.' The Ancyra canon in the version of
   the *Hispana Collection* (PL 84.108B) is quoted by *Excarpsus of Cummean* 3.22
   (S 2.615).
22 'Si quis fornicaberit habens uxorem et presens fuerit uxor eius ...' *Merseburg
   P* 148 (S 2.368). 'If anyone having a wife should commit fornication with his
   wife present ...' I suspect that the word 'present' means that the wife is
   available or at hand; the man is not away at war, for example.
23 See Halitgar 6, Ordo (S 2.292); Regino of Prüm *Libri duo de synodalibus causis
   et disciplinis ecclesiasticis* 2.446, p 389; Burchard of Worms *Decretum* 19.22 (PL
   140.983B).
24 'Si quis cum uxore alterius adulteraverit episcopus XII ann., III ex his in pane
   et aqua et deponatur, presbyter X, III ex his in pane et aqua et deponatur.
   Diaconus et monachus VII, III ex his in pane et aqua et deponatur. Clericus
   et laicus V ann. paenit., II ex his in pane et aqua; hii supra scribti a communione priventur. Post actam paenit. reconcilientur ad communionem, nam ad
   sacerdotium nunquam accedant' *Cap iudiciorum* 7.3 (S 2.222).
25 See *Bobbio Penitential* 11 (S 2.324). This penitential in the editions is taken out

of the liturgical context of the Bobbio Missal; see Lowe [Loew] (ed) *The Bobbio Missal*; Wilmart, Lowe, and Wilson *The Bobbio Missal*; Kottje 'Überlieferung und Rezeption' 520. The *Penitential of Bede* has several canons on adultery (3.12–14), one of which is addressed explicitly to single men: 'Si quis vacans uxorem alterius polluit, II annos' 3.13 (W 222). 'If a single man pollutes another's wife, two years.'

26 See Lindner *Der usus matrimonii* 73–8; Browe *Beiträge zur Sexualethik des Mittelalters* chap 1, 2, 3, 5. The sermons of Caesarius of Arles frequently mention times of sexual abstinence for married couples, particularly prior to major feasts: sermon 44 (CCSL 103.196, 199); sermon 68 (CCSL 103.290); sermon 187 (CCSL 104.765); sermon 188 (CCSL 104.768, 769); sermon 199 (CCSL 104.806); sermon 201 (CCSL 104.813); sermon 225 (CCSL 104.891); sermon 229 (CCSL 104.908, 909).

27 See Appendix B for an overview of these sexual abstinence periods; and see Payer 'Early Medieval Regulations concerning Marital Sexual Relations'; Kottje 'Ehe und Eheverständnis' 33–5.

28 Caesarius of Arles frequently mentions the procreation of children as the purpose of sexual intercourse, often employing the expression 'excepto desiderio filiorum' ('unless there is the desire for children'); see sermon 42 (CCSL 103.187, 188); sermon 44 (CCSL 103.196, 197); sermon 100 (CCSL 103.411); sermon 179 (CCSL 104.725: intercourse for reasons other than procreation among the small sins). See Dubarle 'La contraception chez Césaire d'Arles.'

29 'Oportet enim tres quadragisimas in anno singulo abstinere se *invicem ex consensu ad tempus* ut possint *orationi vacare* pro salute animarum suarum, et in nocte dominica vel sabbati abstineant se ab invicem, et postquam conceperit uxor non intrabit ad eam usquequo genuerit filium *et iterum* ad hoc ipsum conveni[r]ent sicut apostolus dicit' *P of Vinnian* 46 (Bieler 92). The expressions from St Paul (1 Cor 7:5) are italicized.

30 The mention in the parable of the sower (Matt 13:8, 23) of one hundred-fold, sixty-fold, and thirty-fold is used by several patristic authors to rank the various classes in the Church. Invariably the thirty-fold represents the married laity. See Jerome *Adversus Iovinianum* 1:3 (PL 23.223–4), *Commentariorum in Matheum libri* IV (CCSL 77.106), and letter 49 (48), 'Apologeticum ad Pammachium' (CSEL 54.353); Augustine *Quaestionum evangeliorum libri duo* 1.9 (PL 35.1325–26) and *De sancta virginitate* 45–7 (CSEL 41.289–92). And see *Synodus II S Patricii* c 18 (Bieler 190). In the thirteenth century Alexander of Hales uses the text from Matthew in his comparison of marriage and virginity: *Quaestiones disputatae 'Antequam esset Frater'* qu 57, disp 3 membrum 3, 2.1124–7.

31 *P of Cummean* 2.30 (Bieler 116); see Bieler 246, n 12. For Wednesday, Friday, and Saturday as special fast days in the early Church, see Cabrol 'Jeûnes.'

32 *P of Cummean* 2.30; see Lev 15:24 (menstrual period). *P of Cummean* 2.31; see Lev 12:1–5 (purification after childbirth).

33 *Canons of Theodore U* 1.12.3 (Finst 305): 'ante panes propositionis sicut in lege scriptum est.'

34 *Canons of Theodore U* 2.12.1 (Finst 326)

35 *Canons of Theodore* U 1.14.19 (Finst 309)
36 *Canons of Theodore* U 2.12.3 (Finst 326)
37 *Canons of Theodore* U 1.14.20 (Finst 309). For the Sunday abstinence, see the work of W. Thomas, *Der Sonntag im frühen Mittelalter*, particularly appendix 2, 107–10.
38 *Excarpsus of Cummean* 3.18 (S 2.614)
39 For the phrase 'ante plures dies' ('for several days beforehand') in Caesarius of Arles, see sermon 22 (CCSL 103.196); sermons 188, 225, 229 (CCSL 104.768, 891, 908).
40 In the prologue to the *Excarpsus of Cummean* (S 2.604) reference is made to the observance of periods of abstinence as supererogatory works.
41 See *Canons of Theodore* U 1.14.19 (Finst 309) and *Excarpsus of Cummean* 3.16 (S 2.614).
42 *Penitential of Egbert* 7.3 (W 238); cf *P of Cummean* 2.30 (Bieler 116), *Excarpsus of Cummean* 3.18 (S 2.614).
43 'Qui in quadragesima ante pascha cognoscet mulierem suam, noluit abstinere, [ante] peniteat vel suum pretium reddat ad ecclesiam, vel pauperibus dividat aut xx et sex solidos reddat' *P of Egbert* 7.4 (W 238); 'ante' probably should read 'annum.' 'Si per ebrietatem vel aliqua causa accederit sine consuetudine, XL diebus peniteat' *P of Egbert* 7.5 (W 239) 'If this happens because of drunkenness or for some other reason and is not customary, he shall do penance for forty days.'
44 *P of Bede* 3.37 (W 224)
45 See Vaccari 'La tradizione canonica del "debitum" coniugale e la posizione di Graziano'; Makowski 'Conjugal Debt and Medieval Canon Law.'
46 *Merseburg P* 96, 157 (S 2.365, 368) relate back to *Canons of Theodore* U 1.14.23 (Finst 309), and cf *Excarpsus of Cummean* 3.13 (S 2.614); *Merseburg P* 134, 158 (S 2.367, 368) to *Canons of Theodore* U 1.14.18–19 (Finst 309). *Merseburg P* 89 (S 2.365) paraphrases Gregory the Great's response to Augustine in which Gregory says that menstruating women are not to be denied entry to a church; see *Bede's Ecclesiastical History of the English People* ed Colgrave and Mynors, 92; cf *Cap iudiciorum* 10.6 (S 2.229). *Canons of Theodore* U 1.14.23 = *Cap iudiciorum* 9.3 (S 2.226); *Canons of Theodore* U 2.12.3 (Finst 326) = *Cap iudiciorum* 9.1h (S 2.226); *Canons of Theodore* U 1.14.20 = cf *Cap iudiciorum* 9.1j (S 2.226).
47 See, for example, [*Hibernensis*] Wasserschleben *Die irische Kanonensammlung* bk 46.11, p 187; Council of Fréjus (796–7 AD) canon 13, MGH *Concilia* 1.194–5, n 21; *Vetus Gallica* 49.7m, in Mordek *Kirchenrecht und Reform* 564–5.
48 Vogel *La discipline pénitentielle en Gaule des origines à la fin du VIIe siècle* 27; 'Le péché et la pénitence' 198–200; *Les 'Libri Paenitentiales'* 34–5
49 See *Excarpsus of Cummean* prologue 2 (S 2.604) = *Reims P* prologue (Asbach *Das Poenitentiale Remense* appendix, 14); *Merseburg P* 135 (S 2.367) = cf *Vallicellian P* I (S 1.339), *Vienna P* 94 (S 2.356).
50 See *Collection in Nine Books* 9.30(9), Vat lat 1349, fol 201rb (transcribed in S 2.227); *Collection in Five Books* 5.173(12), Vat lat 1339, fol 296ra; Vat Arch S Pietro H 58, canon 43 (fol 114v).
51 See Council of Mainz (852 AD) canon 11, in MGH *Capitularia* 2.189.

52 Council of Worms (868 AD) in Mansi 15.865–84; canon 37 (Mansi 15.876)
53 Canon 30 (Mansi 15.875). For the Council of Worms, see Hartmann *Das Konzil von Worms 868.*
54 The letters were written between 855 and 858; see Pflugk-Harttung *Acta pontificum romanorum inedita* 3.3–4; and Hartmann *Das Konzil von Worms* 49–53.
55 Council of Tribur (895 AD) canon 55, MGH *Capitularia* 2.242
56 Theodore has two canons touching on sexual relations rarely taken up by subsequent works: *Canons of Theodore U* 2.12.30 (Finst 330: husband to wash after intercourse before entering a church); *Canons of Theodore U* 2.12.31 (Finst 330: husband not to see his wife naked).
57 *Canons of Theodore U* 1.14.21 (Finst 309)
58 'Si in tergo nupserit penitere debet quasi ille qui cum animalibus' *Canons of Theodore U* 1.14.22 (Finst 309). The penances for bestiality in Theodore are 10 years (1.2.2; Finst 290) or 15 years (1.2.3). See *Cap iudiciorum* 10.1a (S 2.227), *Merseburg P* 156 (S 2.368).
59 Unfortunately, the translator does not help in this matter; see MHP 197, where *Canons of Theodore U* 1.14.22 is translated, 'For a graver offence of this kind he ought to do penance as one who offends with animals.' Noonan translates 'retro' by 'dorsal intercourse' but understands it to mean 'coitus with the woman on top of the man' *Contraception* 162–3. My interpretation (from behind) seems to be supported by the meaning of the adverb, perhaps explains why some subsequent penitentials confuse the two positions, and would explain Burchard's reference to the position as 'dog-like' ('*canino more*'); see *Decretum* 19.5(52) (S 2.421). Noonan (163, n 21) is incorrect when he says the reference to 'dog-like' is not in Migne; see PL 140.959D.
60 'Qui semen in os miserit VII annos paeniteat. Hoc pessimum malum. Alias ab eo aliter iudicatum est ut ambo usque in finem vitae peniteant vel xv annos vel ut superius VII' *Canons of Theodore U* 1.2.15 (Finst 291). 'Whoever emits semen into the mouth shall do penance for seven years; this is the worst of evils. It has also been judged otherwise by him, namely, that both shall do penance to the end of their lives, or for fifteen years, or for seven years as above.' See Bailey *Homosexuality* 105, and Noonan *Contraception* 164.
61 Immediately after the condemnation of incestuous relations between natural brothers (*Excarpsus of Cummean* 2.3) there follows, 'Sed ad hoc si semen in os miserit VII annos peniteat; alii dicunt usque ad finem vitae' *Excarpsus of Cummean* 2.4 (S 2.609). 'But if he emits semen into the mouth in this case [*ad hoc*], he shall do penance for seven years; others say to the end of his life.' Some mss omit 'ad hoc.'
62 'Effundens semen in os femine, III annos peniteat; si consuetudine adsueti fuerint, VII annos peniteant' *Tripartite of St Gall* (*Cummean*) 8 (S 2.185). Notice that the first clause is in the singular and refers to the male; the second clause is copied from *P of Cummean* 2.8 (Bieler 114) without changing the plural number and so could be understood to embrace both the man and the woman. A modern Latin translation of the *Old-Irish Penitential* 2.23 (Bieler 264) bears a close resemblance to the *Tripartite of St Gall* and is a reasonably

accurate rendering of the original Old Irish, which may be found in Gwynn 'An Irish Penitential' 144.

63 If I am correct, caution should be exercised when consulting Noonan's chart under 'oral intercourse,' *Contraception* 164.

64 In addition to general works on marriage such as Freisen *Geschichte des canonischen Eherechts bis zum Verfall der Glossenlitteratur* and Esmein *Le mariage en droit canonique*, see the well-documented work of Fleury, *Recherches historiques sur les empêchements de parenté dans le mariage canonique*. For some practical implications of these regulations, see Bouchard 'Consanguinity and Noble Marriages.' For a later period see Champeaux '*Ius sanguinis*.'

65 See, for example, *Canons of Theodore U* 2.12.26–9 (Finst 329–30) = *Excarpsus of Cummean* 3.24–6 (S 2.615–16); *Excarpsus of Cummean* 3.42 (S 2.617); *Merseburg P* 136, 146 (S 2.367).

66 See *Canons of Theodore U* 1.2.16 (Finst 291: mother); 1.2.17 (sister; see Basil, letter 217, canon 75, trans Deferarri 257–8); 1.2.19 (brothers).

67 'Si mater cum filio suo parvulo fornicationem imitatur III annos abstineat se a carne et diem unum ieiunet in ebdomada usque ad vesperum' *Canons of Theodore U* 1.2.20 (Finst 292).

68 *Bigotianum P* 2.3.2 (Bieler 221)

69 *Excarpsus of Cummean* 3.21 (S 2.615)

70 See Turner *Ecclesiae occidentalis monumenta iuris antiquissima. Canonum et conciliorum graecorum interpretationes latinae* 2.1.92–9, and PL 84.107B, where the canon is understood to apply in a two-fold sense: 'Sensus autem in hac sententia duplex esse potest, qui ex obiectis coniicitur, aut de his qui cum pecoribus coitu mixti sunt, aut more pecorum incesta cum propinquis sanguine commiserunt.' 'However, there can be a two-fold understanding of this judgment which is conjectured from the subject matter: either it is about those who have coitus with animals, or those who, in the manner of animals, commit incest with blood relations.'

71 'Si matrem, annos VII et quamdiu vivit numquam sine continentia' *P of Bede* 3.18 (W 222). 'If with his mother, seven years and never to be without continence as long as he lives.' But see 'Si matrem, annos VII et quamdiu vivit numquam sine penitentia*' *P of Bede* 1.16 (S 2.655). 'If with his mother, seven years and never to be without penance as long as he lives.' *Three variant readings of *sine continentia*.

72 *P of Egbert* 4.4 (W 234); see *P of Egbert* 4.3 from *Canons of Theodore U* 1.2.16 (Finst 291); *P of Egbert* 4.5–6 from *Canons of Theodore U* 1.2.19–20.

73 'Si quis fornicaberit cum vidua patris sui, aut vidua barbani sui, aut cum germana sua aut cum cognata sua, aut pater turpitudinem filii sui revelaverit*, aut cum filiastra sua, x ann. peregrinus peniteat, II ex his in pane et aqua, et si peregrinare non potest, pro uno anno det solidos XII. Si laicus est, tundatur et dimittat hominem liberum' *Merseburg P* 43 (S 2.362). *See Lev 18:15. For *barbanus* = 'paternal uncle,' see Fournier 'Etudes sur les pénitentiels' RHLR 6 (1901) 310.

74 'Si quis aput suam commatrem fornicaberit, VII ann. pen.' *Merseburg P* 144 (S 2.367). Marrying one's godmother is condemned by the Council of Rome (721 AD) canon 4 (Mansi 12.263).

75 *Merseburg P* 152 (S 2.368). There is a homily appended to the Council of Leptinnes (743 AD) entitled 'Alloquutio sacerdotum de coniugiis inlicitis ad plebem' ('Discourse for priests to be delivered to the people on unlawful sexual relations'), which has been re-edited by Machielsen, 'Fragments patristiques non-identifiés du ms. Vat. Pal. 577' 533–4. Machielsen proposes the beginning of the seventh century as the *terminus ante quem* and associates it with Augustine of Canterbury (p 496). A noteworthy feature of this homily is the paragraph which enumerates various kinds of prohibited sexual relations, using language reminiscent of Leviticus (see p 534 with biblical references). Whatever its date, the work reflects an interest in the same range of sexual offences as the penitentials and, whether meant to be delivered or not, is designed for the practical concerns of the pastoral ministry. The incestuous relations condemned are not those of marriage but of sexual intercourse.

76 'Sic et illa quae semen viri sui cibo miscens ut inde plus amoris accipiat peniteat' *Canons of Theodore U* 1.14.15 (Finst 308); see *Excarpsus of Cummean* 1.36 (S 2.608), *Cap iudiciorum* 23.2b (S 2.241); *Merseburg P* 103 (S 2.366).

77 *P of Vinnian* 19 (Bieler 78). The verb 'gives' has no direct object in the text.

78 'Si autem pro amore quis maleficus sit et neminem perdiderit, annum integrum cum pane et aqua clericus ille paèniteat, laicus dimidium, diaconus duos, sacerdos tres; maxime, si per hoc mulieris partum quis [que] deceperit, ideo vi quadragesimas unus quisque insuper augeat, ne homicidii reus sit' *P of Columbanus* B.6 (Bieler 101).

79 See *Excarpsus of Cummean* 7.2 (S 2.626). For a discussion of potions in the penitentials, see Noonan *Contraception* 155–70.

80 *P of Vinnian* 41, *P of Cummean* 2.28 (Bieler 88, 116). See Caesarius of Arles, sermons 51, 52 (CCSL 103.228, 232); *Cap iudiciorum* 9.2 (S 2.226); *P of Silos* 9.14 (Gonzales Rivas 178); *P of Vigila* 63 (W 531; Gonzales Rivas 193). See Kottje 'Ehe und Eheverständnis' 30–2.

81 'Si vir et mulier coniunxerint se in matrimonio et postea dixerit mulier de viro non posse nubere cum ea, si quis poterit probare quod verum sit accipiat alium' *Canons of Theodore U* 2.12.33 (Finst 330). See the Council of Compiègne (757 AD) canon 20, MGH *Capitularia* 1.39, n 15; Council of Verberi (758–68 AD) canon 17, MGH *Capitularia* 1.41, n 16; Council of Riesbach-Freising-Salzburg (800 AD) canon 46, MGH *Concilia* 1.212, n 24A. For discussion see Freisen *Geschichte des canonischen Eherechts* 330–64; Esmein *Le mariage en droit canonique* 1.259–96.

82 See Noonan *Contraception* 152–70.

83 Noonan *Contraception* 164. I have already remarked on the caution to be used in taking references to oral intercourse in Noonan's chart in a heterosexual sense.

84 'causa filiorum' *P of Vinnian* 46 (Bieler 92); see above, n 28, for the phrase 'excepto desiderio filiorum' in Caesarius of Arles. Noonan *Contraception* 155–6

85 See [*Collectio Hibernensis*] Wasserschleben *Die irische Kanonensammlung* 185–95. Fournier and Le Bras say of this work, '... il nous paraît probable que les manuscrits utilisés par Wasserschleben ne sont que des abrégés de la collec-

tion primitive. Celle-ci dut être composée en Irlande vers l'an 700' *Histoire des collections* 1.62. Fournier points out that book 46 is found alone in several manuscripts; see 'De l'influence de la collection irlandaise sur la formation des collections canoniques' 33. F. Kunstmann has edited one of these excerpts in 'Das Eherecht des Bischofs Bernhard von Pavia mit geschichtlicher Einleitung' 5–10. See Mordek *Kirchenrecht und Reform* 259.

86 *Hibernensis* 46.11 (Wasserschleben ed, 187–8)

87 See *Bede's Ecclesiastical History of the English People* ed Colgrave and Mynors, bk 1.27, 78–103. I have used this edition. See 'Per dilectissimos meos filios,' in *Gregorii I papae registrum epistolarum* bk XI, 56a, 2.331–43.

88 The responses of Gregory the Great to Augustine have been the subject of recent discussion: Deanesly and Grosjean 'The Canterbury Edition of the Answers of Pope Gregory I to St. Augustine'; Meyvaert 'Les "Responsiones" de S. Grégoire le Grand à S. Augustin de Cantorbéry'; Deanesly 'The Capitular Text of the "Responsiones" of Pope Gregory I to St. Augustine'; Kottje 'Exkurs zur Frage nach dem Verfasser der "Responsa Gregorii papae ad Augustinum episcopum,"' in *Studien zum Einfluss des alten Testamentes auf Recht und Liturgie des frühen Mittelalters* 110–16; Meyvaert 'Bede's Text of the *Libellus Responsionum* of Gregory the Great to Augustine of Canterbury,' in *England before the Conquest* ed Clemoes and Hughes, 15–33.

89 *P of Vinnian* (4) (Bieler 74). For the four preliminary canons in Vinnian whose numbers are bracketed and which are given starred line numbers in Bieler's edition, see the remarks of Bieler, p 74, to lines 1*–10*. See *P of Cummean* 10.17 (Bieler 128) and *Cap iudiciorum* 10.1 (S 2.228).

90 'Si autem uxorem non habuit, sed virgo virgini coniunctus est, si volunt parents eius, ipsa sit uxor eius, ita tamen ut anno ante paeniteant ambo et ita sint coniugales' *P of Columbanus* B.16 (Bieler 103) = cf *Excarpsus of Cummean* 3.27 (S 2.616), increasing the penance to five years.

91 Caesarius of Arles frequently preached against the practice of concubinage before marriage and the double standard which allowed freedom to males to indulge their sexual interests before marriage but demanded of females that they be virgins at the time of marriage; see sermon 41 (CCSL 103.182), sermon 42 (CCSL 103.185–8), sermon 43 (CCSL 103.190–2).

92 The Council of Elvira (300–6 AD?) canon 12, in Vives *Concilios Visigóticos e Hispano-Romanos* 4 (PL 84.303c), had condemned prostitution (*lenocinium*), and this condemnation is found in the *P of Silos* 9.43 (Gonzales Rivas 179).

93 'Si quis virginem vel viduam raptus fuerit, .III. ann. peniteat cum pane et aqua' *Burgundian P* 37 (S 2.322) = *Bobbio P* 33 (S 2.325), *Paris P* 29 (S 2.329), *Cap iudiciorum* 8.1 (S 2.224), *Merseburg P* 35 (S 2.362).

94 MHP 277

95 The definition of Isidore does connote sexual relations: 'Raptus proprie est inlicitus coitus, a conrumpendo dictus ...' *Etymologiarum sive originum libri XX* 5.26.14 (ed Lindsay). 'Raptus, in its proper signification, is unlawful sexual intercourse and comes from the word "corrupts."' This text is not often encountered until much later, and certainly the sexual connotation of the term *raptus* which Isidore's definition suggests was never the primary mean-

ing in the Middle Ages. It would be misleading to translate the word by 'rape.' I believe that the Isidorian definition entered the canon law through Ivo of Chartres (*Decretum* 8.26; PL 161.589C); see Gratian *Decretum* C 27, q 2, c 48. For discussion, see Duguit 'Etude historique sur le rapt de séduction'; Freisen *Geschichte des canonischen Eherechts* 587–615; Esmein *Le mariage* 1.434–7; Brundage 'Rape and Marriage in the Medieval Canon Law' (with literature). The Brundage article focuses on the period after Gratian.

96 Council of Chalcedon, canon 27 (PL 84.171D); see the following councils: Orléans (538 AD) canon 19 (CCSL 148A.121); Paris (556–73 AD) canon 5 (CCSL 148A.207); Toledo (589 AD) canon 10 (Vives ed, 128; PL 84.353B); Clichy (626–7 AD) canon 26 (CCSL 148A.296).

97 Council of Rome, canons 10 and 11 (Mansi 12.264). Some later indications in this regard emphasize the abduction aspect of raptus: 'Qui raptum facit, hoc est qui feminam ingenuam trahit contra voluntatem parentum suorum' *Summula de bannis* cap 5 (MGH *Capitularia* 1.224, n 110). 'Whoever commits raptus, that is, whoever bears away a free woman against the will of her parents ...' *Capitula legibus addenda* cap 4 (MGH *Capitularia* 1.281, n 139). 'Raptus enim nec immerito dicimus quae sine consensu parentum vel civitatis episcopi aut ipsae ultra diffugiunt aut nolentes ab aliis abducuntur' Council of Ravenna (877 AD, Mansi 17.338) 'For, with good reason, we say that raptus is when women leave without the consent of their parents or of the bishop of the city or when they are abducted against their will by others.'

98 See *P of Egbert* 5.3–5, 9, 12, 13 (W 236–7).

99 One of Egbert's canons (2.3) has a parallel in Bede, 'Si monachus cum monacha, annos VII' *P of Bede* 3.11 (W 222). 'If a monk with a nun, seven years.'

100 'Si quis fornicaverit cum sanctimoniale vel deo dicata sicut in superiori sententiam unusquisque iuxta ordinem suum peneteat' *Burgundian P* 13 (S 2.321); see *Bobbio P* 12 (S 2.234); *Paris P* 8 (S 2.327); *Merseburg P* 13 (S 2.360).

101 The following canons refer clearly neither to adultery nor to fornication in the strict sense: *Preface of Gildas* 1 (Bieler 60) = *P of Cummean* 2.2 (Bieler 112), *Excarpsus of Cummean* 2.22–5 (S 2.610–11), *Cap iudiciorum* 7.11 (S 2.224). *P of Vinnian* 10–12 (Bieler 76), *P of Columbanus* A.3, B.4 (Bieler 96, 100), *P of Cummean* 2.1 (Bieler 112), *P of Cummean* 2.17 (Bieler 114) = *Excarpsus of Cummean* 3.29 (S 2.616). *Canons of Theodore U* 1.2.1. (Finst 290). *Canons of Theodore U* 1.2.18 (Finst 292) = *Cap iudiciorum* 7.10b (S 2.223). *Canons of Theodore U* 1.8.6 (Finst 301) = *P of Egbert* 5.11 (W 237), *Cap iudiciorum* 7.10.

102 See *Preface of Gildas* 1, Synod of N Britain 1, *Book of David* 5.6.7 (Bieler 60, 66, 70).

103 See *Canons of Theodore U* 1.2.1 (Finst 290) = *Bigotianum P* 2.5.3 (Bieler 220). These texts are as similar as can be without being identical. I do not know why Bieler says (220) that nothing is found in Theodore similar to the Bigotian text.

104 *P of Egbert* 5.10 (W 237).

105 'Qui facit furnicationem in ecclesia, poenitentia est, omnibus diebus vitae suae praebeat obsequium domui Dei' *Paris P* 46 (S 2.330). I am not sure what

this penance means. It suggests that the offender is to be in the service of the Church for the rest of his life, perhaps as a monk or in some servile position. This canon is found in a later manuscript, Vat Arch S Pietro H 58, s xi–xii, fol 114r; for the manuscript, see Kottje *Die Bussbücher Halitgars* 65–9.

106 'Qui sepe fornicaverit, primus canon indicavit x annos penitere, secundus canon vii, sed pro infirmitate hominis per consilium dixerunt iii annos penitere' *Canons of Theodore U* 1.2.18 (Finst 292) = *Cap iudiciorum* 7.10 (S 2.223); cf *P of Bede* 3.27 (W 223).

107 *P of Egbert* 5.1 (W 236), from *Canons of the Apostles* canon 25 (PL 67.144B)

108 For a treatment of homosexuality in the penitentials, see Bailey *Homosexuality and the Western Christian Tradition* 100–10. Boswell pays little attention to the penitentials; see *Christianity, Social Tolerance, and Homosexuality* 180–3; and see Appendix D.

109 Peter Damian's *Liber Gomorrhianus* (PL 145.161–90) seems to be the first extended discussion of clerical homosexuality (ca 1049 AD).

110 'Sodomitae vii annos peniteant et molles sicut adultera' *Canons of Theodore U* 1.2.6 (Finst 290). 'Sodomists shall do penance for seven years and the effeminate shall do the penance imposed on an adulteress.'

111 1 Cor 6:10

112 See *MHP* 185, and Bailey, *Homosexuality* 102 and 104.

113 See *Canons of Theodore U* 1.14.14 (Finst 308). Two early definitions: 'Mollis, quod vigorem sexus enerviati corpore dedecoret, et quasi mulier emolliatur' Isidore *Etymologiarum sive originum libri xx* (ed Lindsay, 10, 179). '*Mollis*, what shames in body the vigor of unnerved sex and is weakened like a woman.' And, 'Molles dicuntur effeminati vel lenes dicti sunt qui putant masculorum concubitores esse [cf 1 Cor 6:10]' Optantius *Commentatio de vitiis ad loca S. Pauli explananda* (PL Supp 4.2200). '*Molles* are called effeminate or they have been called soft who are thought to be the bed companions of males.'

114 See *P of Egbert* 5.17 (W 237), *Excarpsus of Cummean* 2.18 (S 2.610), *Reims P* 4.38 (Asbach *Das Poenitentiale Remense* appendix, 29), *Tripartite of St Gall* (*Theodore*) 20 (S 2.183). It is likely that the one-year penance originates in a different Theodorian tradition from the one we are using; see *Capitula Dacheriana* 154 (Finst 251), *Canones Cottoniani* 161 (Finst 281).

115 In the ninth-century *P of Pseudo-Theodore* 28.3 (W 598) the term is associated with masturbation.

116 See *Preface of Gildas* 1, Synod of N Britain 1, *Book of David* 5 (Bieler 60, 66, 70).

117 'Qui facit scelus virile ut Sodomite, .iiii. annis. Qui vero in femoribus, .iii. annis; manu autem sive alterius sive sua, .ii. annis' Synod of the Grove of Victory 8 (Bieler 68). 'He who commits the male crime as the Sodomists shall do penance for four years. But he who [has relations] between the thighs, two years. However, if by one's own hand or the hand of another, two years.' See *P of Cummean* 2.9 (Bieler 114), *Canons of Theodore U* 1.2.7–9 (Finst 290), *P of Bede* 3.19 (W 222).

118 In translating Synod of the Grove of Victory 8, Bieler glosses over the details: '[In substance:] He who is guilty of sodomy in its various forms shall do penance for four, three, or two years according to the nature of the offence'

(69). Bailey (*Homosexuality* 108) understands 'sodomy' to refer to other kinds of homosexual activity. The Latin noun *sodomia* ('sodomy') is not found in the penitentials at this time.

119 *P of Vinnian* (2) (Bieler 74) = cf *P of Cummean* 10.15 (Bieler 128), *P of Egbert* 5.19 (W 237), *Excarpsus of Cummean* 2.6 (S 2.609), *Cap iudiciorum* 7.15 (S 2.224), *Merseburg P* 155 (S 2.368). *Excarpsus of Cummean* 2.6 and *Merseburg P* 155 read 'crura' ('shanks') for 'terga' ('rear').

120 'Desideria suis labiis conplentes, iii annos. Si in consuetudine fuerint adsueti, vii annos' *P of Vinnian* (3) (Bieler 75). Cummean has two versions of this canon, 2.8 and 10.16 (Bieler 114, 128). Later penitentials adopt their prescriptions against homosexual fellatio from Cummean; see *Bigotianum P* 2.2.4 (Bieler 220), *Cap iudiciorum* 7.15 (S 2.224), *Merseburg P* 56 (S 2.363).

121 See *P of Columbanus* A.3 (Bieler 96).

122 *P of Columbanus* B.3 (Bieler 100)

123 *Burgundian P* 4 (S 2.320); cf *Bobbio P* 3, *Paris P* 37, *St Gall P* 14 (S 2.323, 329, 347), *Cap iudiciorum* 7.1 (S 2.222). Where *P of Columbanus* B.3 has 'non maneat cum alio in aeternum' ('and let him never again live with the other man'), the other penitentials have 'et numquam cum alio dormiat' ('and he shall never again sleep with the other man'). See the Council of Tours (567 AD) canon 15 (CCSL 148A.181).

124 'Si quis vero laicus fornicaverit sodomitico ritu, id est *cum masculo coitu faemineo* peccaverit ...' *P of Columbanus* B.15 (Bieler 102); the underlined expression is from Lev 20:13.

125 Bailey (*Homosexuality* 107–8) outlines the material from Cummean.

126 Fellatio: *P of Cummean* 2.8 (Bieler 114), from *P of Vinnian* (3) (Bieler 74). 'Act of the Sodomites': *P of Cummean* 2.9 (Bieler 114), from Synod of the Grove of Victory 8 (Bieler 68). Femoral intercourse: *P of Cummean* 2.10 (Bieler 114), from Synod of the Grove of Victory 8 (Bieler 68); see *Canons of Theodore U* 1.2.8 (Finst 290).

127 *P of Cummean* 10.4 (Bieler 128), omitted by Bailey. See *Excarpsus of Cummean* 2.15 (S 2.610), *Cap iudiciorum* 10.1 (S 2.227).

128 Mutual masturbation: *P of Cummean* 10.6, 7 (Bieler 114); see *P of Bede* 3.30 (W 223), *Excarpsus of Cummean* 2.16 (S 2.610), *Cap iudiciorum* 10.1K (S 2.228), *Merseburg P* 75 (S 2.364). Femoral intercourse: *P of Cummean* 10.8 (Bieler 114), *P of Bede* 3.31 (W 223), *Cap iudiciorum* 10.1L (S 2.228), *Merseburg P* 75 (S 2.364).

129 'Puer parvulus oppressus a maiore annum aetatis habens decimum, ebdomadam dierum ieiunet; si consentit .xx. diebus' *P of Cummean* 10.9 (Bieler 114). See *P of Bede* 3.22 (W 223), *Excarpsus of Cummean* 2.17 (S 2.610), *Cap iudiciorum* 10.1m (S 2.228), *Merseburg P* 76 (S 2.364). There is ancient precedent for this provision: Council of Elvira (300–6 AD?) canon 71 (Vives ed, 14; PL 84.309B).

130 Femoral intercourse: *P of Cummean* 10.14 (Bieler 114), referred to by Bailey (*Homosexuality* 108) as 'homosexual practices (unspecified).' See *P of Egbert* 5.18 (W 237), *Excarpsus of Cummean* 2.5 (S 2.609), *Cap iudiciorum* 7.15 (S 2.224), *Merseburg P* 154 (S 2.368). Intercourse *in terga*: *P of Cummean* 10.15 (Bieler 114), from *P of Vinnian* (2) (Bieler 74).

131 *P of Cummean* 10.16 (Bieler 114).

132 'Qui coierit cum masculo post xx annum xv annos peniteat' *Canons of Theodore U* 1.2.4 (Finst 290).
133 See above, p 29.
134 'Si mulier cum muliere fornicaverit III annos peniteat' *Canons of Theodore U* 1.2.12 (Finst 291). See *P of Bede* 3.23 (W 223), *Excarpsus of Cummean* 3.35 (S 2.616), *Merseburg P* 95 (S 2.365).
135 Text in Finsterwalder: 'Mulier que se more fornicationis adulterio coniunxerit, III annos peniteat sicut fornicator' *Canons of Theodore U* 1.14.15 (Finst 308). For 'adulterio' Wasserschleben (199) reads 'ad alteram,' and see *Capitula Dacheriana* 85 (Finst 246). McNeill (*MHP* 196) accepts the first reading and translates the text in terms of adultery. Hrabanus Maurus *Paenitentiale ad Heribaldum* canon 25 (PL 110.490A); perhaps from *Martenianum P* 77.3 (von Hörmann ed, 464): see Kottje *Die Bussbücher Halitgars* 205.
136 'Si sanctaemoniales cum sanctaemoniale per machinam, annos VII' *P of Bede* 3.24 (W 223). 'If nuns with a nun, using an instrument, seven years.'
137 *Excarpsus of Cummean* 2.2 (S 2.608), *P of Egbert* 2.2 (W 234), *Merseburg P* 145 (S 2.367)
138 *P of Bede* 3.19–21 (W 222–3)
139 Taylor *Sex in History* 54
140 See Council of Ancyra (314 AD?) canon 16 (PL 84.107B). Regardless of what the texts meant in their original context, canons 16 and 17 of this council will be frequently used by later collections of ecclesiastical law to support censures of homosexuality and bestiality. See Boswell, *Christianity, Social Tolerance, and Homosexuality* 178.
141 *Preface of Gildas* 11, *Synod of the Grove of Victory* 7, *Book of David* 5, 11 (Bieler 62, 68, 70) = cf *P of Cummean* 2.6 (Bieler 114), *P of Bede* 3.25 (W 223), *Cap iudiciorum* 7.12 (S 2.224).
142 *P of Vinnian* (1) (Bieler 74); see *P of Cummean* 10.5 (Bieler 128), *Cap iudiciorum* 10.1j (S 2.228).
143 *P of Columbanus* B.10 (Bieler 100)
144 *P of Columbanus* B.17 (Bieler 102); see *Excarpsus of Cummean* 3.28 (S 2.616).
145 *Canons of Theodore U* 1.2.2 (Finst 290); cf *P of Egbert* 5.20 (W 237).
146 *Canons of Theodore U* 1.2.3 (Finst 290); see *Excarpsus of Cummean* 3.10 (S 2.613), *Cap iudiciorum* 7.10c (S 2.223).
147 'De his qui fornicantur irrationabiliter, id est qui miscentur pecoribus aut cum masculis polluuntur. De his qui irrationabiliter versati sunt sive versantur, quotquot ante vicesimum annum tale crimen commiserint, quindecim annis exactis in poenitentia, communionem mereantur orationum. Deinde quinquennio in hac communione durantes tunc demum oblationis sacramenta contingant. Discutiatur autem et vita eorum qualis tempore poenitudinis extiterit, et ita misericordiam consequantur. Quod si inexplebiliter his herese criminibus, ad agendum poenitentiam prolixius tempus insumant. Quotquot autem peracta viginti annorum aetate, et uxores habentes hoc peccato prolapsi sunt, viginti quinque annis poenitudinem gerentes in communione suscipiantur orationum, in qua quinquennio perdurantes, tunc demum oblationis sacramenta percipiant. Quodsi qui et uxores habentes et transcendentes quinquagesimum annum etatis ita deliquerint ad exitum vite

communionis gratiam consequantur' Council of Ancyra, canon 16 (PL 67.154). See Basil, letter 217, canon 63 (trans Deferrari 251).

148 See *Excarpsus of Cummean* 3.10 (S 2.613) from *Canons of Theodore* U 1.2.3 (Finst 290); *Excarpsus of Cummean* 3.28 (S 2.616) from *P of Columbanus* B.17 (Bieler 102).

149 *Burgundian P* 33 (S 2.322); see *Bobbio P* 29 (S 2.325), *P of Egbert* 4.2 (W 234), *Paris P* 25 (S 2.329), *Cap iudiciorum* 7.7 (S 2.223).

150 'Qui cum pecode peccaverit vel iumento, x. annos, quidam VII., quidam III., quidam unum, quidam C. diebus ut pueri' *P of Egbert* 5.20 (W 237). 'He who has sinned with cattle or a mule, ten years; some [say] seven; some, three; some, one; some, a hundred days as for boys.'

151 *P of Bede* 3.25 (W 223)

152 'Animalia coitu hominum polluta occidantur carnesque canibus proiciantur. Sed quod generant, sit in usu et coria adsumantur. Ubi autem dubium est, non occidantur' *Canons of Theodore* U 2.11.9 (Finst 326); see *P of Bede* 3.26 (W 223), *Excarpsus of Cummean* 1.28 (S 2.607), a variant reading in *Cap iudiciorum* 23.1 (S 2.240), *Merseburg P* 143 (S 2.367).

153 'Oportet discretio esse inter qualitate peccodum vel hominum, sicut supra diximus' *P of Egbert* 5.21 (W 237), 'One ought to distinguish between the quality of the cattle or of the men as we said above.' In the prologue the confessor is instructed to discriminate 'de qualitate pecorum vel hominum' (W 232), 'in regard to the quality of the cattle or the men.'

154 The ninth-century *St Hubert Penitential* (34, 58) distinguishes between bestiality with unclean and clean animals (S 2.336, 338).

155 The preferred terms in the Biblical censures are *iumentum* and *pecus, -oris*; see Exod 22:19; Lev 18:23, 20:15, 16; Deut 27:21.

156 'Sicut est autem plus abhominabile miscere cum iumento quam cum masculo, ita plus est inrationabile crimen cum masculo quam cum muliere. Cum consanguinea et cum sanctimoniale peccare aequale crimen. Ideo lex Moisi morte mori judicat et cum iumento et masculo et cum consanguinea coeuntes' Theodulf of Orleans, Second Diocesan Statute 39 (De Clercq 1.336; PL 105.214D).

157 The act is described in some detail by Burchard, *Decretum* 19.5(123) (S 2.436).

158 'Si sola cum se ipsa coitum habet sic peniteat' *Canons of Theodore* U 1.2.13 (Finst 291). 'If she has coitus alone with herself she shall do penance thus.' The 'sic' refers to the penance of three years in the preceding canon. I suggest the use of an instrument both because of the length of the penance and because of the expression 'coitum habet.' See *Excarpsus of Cummean* 3.34 (S 2.616), *Cap iudiciorum* 10.1c (S 2.227), *Merseburg P* 95 (S 2.365).

159 See *Synod of the Grove of Victory* 8 (Bieler 68), *Canons of Theodore* U 1.8.4 (Finst 300), *P of Egbert* 9.5 (W 240), *Cap iudiciorum* 10.2 (S 2.228).

160 *Synod of N Britain* 2 (Bieler 66), *P of Columbanus* A.7 (Bieler 96), *Canons of Theodore* U 1.2.9, 1.8.11 (Finst 290, 301). A similar expression is in *P of Cummean* 10.13 (Bieler 128); see *Excarpsus of Cummean* 2.7 (S 2.609), *Cap iudiciorum* 7.15 (S 2.224).

161 'Si in femoribus I annum vel III XLmas' *Canons of Theodore* U 1.8.10 (Finst 301).

162 'Si quis corpus suum titille [Wasserschleben in a note: 'titillat, titillaverit?'] in

consurgendo furnicare, XL noctes poeniteat et si pollutus fuerit titillatione, LXX diebus et superpositus VII' *Paris P* 44 (S 2.330), Wasserschleben's note in *Die Bussordnungen* 416. And see 'Si quis propter concupiscentiam vel libidinem per ipsum fornicaverit, annum integrum peneteat' *Burgundian P* 14 (S 2.321). 'If anyone, out of concupiscence or lust, has sexual contact with himself, he shall do penance for a full year,' *Bobbio P* 13 (S 2.324), *Merseburg P* 14 (S 2.360).

163 See the following councils: Toledo I (397–400 AD) canon 6 (Vives ed, 21; PL 84.330); Agde (506 AD) canons 10, 28 (CCSL 148.199, 205); Epaone (517 AD) canon 38 (CCSL 148A.34); Tours (567 AD) canons 16, 17 (CCSL 148A.181–2); Autun (663–80 AD) canon 10 (CCSL 148A.319); Fréjus (796–7 AD) canon 12 (Werminghoff *Concilia aevi karolini* 1.193–4, n 21).

164 See *P of Vinnian* 14, 15 (Bieler 78), *P of Cummean* 2.18 (Bieler 116) = *Merseburg P* 58 (S 2.363); *P of Cummean* 2.20 (Bieler 116) = *Canons of Theodore U* 1.2.22 (Finst 292), *P of Egbert* 9.13 (W 241), *Cap iudiciorum* 7.14 (S 2.224), *Merseburg P* 58 (S 2.363); *P of Cummean* 2.21 (Bieler 116); and see Caesarius of Arles, sermon 14 (CCSL 103.70), sermon 41 (CCSL 103.180).

165 John Chrysostom *Adversus eos qui apud se habent virgines subintroductas* (PG 47.495–514), new edn *Les cohabitations suspectes* ed and trans Dumortier. For the problem in the Irish church see Reynolds '*Virgines subintroductae* in Celtic Christianity.'

166 'Interdixit per omnia magna synodus, non episcopo, non presbytero, non diacono, nec alicui omnino, qui in clero est, licere subintroductam habere mulierem: nisi forte matrem, aut sororem, aut amitam, vel eas tantum personaṣ quae suspiciones effugiunt' (PL 67.147D). The *Hispana* version does not differ substantially from this except for the sanction at the end, 'Qui autem praeter haec agit, periclitabitur de clero suo' (PL 84.94A). 'However, whoever acts outside this [decree] shall be struck from his clerical rank.' For the different Latin versions, see Turner *Ecclesiae occidentalis monumenta iuris antiquissima. Canonum et conciliorum graecorum interpretationes latinae* 1, pars altera (1904) 116–17.

167 See *Book of David* 15 (Bieler 72); *P of Cummean* 2.19 (Bieler 116) = *Merseburg P* 58 (S 2.363); *Canons of Theodore U* 1.8.2 (Finst 300) = *P of Egbert* 9.3 (W 240), *Excarpsus of Cummean* 3.39 (S 2.617), *Cap iudiciorum* 10.2 (S 2.228), *Merseburg P* 100 (S 2.365).

168 'Si autem perseveranter concupivit et non potuit, sed non suscipit eum mulier, sive erupit dicere, iam mechatus est eam in corde suo, sed in corde non in corpore; unum est peccatum per corpus et animam sed non eadem penitentia. Penitentia eius haec est: xl dies [peniteat] cum pane et aqua' *P of Vinnian* 17 (Bieler 79), based on Matt 5:28. A canon of Cummean is also used by later penitentials: 'Qui concupiscit mente tantum fornicari sed non potuit, .i. ann(o) peniteat, maxime in tribus xlmis' *P of Cummean* 2.11 (Bieler 114). The text is found in later works with 'tantum' omitted. But see the Council of Neocaesaria (314 AD?) canon 4: 'Si quis mulierem concupiscens proposuerit cum eo concumbere, et cogitatio eius non perveniat ad effectum, apparet quod Dei gratia liberatus sit' (PL 67.155D). 'If anyone, desiring a woman,

proposed to go to bed with her and his thought comes to nothing, it is clear that he was freed by the grace of God.' The ninth-century *Penitential of Pseudo-Gregory* 6 adds to its citation of this conciliar text, 'Ridiculosum est, ut pro tactu vel osculo et amplexu mulierum quis damnatus inveniatur' (W 539). 'It is ridiculous that one be found condemned for touching, kissing, or embracing women.'

169 See *Cap iudiciorum* 7.8 (S 2.223).

170 For boys kissing, see *P of Cummean* 10.2 (Bieler 126); for priests, *Cap iudiciorum* 10.2 (S 2.228), *Merseburg P* 100 (S 2.365).

171 'Über die Kommunion der Eheleute, Wöchnerinnen und menstruierenden Frauen ist wahrend des M.A. viel geschrieben und gestritten worden, aber doch nur wenig im Vergleich zur Frage, ob die Männer nach einer Pollution zum Tische des Herrn gehen dürften' Browe *Beiträge zur Sexualethik* 80.

172 Browe deals with the penitentials (ibid, 92–5), citing *Capitula iudiciorum*, *Canons of Theodore*, *Vallicellian Penitential* I (Schmitz), *St Gall P*, *P of Bede*; he cites the *Tripartite of St Gall (Canons)* 32 (Browe 90, n 28); for a thorough treatment of the subject in the period after Gratian, see Müller 'Ein sexual-ethisches Problem der Scholastik' 442–97, with a very brief historical introduction, 442–4.

173 I shall deal with the first and third group of canons in turn. Those of the second group will be appended to the canons which they most closely resemble.

174 See Lev 15:2; Deut 23:10; Caesarius of Arles, sermon 177 (CCSL 104.720).

175 'Qui in sompnis cum voluntate pollutus est surgat canatque .vii. psalmos et in die illo in pane et aqua vivat; sin autem, .xxx. psalmos canat' *Book of David* 8 (Bieler 71, translation modified).

176 Bieler 71; see MHP 173.

177 *P of Cummean* 2.15 (Bieler 114); cf *P of Egbert* 9.7 (W 240), *Cap iudiciorum* 10.3d (S 2.228), *Merseburg P* 59 (S 2.363). *Bobbio P* 38 (S 2.325) seems to derive from *P of Cummean* 2.15, adding 'et ad altare non accedat usque mane' ('and he shall not approach the altar until morning'), and see, 'Et qui acciperit sacrificium pollutus somno, sic paenit' *Cap iudiciorum* 34.1p (S 2.249). 'And he who receives the sacrifice after being polluted in sleep shall do a similar penance.'

178 'Volens in sompnis peccare sed non potuit, .xv. psalmos. Si autem peccavit sed non pollutus est, .xxiiii. Si sine voluntate pollutus est, .xvi.' *Book of David* 9 (Bieler 70).

179 See MHP 173; Bieler 71.

180 *P of Cummean* 2.16 (Bieler 114), *Bigotianum P* 2.1.8 (Bieler 220), *P of Egbert* 9.8 (W 241), *Excarpsus of Cummean* 2.20 (S 2.610), *Cap iudiciorum* 10.3 (S 2.228); cf *Bobbio P* 40 (S 2.325).

181 'Qui per turpiloquium vel aspectu coinquinatus est, non tamen voluit fornicari corporaliter, .xx. vel .xl. diebus iuxta qualitatem peccantis peniteat' *P of Cummean* 2.12 (Bieler 114). 'He who is polluted by an evil word or glance, yet did not wish to commit bodily fornication, shall do penance for twenty or forty days according to the state of the sinner.'

182 See *P of Egbert* 9.2 (W 240), *Excarpsus of Cummean* 2.9 (S 2.609), *Cap iudiciorum* 10.3 (S 2.228), *Merseburg P* 57 (S 2.363); cf *P of Bede* 3.35 (W 223).

183 *P of Cummean* 2.13 (Bieler 114); see *P of Bede* 3.36 (W 224), *P of Egbert* 9.6 (W 240), *Paris P* 39 (S 2.329), *Cap iudiciorum* 10.3 (S 2.228).

184 'Sacerdos si tangendo mulierem aut osculando coinquinabitur, XL dies poeniteat' *Canons of Theodore U* 1.8.1 (Finst 300). 'If a priest is defiled when touching or kissing a woman, he shall do penance for forty days.' See *Excarpsus of Cummean* 3.40 (S 2.617).

185 'Presbiter quoque si per cogitationem semen fuderit, ebdomadam ieiunet' *Canons of Theodore U* 1.8.3 (Finst 300). 'Again, if a priest emits a flow of semen as a result of his thoughts, he shall fast for a week.' See *P of Egbert* 9.5 (W 240), *Excarpsus of Cummean* 3.41 (S 2.617), *Cap iudiciorum* 10.2 (S 2.228).

186 See *Canons of Theodore U* 1.8.7 (Finst 301), *Cap iudiciorum* 10.2 (S 2.228) and *Canons of Theodore U* 1.8.8 (Finst 301), *P of Egbert* 9.11 (W 241), *Excarpsus of Cummean* 2.21 (S 2.610), *Cap iudiciorum* 10.3f (S 2.228), *Merseburg P* 142 (S 2.367).

187 'Si per somnum peccaverit quasi cum femina, viginti quinque psalmos cantet' *Bobbio P* 39 (S 2.325). See Ivo of Chartres *Decretum* 9.113 (PL 161.687D).

188 See *Cap iudiciorum* 10.4 (S 2.228).

189 *Bobbio P* 41 (S 2.325).

190 See *P of Egbert* 9.12 (W 241).

191 *P of Bede* 3.33 (W 223)

192 'Si post inlusionem, quae per somnium solet accedere, vel corpus Domini quislibet accipere valeat vel, si sacerdos sit, sacra mysteria celebrare?' *Bede's Ecclesiastical History* ed Colgrave and Mynors 99. 'Can anyone receive the Body of the Lord after an illusion such as is wont to occur in a dream; and if he is a priest can he celebrate the holy mysteries?'

193 See *Merseburg P* 90 (S 2.365).

194 *P of Vinnian* 46 (Bieler 90–2), with suggestions of Gen 2:24; 1 Cor 7:5; 1 Cor 11:27–9; Matt 13:8

195 *Canons of Theodore U* 1.12.3 (Finst 305), alluding to 1 Sam 21:4–5

196 *P of Egbert* 5.1 (W 236) names the *Canons of the Apostles*.

197 The question of the non-penitential sources of penitential canons has barely been broached by contemporary scholars, but I assume it will be tackled in the editions scheduled to appear in CCSL. Schmitz's edition and commentary on *Vallicellian P* 1 (S 1.247–342) is sometimes helpful but is frequently wrong. The edition by von Hörmann of the *Martenianum Penitential*, really a mix of penitential canons, decretals, and conciliar sources, is useful.

CHAPTER 2: THE NINTH CENTURY

1 See Hoyt 'The Carolingian Episcopate'; McKitterick *The Frankish Church and the Carolingian Reforms*. For an example of canonical activity around Salzburg, see Reynolds 'Canon Law Collections in Early Ninth-Century Salzburg.'

2 See 'Interrogationes examinationis' c 3 (MGH *Capitularia* 1.234, n 116; De

Clercq 1.225); 'Quae a presbyteris discenda sint' c 7 (MGH *Capitularia* 1.235, n 117; De Clercq 1.226); 'Capitula in diocesana quadam synodo tractata' c 4 (MGH *Capitularia* 1.237, n 119; De Clercq 1.291).

3 For a fine discussion of earlier diocesan statutes see Gaudemet 'Les statuts épiscopaux de la première décade du ixe siècle.' See Vykoukal 'Les examens du clergé paroissial à l'époque carolingienne'; Devailly 'La pastoral en Gaule au ixe siècle'; Brommer 'Capitula episcoporum. Bemerkungen zu den bischöflichen Kapitularien.'

4 See Gerbald 1.9 (De Clercq 1.354); Waltcaud, c 11 (De Clercq 1.364); Freising, c 32, in Seckel 'Studien zu Benedictus Levita ii–v' 294; Hatto of Basel *Capitula* c 6 (MGH *Capitularia* 1.363, n 177).

5 Theodulf of Orleans wrote two sets of diocesan statutes: *Capitula ad presbyteros parochiae suae* (PL 105.191–208) and the Second Diocesan Statute (PL 105.207–24; De Clercq 1.321–51). Gaudemet says of the second that it 'prend, à partir du c. 12 et jusqu'à la fin (c. 85), l'allure d'un pénitentiel, avec de nombreuses applications des systèmes des pénitences tarifées' ('Les statuts épiscopaux' 306). For a study of Theodulf's statutes see Brommer 'Die bischöfliche Gesetzgebung Theodulfs von Orléans.'

6 'Sed tamen non omnia crimina debet ei innotescere, quoniam multa vitia recitantur in paenitentiale quae non decent hominem scire. Ideo non debet eum sacerdos de omnibus interrogare, ne forte cum ab illo recesserit, suadente diabolo in aliquod crimen de his quae ante nesciebat cadat' Theodulf of Orleans, Second Diocesan Statute 2.65 (De Clercq 1.345; PL 105.219B).

7 Gaudemet 'Les statuts épiscopaux' 338–49

8 See Brommer 'Die Rezeption der bischöflichen Kapitularien Theodulfs von Orléans,' an extensive treatment of the use made of Theodulf's work in subsequent centuries.

9 'Ammonendi sunt sacerdotes et intruendi [sic] ut primum ipsi ab omni fornicatione carnis sint alieni, et tunc plebibus sibi subiectis et verbis praedicent et exemplum ostendant ut ab omni se fornicatione et ab omni inrationabili, veluti pecudum, luxuria et pollutione abstineant, et mundos se corpore et mente Deo praeparent' Theodulf of Orleans, Second Diocesan Statute 2.14 (De Clercq 1.327–8; PL 105.211A).

10 Theodulf of Orleans, Second Diocesan Statute, 7.34–44 (De Clercq 1.335–8; PL 105.214A–215D)

11 See Turner *Ecclesiae occidentalis monumenta* 2, 1.92.

12 'Si, quod absit, in locis sanctis tale crimen admiserit aliquis, duplicetur ei poenitentia. Vocatur autem in Scripturis crimen pessimum tam de iumento quam de masculo quam de consanguinea. Vocatur autem immunditia vel detestabile peccatum cum femina non naturaliter concumbere, unde Onas filius Iudae a Deo percussus legitur qui semen fundebat in terram ingressus ad mulierem. Simul etiam vocatur immunditia mollicies vel propter tactum vel visum vel recordationem mulieris, vel aliqua delectatione accidens vigilanti, vel qui inter femora sua impuritatem solus cum se ipso vel cum alio exercet' Theodulf of Orleans, Second Diocesan Statute 7.44 (De Clercq 1.338; PL

105.215C). The passage ends with several texts from St Paul; cf Gal 5:20, Eph 5:3, 1 Cor 6:10. For Onan see Gen 38:9–10. I translate 'mollicies' by 'masturbation' since the text seems to demand this translation, although the word had not yet acquired such a definite meaning and would not do so until the thirteenth century. By the time of J. Gerson (d 1429) the meaning of masturbation had been acquired by the term, and we find Gerson writing a small tract entitled 'De confessione mollitiei' ('On the Confession of Masturbation'). See Jean Gerson *Oeuvres complètes* ed Glorieux, 8.71–4.

13 See Theodulf of Orleans, Second Diocesan Statute 1.9 (De Clerq 1.326; PL 105.210B), and see the First Statute 1.43–4 (PL 105.205). Later (10.70) Theodulf reports the claim that to have sexual relations during these times is a minor (venial?) sin (De Clercq 1.346; PL 105.219D).

14 'Si qua mulier non habens virum, aut vir non habens uxorem fornicati fuerint, quinque annos poeniteant. Quod si vir non habens uxorem cum alterius uxore adulteraverit, aut si qua mulier non habens virum cum alterius viro adulteraverit ...' Theodulf of Orleans, Second Diocesan Statute 5.29–30 (De Clercq 1.334; PL 105.213D). 'If a woman not having a husband or a man not having a wife commits fornication, they shall do penance for five years. But if a man not having a wife commits adultery with another's wife, or if a woman not having a husband commits adultery with another's husband ...'

15 'De iudicio poenitentiae ad interrogandum reliquimus per quem poenitentialem vel qualiter iudicentur poenitentes' (MGH *Capitularia* 1.179, n 8, chap 20; see De Clercq 1.291, n 1). 'As to the judgment regarding penance, we leave aside the question by what penitential and how penitents are to be judged.'

16 See MGH *Concilia* 1.248–93, nos 34–8.

17 'Modus autem paenitentiae peccata sua confitentibus aut per antiquorum canonum institutionem aut per sanctarum scripturarum auctoritatem aut per ecclesiasticam consuetudinem, sicut superius dictum est, imponi debet, repudiatis ac penitus eliminatis libellis, quos paenitentiales vocant, quorum sunt certi errores, incerti auctores ... Qui dum pro peccatis gravibus leves quosdam et inusitatos imponunt paenitentae modos ...' Council of Châlons (813 AD) canon 38 (MGH *Concilia* 1.281, n 37). See Wasserschleben *Die Bussordnungen* 77–80; Le Bras 'Pénitentiels' DTC 12.1172; Fournier and Le Bras *Histoires des collections canoniques* 1.98–100; Frantzen 'The Significance of the Frankish Penitentials.'

18 See Council of Tours (813 AD) canon 22 (MGH *Concilia* 1.289, n 38).

19 Neither in the 'Excerpta' nor in the 'Concordia episcoporum,' printed by Werminghoff (MGH *Concilia* 1.294–306) as 'Appendices ad concilia anni 813,' is there mention of the Châlons canon condemning the penitentials.

20 'Ut codicelli, quos penitentiales vocant, quia canonicae auctoritati refragantur, poenitus aboleantur. Quoniam multi sacerdotum partim incuria, partim ignorantia modum paenitentiae reatum suum confitentibus secus, quam iura canonica decernant, imponunt, utentes scilicet quibusdam codicellis contra canonicam auctoritatem scriptis, quos paenitentiales vocant, et ob id non vulnera peccatorum curant, sed potius foventes palpant ... omnibus nobis

salubriter in commune visum est, ut unusquisque episcoporum in sua
parroechia eosdem erroneos codicellos diligenter perquirat et inventos igni
tradat, ne per eos ulterius sacerdotes imperiti homines decipiant' Council of
Paris (829 AD) canon 32 (MGH *Concilia* 2.633, n 50).

21 Council of Mainz (847 AD) canon 31 (MGH *Capitularia* 2.183–4, n 248)
22 Rodulph of Bourges *Capitula* c 33 (PL 119.719D) = Council of Châlons (813
AD) canon 38.
23 See Rather of Verona, letter 25, in *Die Briefe* ed Weigle, 135.
24 See Vat Ottobonianus 261, c 8, regarding clerical cohabitation, in Werminghoff 'Reise nach Italien ...' 582; Rodulph of Bourges *Capitula* c 9, 16: clerical
cohabitation (PL 119:708, 711), cc 41–3: incest, adultery, homosexuality, nocturnal emission (PL 119:723); Herard of Tours *Capitula* c 11: homosexuality
and incest, c 19: clerical cohabitation, c 62: periods of sexual abstinence, c 89:
sexual abstinence of newly-weds for first two or three days, c 124: sexual
abstinence (PL 121:765, 768, 770, 773); Walter of Orleans *Capitula* c 3: clerical
cohabitation (PL 119: 732).
25 Isaac of Langres *Canones* (PL 124.1075C–1110C)
26 See Hincmar of Reims *Capitula* c 21: 'De illicito clericorum accessu ad feminas
et qua ratione de illo arguendi vel purgandi sint' (PL 125.780–4): 'On the
unlawful approach of clerics to women, and the reasons for accusing them
or for punishing them'). Referring to this work, he says later, 'Sed video
quosdam vestrum illud parvipendere. Unde iterum illud in conventu vestro
volo recitari' (PL 125.797D). 'But I see that some of you make light of it.
Consequently, I wish it to be recited again in your assembly.' For a discussion of Hincmar's statutes, see Devisse *Hincmar* 2.872–89.
27 Devisse *Hincmar* 3.1431
28 See De Clercq 2.345–6 (Rodulph of Bourges) and Brommer 'Die Quellen der
"Capitula" Radulfs von Bourges'; De Clercq 2.353 (Herard of Tours), 2.373–4
(Isaac of Langres). For the later tenth-century *Capitulare* of Atto of Vercelli,
see Wemple *Atto of Vercelli*.
29 Kottje 'Überlieferung und Rezeption' 516–17
30 For St Gall, Stiftsbibliothek 150, see Bieler *Irish Penitentials* 15, and Kottje
'Überlieferung und Rezeption' 516, n 34. For Vienna Österreichische
Nationalibliothek Cod lat 2223, containing the Bede and Egbert penitentials,
see Kottje *Die Bussbücher Halitgars* 207, n 180. Appendix V in MHP has a
useful list of manuscripts of penitentials whose dates, however, should be
checked against more recent scholarship. See, for example, the description
of manuscripts with literature in Asbach *Das Poenitentiale Remense* 18–40,
and Kottje *Die Bussbücher Halitgars* 14–83 and passim.
31 For dating the *Bede-Egbert Double Penitential* to the second third of the ninth
century, see R. and M. Haggenmüller 'Ein Fragment des Paenitentiale
Ps.-Bedae in der Ottobeurer Handschrift Ms. O. 28'; Kottje *Die Bussbücher
Halitgars* 120–8.
32 See Wasserschleben *Die Bussordnungen* 58; Schmitz *Die Bussbücher und das
Bussverfahren* 331–3; MHP 292. Kottje seems to favour the more recent date
(*Die Bussbücher Halitgars* 238).

33 'Si quis fornicaverit cum his feminis, qui cum aliis fornicaverunt et virginitatem amiserunt vel viduis, III annis poeniteat, monachus vero VII' *St Hubert*
P 12 (S 2.334).
34 *St Hubert P* 34: unclean animals, 58: clean animals (S 2.336, 338). See Lev
11.1–8.
35 'Si quis virginem vel viduam raptus fuerit et contra voluntatem eius eam sibi
aut alteri sociaverit per vim, III annis poeniteat' *St Hubert P* 38 (S 2.337). 'If
anyone has abducted a virgin or a widow and has forced her against her will
to associate with himself or another, he shall do penance for three years.'
36 *St Hubert P* 44 (S 2.337); see *P of Bede* 3.33 (W 223).
37 *St Hubert P* 47 (S 2.337); see Council of Laodicaea (ca 365 AD?) canon 30 (PL
84.132C).
38 *St Hubert P* 49 (S 2.338); see *Silos P* 9.25 (Gonzales Rivas 178).
39 *St Hubert P* 57 (S 2.338); see *Canons of Theodore U* 2.12.30 (Finst 330).
40 See MHP 430; Le Bras (DTC 12.1173) accepts the date of von Hörmann – that
is, between 830 and 847. One of the peculiarities of this work is its use of the
verb *imito* in such expressions as 'fornicationem imitatur' to denote the acts
themselves. For a discussion of the penitential see von Hörmann 'Ueber die
Entstehungsverhaltnisse des sogen. Poenitentiale Pseudo-Theodori.' See
Kottje *Die Bussbücher Halitgars* 246.
41 *P of Pseudo-Theodore* 16.4 (W 574); see *Bede-Egbert Double P* 9.1 (S 2.688).
42 '... quia christiana religio fornicationem in utroque sexu pari ratione con-
dempnat' *P of Pseudo-Theodore* 16.25 (W 575), and see *P of Pseudo-Theodore*
18.7 (W 579) for the same expression.
43 *P of Pseudo-Theodore* 16.26 (W 575); see Halitgar 6.87 (S 2.299).
44 *P of Pseudo-Theodore* 16.27 (W 576)
45 *P of Pseudo-Theodore* 17.1, 17.11 (W 577, 578): after communion; 17.4 (W 577):
after Pentecost; 17.6 (W 577): feasts of saints
46 'Mollis vero vir semetipsum coinquinans, primo C dies poeniteat, et si
iterans, annum I poeniteat' *P of Pseudo-Theodore* 28.3 (W 598). 'Indeed, an
effeminate man who defiles himself shall do penance for a hundred days for
the first occurrence, and if he repeats it, he shall do penance for a year. If he
has clerical rank there will be an additional penance.' Cf *Excarpsus of Cummean* 2.7 (S 2.609).
47 See Fournier and Le Bras *Histoire des collections canoniques* 1.145–233; Fuhrmann *Einfluss und Verbreitung der pseudoisidorischen Fälschungen.*
48 *Collectio antiqua canonum poenitentialium,* in d'Achéry *Spicilegium sive collectio
veterum aliquot scriptorum qui in Galliae bibliothecis delituerant.* See Maassen,
Geschichte der Quellen 848–52 (not before 774 or after 831); Fournier and Le
Bras *Histoire des collections canoniques* 1.104–7; Mordek *Kirchenrecht und Reform*
259 (about 800); Haenni 'Note sur les sources de la Dacheriana.'
49 See Le Bras 'Les deux formes de la *Dacheriana*' 397.
50 See Maassen *Geschichte der Quellen* 852–63; Bateson 'The Supposed Latin
Penitential of Egbert and the Missing Work of Halitgar of Cambrai'; Le Bras
'Manuscrit vendômois du "Quadripartitus"'; Fournier and Le Bras *Histoire
des collections canoniques* 1.110–11, 318. In regard to Vat lat 1347 see Mordek

Kirchenrecht und Reform 172, n 356 (s ix²), and 263; Kottje *Die Bussbücher Halitgars* 184, n 41 (s ix³/⁴). I have not had an opportunity to examine F. Kerff *Der Quadripartitus.*

51 '... ex sacrorum canonum orthodoxorumque patrum libris vel [marg.] institutis' Vat lat 1347, fol 144r

52 'LXXXIIII. Monachus faciens fornicationem VII ann. poeniteat. Si vero monachus quaerens fornicationem et non inveniens ann. .1. et dimidium poeniteat' Vat lat 1347, fol 157v. 'LXXXIIII. A monk committing fornication shall do penance for seven years. If, however, a monk looks to commit fornication and is not successful, he shall do penance for a year and a half.' See *Bede-Egbert Double P* 1.2h (S 2.685).

53 Vat lat 1347, fol 178v; cf *Martenianum P* 70.1 (von Hörmann 441).

54 See PL 106.167–204. Some of the material from the second book of the *De institutione laicali* seems to have been incorporated into the Council of Paris (829 AD); see MGH *Concilia* 2.670–1, n 50, with notes.

55 Jonas of Orleans *De institutione laicali* 1.10 (PL 106.138–43)

56 'Hanc institutionem conlationum constituerunt sancti apostoli, deinde sancti patres et sanctus Punifius deinde canones sanctorum patrum, deinde alii atque alii ut Hyeronimus et Agustinus et Gregorius et Teodorus ...' *P of Egbert* prologue (W 232).

57 See, for example: *P of Vinnian* epilogue (Bieler 92, 94); *P of Columbanus* A.1 (Bieler 96); *P of Columbanus* B, preface (Bieler 98); *P of Cummean* prologue (a variant incipit attributes the work to St Basil: Bieler 108); *P of Cummean* prologue 1, 14 (Bieler 108, 110); *Bigotianum P* preface (Bieler 198).

58 See PL 105.651–710. For books 3–6 I have used the edition by Schmitz (2.275–300). For Halitgar now, see Kottje *Die Bussbücher Halitgars*; see p 5 for approximate date.

59 Halitgar 4.24 (S 2.284); see *Canons of Theodore U* 2.12.1–3 (Finst 326). Halitgar's rubric corresponds to the title of Theodore's twelfth chapter. See Kottje *Die Bussbücher Halitgars* 183, n 35.

60 See Halitgar 5.17 (S 2.289–90), which cites the entire text of Gregory's reply.

61 'Et hoc est, quod in hac re me valde sollicitat, quum ita confusa sunt iudicia penitentum in presbyterorum nostrorum opusculis atque ita diversa et inter se discrepantia et nullius auctoritate suffula, ut vix propter dissonantiam possint discerni 'Ebbo to Halitgar (S 2.265). 'And this is what troubles me greatly, the judgments for penitents are so confused in the books of our priests and they are so diverse and at odds with one another without the support of any authority that they cannot be distinguished because of the lack of agreement.'

62 'Addidimus etiam huic operi excerptionis nostrae paenitentialem romanum alterum quod de scrinio romane ecclesie adsumpsimus, attamen, a quo sit editus, ignoramus. Idcirco adnectendum prescriptis canonum sententiis decrevimus, ut si forte he prolate sentente alicui superfluum sunt visae aut penitus que desiderat ibi de singulorum criminibus nequiverit invenire, in hac saltem brevitate novissima omnium scelera forsitan inveniet explicata' Halitgar 6, preface (S 2.290). The work, which bears no title, will be referred

to as Halitgar 6. See Kottje *Die Bussbücher Halitgars* 157–67. For a study of the sources of the sixth book of Halitgar, see Fournier 'Etudes sur les pénitentiels, iv. Le livre vi du pénitentiel d'Halitgaire' *RHLR* 8 (1903) 528–53; Kottje *Die Bussbücher Halitgars* 185–90.

63 'Sextus quoque ponitur libellus de paenitentia qui non est ex labore nostre excerpsionis sed adsumptus de scrinio romane ecclesiae in quo multa ac diversa continentur, que in canonibus non habentur' Halitgar 6, preface (S 2.266).

64 Clerical adultery, Halitgar 6.7 (S 2.294); magic, Halitgar 6.32 (S 2.296). Halitgar 4.24 has provisions on periods of sexual abstinence taken from Theodore, as we have seen. There are a number of canons in Halitgar's penitential dealing with incest, as there are in book four, but they are concerned with marital incest.

65 Halitgar 6.16 (S 2.295)

66 Halitgar 6.17 (S 2.295)

67 See Halitgar 6.56, 57 (S 2.297–8), and: 'Propter fornicationem autem multi nesciunt numerum mulierum cum quibus fornicati sunt, illi ieiunent hebdomadas quinquaginta' Halitgar 6.87 (S 2.299). 'On account of their sexual activity, however, many do not know the number of women with whom they have committed fornication. These shall fast for fifty weeks.' Notice that this is a considerably milder penance for such memory lapses than the penance of ten years imposed by *P of Pseudo-Theodore* 16.26 (W 575).

68 Halitgar 6.6, 13 (S 2.294, 295)

69 Halitgar 4.7 (S 2.280–1)

70 Halitgar 6.10 (S 2.294); but see PL 105.698A. See *P of Columbanus* B.10 (Bieler 100).

71 Halitgar 6.18 (S 2.295); see *P of Columbanus* B.17 (Bieler 102).

72 Halitgar 6.54 (S 2.297)

73 Halitgar 5.17 (S 2.289–90)

74 There is a canon borrowed from Cummean, in regard to small boys who kiss one another, in which the occurrence of seminal emission warrants a more severe penance: Halitgar 6.67 (S 2.298); see *P of Cummean* 10.2 (Bieler 126).

75 Hrabanus Maurus 'Response to Regimbald 1' (PL 110.1187–96; MGH *Epistolae Karolini aevi* 3, n 30, dated –842); *Paenitentiale ad Otgarium* (PL 112.1397–1424; MGH *Epistolae Karolini aevi* 3, n 32); accompanying the latter work were *De consanguineorum nuptiis* (PL 110.1087–96) and *De magorum praestigiis falsisque divinationibus* (PL 110.1095–1110; see MGH *Epistolae Karolini aevi* 3, n 31, dated 842); 'Quota generatione licitum sit connubium' (PL 110.1083–8; MGH *Epistolae Karolini aevi* 3, n 29, dated after 842); 'Response to Regimbald 2' (PL 112.1507–10; MGH *Epistolae Karolini aevi* 3, n 41, dated –847); *Paenitentiale ad Heribaldum* (PL 110.467–94; MGH *Epistolae Karolini aevi* 3, n 56). The *Paenitentiale ad Otgarium* is dated to the second half of 841 – beginning of 842, the *Paenitentiale ad Heribaldum* to 853, by Kottje *Die Bussbücher* 6–7. In an appendix Kottje edits a Collection in Sixty Chapters which he sees as an expansion of Halitgar's fourth book and which he believes comes from Hrabanus himself or from those working in association with him. Kottje's book arrived too

late for careful analysis; see *Die Bussbücher Halitgars* 253 and appendix 1 (255–75).

76 '... ideoque iussistis mihi ut de canonibus et sanctorum patrum sententiis breviter excerperem atque in unum colligerem quae a magistris ecclesiae huiusmodi personis ad emendationem vitiorum promulgata sunt' prefatory letter to Otgar (MGH *Epistolae Karolini aevi* 3.462). 'Therefore, you have commanded me to make brief excerpts from the canons and the opinions of the holy Fathers and to gather into one what was promolgated by the masters in the Church for the emendation of the vices of the persons you mentioned.' 'Dehinc quoque ad interrogata, quantum possumus breviter iuxta canonum instituta respondere curemus' prefatory letter to Heribald (MGH *Epistolae Karolini aevi* 3.512). 'So we take care to reply to the questions as far as we are able according to the institutions of the canons.' For a new edition of this letter, see Kottje *Die Bussbücher Halitgars* 276–8.

77 *Paenitentiale ad Otgarium* epilogue (MGH *Epistolae Karolini aevi* 3.465)

78 See Kottje *Die Bussbücher Halitgars* 9.

79 Presented as a continuous passage: Lev 20:7; 19:35; 19:16–18; 20:9–11; 20:13, 12; 20:14–21; 20.25–7; 20.22–3 (MGH *Epistolae Karolini aevi* 3.511). For use of the Bible, see Kottje *Die Bussbücher Halitgars* 213–16.

80 Gal 5:16–26; 6:7–9 (MGH *Epistolae Karolini aevi* 3.512)

81 'Theodori archiepiscopi gentis Anglorum' *Paenitentiale ad Heribaldum* c 30 (PL 110.491B–C); see *Canons of Theodore U* 1.14.15 (Finst 308). For a favourable use of Theodore by Hrabanus, see his letter to Humbert, 'Quota generatione licitum sit connubium' (MGH *Epistolae Karolini aevi* 3.446–7). For Hrabanus's use of the penitentials, see Kottje *Die Bussbücher Halitgars* 204–12.

82 At chapter 18 (PL 110.484D) Hrabanus quotes 'Ecbertus Anglorum episcopus'; see *P of Egbert* 6.1–6 (W 238); Kottje *Die Bussbücher Halitgars* 210–11.

83 'De feminis quae inter se fornicantur in Ancyrano concilio scriptum est ...' *Paenitentiale ad Heribaldum* c 25 (PL 110.490A); see *Canons of Theodore U* 1.2.12 (Finst 291), 1.14.15 (Finst 308), 1.2.13 (Finst 291); and see Kottje *Die Bussbücher Halitgars* 205–6 for suggestion that the immediate source for this chapter is probably the *Martenianum P* 77.3 and 77.5 al 2 (von Hörmann 464, 465).

84 '... non cum auctoritate, sed de quorumdam statutis respondemus' *Paenitentiale ad Heribaldum* c 29 (PL 110.491A); see *Canons of Theodore U* 2.12.33 (Finst 330); Kottje *Die Bussbücher Halitgars* 206.

85 See Lev 20:10–12, 14, 17, 19–20.

86 'Igitur Theodorus iudicavit eum, qui incestum fecerit, duodecim annos paenitere debere' – 'Response to Regimbald 1' n 4 (MGH *Epistolae Karolini aevi* 3.451).

87 *Tripartite of St Gall* (*Theodore*) 10 (S 2.183); see *Canons of Theodore U* 1.2.16 (Finst 291).

88 'Response to Regimbald 1' n 4 (MGH *Epistolae Karolini aevi* 3.451)

89 'Tertia quaestio de eo fuit qui cani feminae inrationabiliter se commiscuit; et quarta de illo qui cum vaccis sepius fornicatus est' – 'Response to Regimbald 2' (MGH *Epistolae Karolini aevi* 3.480). 'The third question concerned the man

who mixed irrationally with a female dog; and the fourth concerned the man who committed fornication with cows.'

90 Lev 20:15–16

91 'De vitulis quoque qui a vaccis illis pollutis nati sunt, nescio quid obsit, ne eorum usus hominibus deserviat' – 'Response to Regimbald 2' (MGH *Epistolae Karolini aevi* 3.480). 'Again, in regard to calves born of those polluted cows, I don't know what would stand in the way of their being used by men.' See *Canons of Theodore U* 2.11.9 (Finst 326), and see above, chap 1, n 152.

92 Finsterwalder discusses Hrabanus's references to Theodore, *Die Canones Theodori Cantuariensis* 81–2.

CHAPTER 3: PENITENTIAL TEXTS IN CANONICAL COLLECTIONS

1 Regino of Prüm *De synodalibus causis* ed Wasserschleben 2.135 (p 266), 2.133 (265)

2 Burchard *Decretum* 9.68 (PL 140.826D); Ivo of Chartres *Decretum* 8.205 (PL 161.626C); *Polycarpus* (Paris Bibl nat lat 3881, fol 134r)

3 Machielsen 'Les spurii de S. Grégoire le Grand en matière matrimoniale ...' Fournier records several of these apocryphal texts in 'Un groupe de recueils canoniques italiens des xe et xie siècles' 149–51 (for Vat lat 1349), 178–80 (for Vat lat 1339).

4 Collection in Two Books: ed Bernhard 'La collection en deux livres (Cod Vat lat 3832)'; see Gilchrist 'The Collection of Cod. Vat lat. 3832, a Source of the Collection in Seventy Four Titles?' Collection in Seventy-four Titles: ed Gilchrist *Diversorum patrum sentratie sive Collectio in LXXIV titulos digesta*. Deusdedit: ed von Glanvell *Die Kanonessammlung des Kardinals Deusdedit*.

5 See Peter Damian *Liber Gomorrhianus* (c 1049 AD) chaps 10–12 (PL 145.169–72). It should be noted that Peter Damian's harsh remarks are indeed levelled at what are in fact penitential texts. However, he nowhere attacks penitentials as such; his concern is with texts which do not seem to him to be consonant with ecclesiastical tradition. It is later scholars who have tended to interpret Damian's remarks as censures of penitentials *tout court*.

6 See Cardinal Atto's reservations about a Roman penitential quoted in Ryan *St. Peter Damiani and his Canonical Sources* 11, n 13. Mai's edition of Cardinal Atto was not available to me.

7 For example, in regard to Deusdedit, 'Que Deusdedit ait composé son œuvre avec le dessein d'élever un monument au pouvoir suprême du Pontife romain, fondement nécessaire et indispensable instrument de la Réforme ecclésiastique, c'est là un fait trop évident pour qu'il soit besoin d'y insister' Fournier and Le Bras *Histoire des collections canoniques* 2.51. See Gilchrist 'Canon Law Aspects of the Eleventh Century Gregorian Reform Programme.'

8 *Collectio Barberiniana*: ed Fornasari 'Collectio canonum Barberiniana.' Fornasari dates the work to the second half of the eleventh century (p 128). Two other works belonging to this group of collections depending on Burchard are the *Summa de iudiciis omnium peccatorum* (S 2.468–505, edn 480–505) and

the Collection in Seventeen Books (Reims Bibl municipale 675 [G 528]). Both collections make ample use of acknowledged penitential sources.

9 See Bonizo: ed Perels *Bonizo. Liber de vita christiana*; Berschin *Bonizo von Sutri* 57–75.

10 See Fournier and Le Bras *Histoire des collections canoniques* 2.176–7.

11 See fol 134r for the canon on fornication, 'Si laicus cum laica ...,' attributed to a Council of Meaux = cf Burchard *Decretum* 9.68 (PL 140.826D). The *Polycarpus* (fol 134r) has an interesting excerpt from the letter of Leo IX to Peter Damian in regard to the treatment of clerics committing masturbation and homosexual acts: 'Quo enim modo ... se noverit periculo agere' (PL 145.159C).

12 For Magister A see Le Bras 'Alger de Liége et Gratien' 21–6.

13 Collections of Milan: ed Picasso *Collezioni canoniche Milanese del seculo XII*, and by the same author, 'Atteggiamenti verso i laici in collezioni canoniche milanesi del secolo XII.'

14 *Collezioni canoniche Milanesi* ed Picasso, 218.

15 Edition used is that of Wasserschleben; an older edition may be found in PL 132 but the chapter numbers do not correspond in the two editions. The date is deduced from the two formularies at Regino 1.450, 451 (Wasserschleben 201, 202), which bear the date 906.

16 See Fournier and Le Bras *Histoire des collections canoniques* 1.245; Hellinger 'Die Pfarrvisitation nach Regino von Prüm.'

17 'Si feria quarta ante quadragesimam plebem sibi commissam ad confessionem invitet, et ei iuxta qualitatem delicti poenitentiam iniungat, non ex corde suo, sed, sicut in poenitentiali scriptum est' Regino 1, interrogatory 59 (Wasserschleben 23). These questions seem to be from a document widely circulating at the time which outlines the questions to be asked during pastoral visitations. See ['Admonitio synodalis'] Amiet 'Une "Admonitio Synodalis" de l'époque carolingienne: Etude critique et édition'; for Regino's question 59 see n 63 in Amiet, p 58. See Brommer 'Die bischöfliche Gesetzgebung Theodulfs von Orleans' 116–18 (sources for Regino's interrogatory), 35, n 221, and 119–120 (on the 'Admonitio synodalis'); in this same article Brommer edits a diocesan statute from the beginning of the eleventh century which recommends the use of a penitential (Florence Bibl Med Laur, Plut IV sin. Cod 4, fol 56v–57v [35, n 219, literature; 108–13, edn] c 6 [109], recommending the use of a penitential). Later in the tenth century we find Rather of Verona (before 966 AD) using the 'Admonitio synodalis' with its recommendations about a penitential; see Rather of Verona *Briefe* ed Weigle, 133, 135; also in PL 136.562, 564.

18 Regino 1, interrogatory 96 (Wasserschleben 26). This text seems to be original with Regino.

19 See *MHP* 217.

20 See Regino 1.309, 1.339, 2.266, 2.376, 2.446 (Wasserschleben 149, 159, 317, 358, 389).

21 See Regino 1.301, 2.247 (Wasserschleben 139, 310).

22 See above, Introduction, n 43; Kottje *Die Bussbücher Halitgars* 120–31. Wasserschleben, in his edition of Regino, refers to Regino's source as the *Darmstadt*

Penitential (Darmstadt Cod 2117, now Cologne 118), which is in reality the *Bede-Egbert Double Penitential*, which he calls *Poenitentiale Pseudo-Bedae* in *Die Bussordnungen* (248). The Schmitz edition (S 2.679–701) of this work is used here. On Cologne 118 not being the manuscript used by Regino, see Kottje *Die Bussbücher Halitgars* 128–9.

23 See S 2.681–3. A similar interrogatory may be found in the Romano-German Pontifical cxxxvi, 13, ed Vogel and Elze, 2.237–40.

24 See in particular Regino 2.5 (questions 15–37), 'Deinde interrogandum de adulteriis et fornicationibus' (Wasserschleben 210–11).

25 'Capitula haec quae per ordinem adnotavimus, canonicis oportet roborari decretis' Regino (Wasserschleben 216).

26 See the fundamental discussion by P. Fournier, 'Un groupe de recueils canoniques italiens des xe et xie siècles.' Fournier dates the *collection* 'between 911 and 930, approximately in the vicinity of the year 920' (155). On palaeographical grounds E.A. Loew dates the *manuscript* to the middle of the eleventh century (*The Beneventan Script* 39, 213–15, 226, n 4). See Fournier and Le Bras *Histoire des collections canoniques* 1.341–7; Fuhrmann 'Eine im Original erhaltene Propagandaschrift des Erzbischofs Gunthar von Köln (865)' 30–3; Mordek *Kirchenrecht und Reform* 138, n 185.

27 Fournier provides some useful observations on this penitential in 'Etudes sur les pénitentiels v' *RHLR* 9 (1904) 98–9. Until recently no manuscripts have been known to contain the *Penitential of Pseudo-Gregory*. Professor F. Kerff kindly sent me an offprint of a recently published article which I have been unable to use in this study, 'Das Paenitentiale Pseudo-Gregorii iii. Ein Zeugnis karolingischer Reformbestregungen' *ZSavRG.KA* 79 (1983) 46–67.

28 Fournier seems correct in the view that Vat lat 1349 obtains many of its texts from the manuscript Rome Bibl Vall, T xviii, particularly from the version of the *Collectio Hibernensis* found in this manuscript. However, I was unable to find any penitential texts in the Vallicellian manuscript which were taken up by Vat lat 1349. There is a text on sexual abstinence, Bibl Vall, T xviii, fol 55va, but it is not incorporated in that form into the Collection in Nine Books. See the detailed description in Giorgetti Vichi and Mottironi *Catalogo dei manoscritti della Biblioteca Vallicellana* 1.243–52.

29 '... ex sanctorum patrum sententiis quam canonicis scripturis vel ab comprobatis poenitentium exemplis' *Decretum*, prefatory letter (PL 140.537A). The *Decretum* is dated to 1008–12. It is the view of E. Van Balberghe that the authentic preface of Burchard is not the one printed in the edition (PL 140.537–40) but the text published by the Ballerini in the introductory remarks to the edition (PL 140.499C–502C); see 'Les éditions du Décret de Burchard de Worms' 16. If he is correct, then the quoted passage would read, '... tam ex sententiis sanctorum patrum quam ex canonibus seu ex diversis poenitentialibus' (PL 140.499C). There is considerable literature on Burchard, but the most directly relevant work is the early study by Fournier of Burchard's sources, 'Etudes critiques sur le Décret de Burchard de Worms.' See *MHP* 321–3.

30 See *Decretum* 2.2 (PL 140.625D). This text will have a long history in the

collections and *summae confessorum.* I discuss it in an article to appear in *Mediaeval Studies,* 'The Humanism of the Penitentials and the Continuity of the Penitential Tradition.'

31 'Ad haec autem suum poenitentialem, qui et secundum canonum auctoritatem, et iustas sententias trium poenitentialium, Theodori episcopi, et Romanorum Pontificum, et Bedae ordinetur. Sed in Poenitentiali Bedae plura inveniuntur utilia; plura autem inveniuntur ab aliis inserta, quae nec canonibus nec aliis penitentialibus conveniunt' *Decretum* 19.8 (PL 140.979D); see the prefatory letter printed from the Ballerini (PL 140.502C). I assume that the *Penitential of the Roman Pontiffs* is the same as the Roman penitential referred to later (PL 140.980B). The *Penitential of Monte Cassino* bears the title 'Poenitentiarium Summorum Pontificum' (S 1.397), but there are no indications that Burchard used this penitential.

32 The title of the book is 'De poenitentia,' but see the introductory note, 'Liber hic Corrector vocatur et Medicus' (PL 140.949A). 'Medicus' is omitted from the index (PL 140.542A), but see the index printed from the Ballerini (PL 140.501C). See Fournier's discussion of book 19 in 'Etudes critiques ...' 213–21.

33 'Quamvis hae praedictae interrogationes foeminis et viris sint communes, tamen hae sequentes specialiter ad foeminas pertinent' (S 2.442, siglum α). See *Penitential of Monte Cassino* 'Inquisitio de mulieribus' 49–64 (S 1.411–13) and 'Item capita quae dicenda sunt ad viros seu ad mulieres' 65–74 (S 1.413–14).

34 At the end of *Decretum* 19.8 Burchard says, 'Haec omnia de canonibus, et de sanctorum patrum sententiis, et de Hieronymo, de Augustino, Gregorio, Theodoro, Beda, et ex Poenitentiali Romano vera collegimus' (PL 140.980A).

35 The seventh book, entitled 'De incestu,' deals primarily with marital incest.

36 See Fournier's discussion, entitled 'Les "inscriptions" imaginées par Burchard,' in 'Etudes critiques' 308–31.

37 The manuscript Vat Pal lat 294 is used by Schmitz for an edition of the *Penitential of Bede* (S 2.654–9), and its variants under siglum γ are given for his edition of the *Excarpsus of Egbert* (S 2.661–74). For his edition of the *Bede-Egbert Double Penitential* Albers provides variant readings from Vat Pal lat 294; see Albers 'Wann sind die Beda-Egbert'schen Bussbücher verfasst worden?' 401ff.

38 See Fransen 'Le Décret de Burchard de Worms. Valeur du texte de l'édition. Essai de classement des manuscrits' 8.

39 Collection in Five Books: ed Fornasari *Collectio canonum in v libris (Lib I–III)*. This edition has been severely criticized by Fransen, 'Principes d'édition des collections canoniques.' Fournier's discussion of this work is still the fundamental study: 'Un groupe de recueils canoniques italiens des xe et xIe siècles' 159–89. See Fournier and Le Bras *Histoire des collections canoniques* 1.421–31; Dold 'Eine alte Bussliturgie aus Codex Vaticanus latinus 1339'; Fornasari 'Un manoscritto e una collezione canonica del secolo XI provenienti da Farfa'; Fuhrmann 'Eine im Original erhaltene Propagandaschrift des Erzbischofs Gunthar von Köln (865)' 30–3.

40 See Fornasari *Collectio canonum in V libris* CC.CM 6.XIV; Fournier 'Un groupe de recueils' 169–74; Mordek *Kirchenrecht und Reform* 138, n 187; Fransen: '... mais nous montrerons qu'il n'y a pas de motif de s'écarter de l'opinion de Fournier' ('Principes d'édition' 131). It would perhaps be more accurate to say that the Coll 5 Bk made use of the Coll 9 Bk and so not presume manuscript affiliations which have not been demonstrated.

41 See Fournier 'Un groupe de recueils' 196–7 (Burchard), 195–208 (a general discussion of the influence of the Coll 5 Bk). This version of Burchard, *Decretum* 19.5, is edited by Wasserschleben, *Die Bussordnungen* 624–82.

42 See Walter *L'iconographie des conciles dans la tradition Byzantine* 61–7. I am grateful to Sister W. Fitzgerald for this reference. See Reynolds 'Excerpta from the Collectio Hibernensis in three Vatican Manuscripts' 1, n 3.

43 The work is partially edited (to book 11.15) by F. Thaner, *Anselmi ep. Lucensis, Collectio canonum una cum collectione minore.*

44 See above, nn 4, 7.

45 See Fournier, 'Les collections canoniques romaines de l'époque de Grégoire VII' 28(294)–61(327); Fournier and Le Bras *Histoire des collections canoniques* 2.25–37.

46 See Fournier 'Les sources canoniques du "Liber de vita christiana" de Bonizo de Sutri' 122; Fournier and Le Bras *Histoire des collections canoniques* 2.29–30, 35.

47 See Fournier 'Les collections canoniques romaines' 36(302)–7(303), and Fournier and Le Bras *Histoire des collections canoniques* 2.29.

48 The *Collectio tripartita* is unedited; *Decretum* (PL 161.47–1022); *Panormia* (PL 161.1041–1344). The *Decretum* is dated to 1091–5 by L. Chevailler, 'Yves de Chartres' 1647. See Fournier 'Les collections canoniques attribuées à Yves de Chartres.' The *Collectio tripartita* was examined in the manuscript Paris BN lat 3858B. There is a most sparing use of the penitentials in this work. An interesting feature is the use of the full inscription, 'Ex penitentiali Theodori Cantuariensis archiepiscopi,' at fols 177vb, 196rb, 200rb, 200vb.

49 'Theodorus archiepiscopus, et Adrianus abbas vir aeque doctissimus, a Vitaliano papa missi Britanniam, plurimas ecclesias Anglorum doctrinae ecclesiasticae fruge fecundarunt. E quibus Theodorus peccantium iudicia, quantis scilicet annis pro unoquoque peccato quis poenitere debeat, mirabiliter scripsit' Ivo *Decretum* 4.146 (PL 161.299); see Paul the Deacon *Historia Langobardorum* ed Bethmann and Waitz, 154 (PL 95.611A), and Sigebert of Gembloux *Chronica* ed L. Bethmann Scriptores 6.326.

50 See Ivo *Decretum* 6.22 (PL 161.450) = Burchard *Decretum* 2.2 (PL 140.625).

51 'Quod secundum canonum et poenitentialium statuta poenitentiae dandae sunt' Ivo *Decretum* 15.157 (PL 161.893) = Burchard *Decretum* 19.147 (PL 140.1011).

52 For Gratian I used Friedberg ed *Corpus iuris canonici*. The editor lists sixty-one canons of Gratian which he claims are from various penitential sources; see prolegomena, col XXXIX, twenty-five of which are attributed to the unlikely source of the *P of Pseudo-Theodore*.

53 One still finds in Gratian D.38, c 5 (Friedberg 141), the text's pointing out the

need of having a penitential, which was encountered already in Burchard and Ivo of Chartres.

54 Books 17 and 19 of the *Decretum* of Burchard were widely used, even into the thirteenth century, for prescriptions on sexual matters. A manuscript examined but not incorporated into our discussion (Reims Bibl mun 675 [G 528]) contains a Collection in Seventeen Books which relies heavily on Burchard; see Fournier 'De quelques collections canoniques issues du Décret de Burchard' 205–7; Fournier and Le Bras *Histoire des collections canoniques* 1.230–5; dated to the twelfth century, H. Loriquet *Catalogue général des manuscrits de bibliothèques publiques de France* Départements XXXIX Reims (Paris 1904) 11.27; and see Reynolds 'The "Isidorian" *Epistula ad Leudefredum'* 296. In general, see Fournier 'Le Décret de Burchard de Worms.' In a thirteenth-century work attributed to Robert Grosseteste, there is an interrogatory of eighty-four questions which seems to depend on the questions in Burchard *Decretum* 19.5; see London Lambeth Palace Library 144, fols 138ra–140rb.

55 See Kuttner 'The Father of the Science of Canon Law.'

56 For insightful comment on this literature, see Boyle 'Summae confessorum.'

57 [Bartholomew of Exeter] ed Morey *Bartholomew of Exeter, Bishop and Canonist.* Morey calls Bartholomew's work a penitential, but it seems to be more in the tradition of the *summae confessorum.* See chapters 61 (227), 66 (231), 67 (234), 69 (236), 70 (237), for texts on sexual offences taken from Gratian or Ivo of Chartres which are actually penitential canons.

58 See *Robert of Flamborough* ed Firth, bk 5, chap 3, 'De fornicatione' (229–44), and the interesting interrogatories in appendix B (296–9). Much of the chapter on sexual offences is taken from Bartholomew of Exeter and Ivo of Chartres.

59 I discuss the subject in a forthcoming article in *Mediaeval Studies*, 'The Humanism of the Penitentials and the Continuity of the Penitential Tradition.'

60 See *Poenitentiale ecclesiarum Germaniae* (= *Corrector* 1–33): general remarks (S 2.381–92), manuscripts (S 2.393–402), text (S 2.403–467). Wasserschleben (*Die Bussordnungen* 624–82) has edited a longer form of the *Corrector* from Rome Bibl Vallicelliana, Cod F 8. I believe that this manuscript incorporates additions made to the *Corrector.*

61 Basically an expansion and commentary on Burchard 9.69 (PL 140.826), which Burchard attributes to a Mainz council but which is from the Council of Elvira, canon 70 (Vives 13); see Regino 2.139 (Wasserschleben 267–8).

62 I include questions 105–12, 114–15, 119, since they deal with sexual incest. They have parallels in the seventeenth book of Burchard, but there they are based on conciliar texts, not on penitential sources. That is why they were not noted in the treatment of that book. In some cases the primary concern seems not to be the incest as such but the disqualifying results from the particular incestuous relationship. While the wording of the question focuses on fornication or sexual incest, the interest is often in marital incest.

63 *Arundel P* (S 1.432–65); see Fournier 'Etudes sur les penitentiels V' RHLR 9 (1904) 97–8 (not before the tenth century; rather, of the eleventh century); Liebermann 'Zum Poenitentiale Arundel' (Frankish empire, tenth century).

CHAPTER 4: GENERAL CONCLUSION

1 See Brundage 'Prostitution in the Medieval Canon Law' (with literature).
2 Vogel 'Pratiques superstitieuses au début du xie siècle d'après le *Corrector sive medicus* de Burchard évêque de Worms (965–1025).'
3 See above, p 13.
4 See above, p 3, n 4.
5 See above, p 69.
6 See Peter Damian *Liber Gomorrhianus* chaps 10–12 (PL 145.169–72).
7 See the interesting tracts on celibacy from the end of the eleventh century in MGH *Libelli de lite imperatorum et pontificum* 1.254–60; 2.7–26, 436–48; 3.1–11, 573–8, 579–83, 584–7, 588–96. See also Mirbt *Die Publizistik im Zeitalter Gregors* vii 239–342 ('Der Kampf um den Priestercölibat').
8 In *The History of Sexuality* vol 1, Michel Foucault attempts to link the development of more recent attitudes and beliefs about sexuality with the development of the history of penance since the Fourth Lateran Council (1215 AD). I offer some critical comment on this thesis in a forthcoming article in *Studies in Religion*, 'Foucault on Penance and the Shaping of Sexuality.'

Bibliography

MANUSCRIPTS (Microfilm)

London Lambeth Palace Library 144 (Robert Grosseteste)
Paris Bibliothèque nationale lat 3858B (Ivo of Chartres, *Collectio tripartita*)
– Bibliothèque nationale lat 3881 (*Polycarpus*)
– Bibliothèque nationale lat 12519 (Anselm of Lucca)
Reims Bibliothèque municipale 675 (G 528) (Collection in Seventeen Books)
Rome Biblioteca Vallicelliana, T XVIII (*Hibernensis*)
Vatican City Biblioteca Apostolica Vaticana
– Arch S Pietro H 58 (collection of penitential canons)
– Vat lat 1339 (Collection in Five Books)
– Vat lat 1347 (*Quadripartitus*)
– Vat lat 1349 (Collection in Nine Books)

EDITIONS OF PENITENTIALS

Albers, B. 'Wann sind die Beda-Egbert'schen Bussbücher verfasst worden, und wer ist ihr Verfasser?' *AkK* 81 (1901) 393–420
Asbach, F.B. *Das Poenitentiale Remense und der sogen. Excarpsus Cummeani: Überlieferung, Quellen und Entwicklung zweier kontinentaler Bussbücher aus der 1. Hälfte des 8. Jahrhunderts* Regensburg [1979]
Bieler, L. *The Irish Penitentials* appendix D.A. Binchy. Scriptores latini Hiberniae 5. Dublin 1963.
Caput de poenitentiae agendae ratione ex codice legum patrum. PL Supp 4.2206–14
Finsterwalder, P.W. *Die Canones Theodori Cantuariensis und ihre Überlieferungsformen* Weimar 1929
Gonzales Rivas, S. *La penitencia en la primitiva iglesia española. Estudio histórico, dogmático y canónico de la penitencia en la Iglesia española, desde sus orígenes hasta los primeros tiempos de la invasión musulmana* np 1949
Gwynn, E.J. 'An Irish Penitential' *Ériu* 7 (1914) 121–95
Hörmann, W. von *Bussbücherstudien* 1 *Das sogenannte poenitentiale Martenianum* Weimar nd. Sonderdruck aus der *Zeitschrift der Savigny-Stiftung für Rechtsgeschichte. Kan Abt* 1911–14

Hrabanus Maurus *Paenitentiale ad Heribaldum.* PL 110.467–94
– *Paenitentiale ad Otgarium.* PL 112.1397–1424
Iudicium penitentis. PL 138.959–80
Laporte, J. *Le Pénitentiel de Saint Colomban* Introduction et édition critique. Tournai 1958
Lowe [Loew], E.A. *The Bobbio Missal. A Gallican Mass-Book* (MS. *Paris lat. 13246*) *Text* Henry Bradshaw Society 58. London 1920
– 'The Vatican MS of the Gelasian Sacramentary and its Supplement at Paris' *The Journal of Theological Studies* 27 (1925–6) 357–73
Madoz, J. 'Una nueva recension del Penitencial "Vallicellanum I"' *Analecta sacra Tarraconensia* 18 (1945) 27–58
Mohlberg, L.C., L. Eizenhöfer, P. Siffrin *Liber sacramentorum romanae aecclesiae ordinis anni circuli* (Cod Vat Reg lat. 316 / Paris BN 7193, 41–56) (Sacramentarium Gelasianum). Rerum ecclesiasticarum documenta. Series maior, fontes IV. Rome 1960
Pseudo-Jerome *Canones poenitentiales.* PL 30.425–34
Schmitz, H.J. *Die Bussbücher und die Bussdisciplin der Kirche nach handschriftlichen Quellen dargestellt* Mainz 1883
– *Die Bussbücher und das kanonische Bussverfahren nach handschriftlichen Quellen dargestellt* Düsseldorf 1898
Urbel Perez, J. de and L. Parga Vazquez 'Un nuevo penitencial Español' *Annuario de Historia del Derecho Español* 14 (1942) 5–32
Walker, G. *Sancti Columbani opera* Scriptores latini Hiberniae 2. Dublin 1957
Wasserschleben, H. *Die Bussordnungen der abendländischen Kirche* Halle 1851

MEDIEVAL SOURCES

Admonitio synodalis: R. Amiet 'Une "Admonitio Synodalis" de l'époque carolingienne: Etude critique et édition' *Mediaeval Studies* 26 (1964) 12–82
Alexander of Hales *Quaestiones disputatae 'Antequam esset frater'* Vol 2. Florence 1960
Ansegisus *Ansegisi abbatis capitularium collectio.* MGH *Capitularia* 1.382–450 (PL 97.503–84)
Anselm of Lucca: F. Thaner *Anselmi ep. Lucensis. Collectio canonum una cum collectione minore* Innsbruck 1906–15
Atto of Vercelli *Capitulare.* PL 134.27–52
Augustine *De bono coniugali* ed. J. Zycha. CSEL 41.187–231. Vienna 1900. *The Good of Marriage* trans C.T. Wilcox. The Writings of Saint Augustine 15. The Fathers of the Church 27. New York 1955
– *De sancta virginitate* ed J. Zycha. CSEL 41.235–302. Vienna 1900. *Holy Virginity* trans J. McQuade. The Writings of Saint Augustine 15. The Fathers of the Church 27. New York 1955
– *Quaestionum evangeliorum libri duo.* PL 35.1321–64
Bartholomew of Exeter: A. Morey *Bartholomew of Exeter, Bishop and Canonist. A Study in the Twelfth Century* Cambridge 1937
Basil *The Letters* trans Roy J. Deferrari. 4 vols, Loeb Classical Library. Vol 3. London, Cambridge Mass 1930

Bede: C. Plummer *Venerabilis Baedae opera historica. Venerabilis Baedae Historiam ecclesiasticam gentis anglorum. Historiam abbatum. Epistolam ad Ecgberctum una cum Historia abbatum auctore anonymo* Tomus prior, prolegomena et textum continens. Oxford 1896
– B. Colgrave and R.A.B. Mynors *Bede's Ecclesiastical History of the English People* Oxford 1969
'Benedictus Levita' *Capitularium collectio.* PL 97.699–912
Boniface *Die Briefe des heiligen Bonifatius und Lullus* ed M. Tangl. MGH *Epistolae selectae* 1. Berlin 1916
Bonizo of Sutri: E. Perels *Bonizo. Liber de vita christiana* Berlin 1930
Burchard of Worms *Decretum.* PL 140.537–1058
Caesarius of Arles *Sermones* ed G. Morin. 2nd edn. CCSL 103–4. Turnhout 1953. *Sermons* trans M.M. Mueller. Vol 1 (1–80) The Fathers of the Church 31. New York 1956. Vol 2 (81–186) The Fathers of the Church 47. Washington 1964. Vol 3 (187–238) The Fathers of the Church 66. Washington 1973
Capitularia regum francorum. MGH Legum sectio 2, vol 1, ed A. Boretius. Hannover 1883
Capitularia regum francorum. MGH Legum sectio 2, vol 2, ed A. Boretius and V. Kraus. Hannover 1890–3
Codex Carolinus ed W. Gundlach. MGH *Epistolae Merowingici et Karolini aevi* 1.469–657. Berlin 1892
Collectio Anselmo dedicata: J.C. Besse *Histoire des textes du droit de l'église au moyen âge de Denis à Gratien. Collectio Anselmo dedicata* Etude et texte. Paris 1957
Collectio Barberiniana: M. Fornasari 'Collectio canonum Barberiniana' *Apollinaris* 36 (1963) 127–41, 215–97
Collectio Dacheriana: Luc d'Achéry *Spicilegium sive collectio veterum aliquot scriptorum qui in Galliae bibliothecis delituerant* 1.509–64. Paris 1723
Collectio Dionysio-Hadriana. PL 67.139–346
Collectio Hibernensis: H. Wasserschleben *Die irische Kanonensammlung* 2nd edn. Leipzig 1885
Collectio Hispana. PL 84.93–848
Collectio Vetus Gallica: H. Mordek *Kirchenrecht und Reform im Frankenreich. Die Collectio Vetus Gallica, die älteste systematische Kanonessammlung des fränkischen Gallien* Studien und Edition. Beiträge zur Geschichte und Quellenkunde des Mittelalters 1. Berlin, New York 1975
Collection in Two Books: J. Bernhard 'La Collection en deux livres (Cod. Vat. lat. 3832)' RDC 12 (1962) 9–601
Collection in Five Books: M. Fornasari *Collectio canonum in v libris (Lib. I–III).* CC.CM 6. Turnhout 1970
Collection in Seventy-four Titles: J.T. Gilchrist *Diversorum patrum sententiae sive Collectio in LXXIV titulos digesta* Monumenta iuris canonici series B: Corpus collectionum. Vol 1. Vatican City 1973. *The Collection in Seventy-Four Titles: A Canon Law Manual of the Gregorian Reform* trans J. Gilchrist. Toronto 1980
Collections of Milan: G. Picasso *Collezioni canoniche Milanesi del secolo XII* Milan 1969
Concilia aevi Karolini. MGH Legum sectio 3, tome 2, vol 1, parts 1 and 2, ed A. Werminghoff. Hannover 1906–8

De Clercq, C. *Concilia Galliae A. 511 – A. 695.* CCSL 148A. Turnhout 1962
Deusdedit: V. Wolf von Glanvell *Die Kanonessammlung des Kardinals Deusdedit* Bd 1 *Die Kanonessammlung selbst* Paderborn 1905
Diocesan statutes (anonymous):
– *Capitula Frisingensia*: E. Seckel 'Studien zu Benedictus Levita II–IV' *Neues Archiv* 29 (1904) 287–94
– Florence Bibl Med Laur, Plut IV sin. Cod 4 (XI in), fols 56v–57v: P. Brommer in *ZSavRG.KA* 60 (1974) 108–12
– Pokorny, R. 'Zwei unerkannte Bischöfskapitularien des 10. Jahrhunderts' *Deutsches Archiv* 35 (1979) 487–513
– St Gall, Stiftsbibliothek 679: P. Finsterwalder 'Zwei Bischofskapitularien der Karolingerzeit' *ZSavRG.KA* 14 (1925) 375–81
– Unknown bishop before Herard of Tours: C. De Clercq *La législation religieuse* 2.411–14
– Vat Ottob lat 261: A. Werminghoff 'Reise nach Italien im Jahre 1901' *Neues Archiv* 27 (1902) 580–7
– Vat Reg lat 612: P. Finsterwalder 'Zwei Bischofskapitularien ...' 350–67
– Vesoul Bibl publ 73: C. De Clercq *La législation religieuse* 1.367–74
Fulgentius of Ruspe *Opera* ed J. Fraipont. CCSL 91. Turnhout 1968
Gerbald of Liége *Capitula*: C. De Clercq *La législation religieuse* 1.352–6, 357–62
– *Capitula a sacerdotibus proposita*: W. Eckhardt *Die Kapitulariensammlung Bischof Ghaerbalds von Lüttich* Germanenrechte neue Folge deutschrechtliches Archiv, Heft 5. Göttingen 1955
Gerson, J. *De confessione mollitiei Œuvres complètes* ed P. Glorieux, 8.71–4. Paris 1971
Gratian: A. Friedberg *Corpus iuris canonici. Pars prior, Decretum Magistri Gratiani* Leipzig 1879
Gregory I *Gregorii I papae registrum epistolarum* ed L.M. Hartmann. MGH *Epistolae* I–II. Berlin 1899
Gregory II 'Desiderabilem mihi,' in *Die Briefe des heiligen Bonifatius und Lullus* ed M. Tangl, n 26
Guillebertus *Capitula*: S. Baluze *Capitularia regum francorum* 2.1377–8. Paris 1677.
Haddan, A.W. and W. Stubbs *Councils and Ecclesiastical Documents relating to Great Britain and Ireland* 3 vols. Oxford 1869–78
Halitgar of Cambrai *De vitiis et virtutibus et de ordine poenitentium.* PL 105.651–710. Bks 3–6 in S 2.275–300
– W. Hartmann 'Neue Texte zur bischöflichen Reformgesetzgebung aus den Jahren 829/31: Vier Diözesansynoden Halitgars von Cambrai' *Deutsches Archiv* 35 (1979) 368–94
Hatto of Basel *Capitula ecclesiastica.* MGH *Capitularia* 1, n 177
Herard of Tours *Capitula.* PL 121.763–74
Hincmar of Reims *Capitula presbyteris data anno 852.* PL 125.773–8
– *Capitula.* PL 125.777–92
– *Capitula anno XII episcopatus superaddita.* PL 125.793–4
– *Capitula in synodo Rhemis data anno 874.* PL 125.795–800
– *Capitula archidiaconibus presbyteris data.* PL 125.799–804

– *De divortio Lotharii regis et Tetbergae reginae.* PL 125.619–772
Hrabanus Maurus *De consanguineorum nuptiis.* PL 110.1087–96
– *De magorum praestigiis falsisque divinitationibus.* PL 110.1095–1110
– *Epistolae* ed E. Dummler. MGH *Epistolae Karolini aevi* 3.379–533. Berlin 1889
– 'Quota generatione licitum sit connubium' PL 110.1083–8 and MGH *Epistolae Karolini aevi* 3, n 29
– 'Response to Regimbald 1' PL 110.1187–96 and MGH *Epistolae Karolini aevi* 3, n 30
– 'Response to Regimbald 2' PL 112.1507–10 and MGH *Epistolae Karolini aevi* 3, n 41
Isaac of Langres *Canones.* PL 124.1075–1110
Isidore of Seville *Etymologiarum sive originum libri xx* ed W.M. Lindsay. Oxford 1911
Ivo of Chartres *Decretum.* PL 161.47–1022
– *Panormia.* PL 161.1041–1344
Jerome *Adversus Iovinianum libri duo.* PL 23.221–352. *St. Jerome. Letters and Select Works* trans W.H. Freemantle. A Select Library of Nicene and Post-Nicene Fathers of the Christian Church, second series, 6.346–416. New York 1892
– *Commentariorum in Matheum libri IV* ed D. Hurst and M. Adriaen. CCSL 77. Turnhout 1969
– *Epistolae* 1 (1–70) ed I. Hilberg. CSEL 54. Vienna 1910. See: *Selected Letters of St. Jerome* trans F.A. Wright. Loeb Classical Library. London, Cambridge Mass 1963
John Chrysostom *Adversus eos qui apud se habent virgines subintroductas* (PG 47.495–514). *Les cohabitations suspectes. Comment observer la virginité* ed J. Dumortier. Paris 1955
Jonas of Orleans *De institutione laicali libri tres.* PL 106.121–278
Leo I 'Epistolas fraternitatis tuae' (to Rusticus of Narbonne) PL 54.1197–1211
Leo IV 'Quanto studio' MGH *Epistolae* 5.593–6
Liebermann, F. *Die Gesetze der Angelsachsen* 3 vols. Halle 1903–16
Mansi, J.D. *Sacrorum conciliorum nova et amplissima collectio* 31 vols. Florence and Venice 1759–98
MGH *Libelli de lite imperatorum et pontificum saeculis XI. et XII. conscripti* 3 vols. Hannover 1891–7
Munier, C. *Concilia Galliae A. 314 – A. 506.* CCSL 148. Turnhout 1963
Optantius *Commentatio de vitiis ad loca S. Pauli explananda.* PL Supp 4.2197–203
Paul the Deacon *Historia Langobardorum* ed L. Bethmann and G. Waitz. MGH *Scriptores rerum Langobardicarum et Italicarum saec VI–IX.* Hannover 1878. PL 95.433–682
Peter Damian *Liber Gomorrhianus.* PL 145.161–90. *Book of Gomorrah. An Eleventh-Century Treatise against Clerical Homosexual Practices* trans, intro, and notes P. Payer. Waterloo Ont 1982
Pflugk-Harttung, J. von *Acta pontificum romanorum inedita. Urkunden der Päpste 590–1197* Vol 3. Stuttgart 1886
Pirmin: U. Engelmann *Der heilige Pirmin und sein Pastoralbüchlein* 2nd edn. Sigmaringen 1976
Pseudo-Isidore: P. Hinschius *Decretales Pseudo-Isidorianae et Capitula Angilramni* Leipzig 1863

Rather of Verona *Die Briefe des Bischofs Rather von Verona* ed F. Weigle. MGH
Die deutschen Geschichtsquellen des Mittelalters 500–1500. Die Briefe der
deutschen Kaizerzeit. 1 Bd. Weimar 1949
Regino of Prüm: H. Wasserschleben *Reginonis abbatis Prumiensis, libri duo de
synodalibus causis et disciplinis ecclesiasticis* Leipzig 1840
Riculph of Soissons *Constitutio* Mansi 18A.81–90
Robert of Flamborough: J.J.F. Firth *Robert of Flamborough, Canon-Penitentiary of
Saint-Victor at Paris. Liber Poenitentialis* Critical edn with intro and notes.
Toronto 1971
Rodulph of Bourges *Capitula*. PL 119.703–26
Romano-German Pontifical: C. Vogel and R. Elze *Le Pontifical Romano-Germanique
du dixième siècle* Studi e Testi, 226, 227, 269. 3 vols. Vatican 1963, 1972
Sigebert of Gembloux *Chronica* ed L.C. Bethmann. MGH *Scriptores* 6.300–74
Siricius 'Directa ad decessorem' (to Himerius of Tarragona) PL 13.1131–47. Trans
in J.T. Shotwell and L.R. Loomis *The See of Peter* Records of Civilization. Sources
and Studies. New York 1927
Stephen II 'In epistola Leonis' PL 89.1024–30
Theiner, A. *Disquisitiones criticae in praecipuis canonum et decretalium collectiones seu
sylloges ...* Index. Rome 1836
Theodulf of Orleans *Capitula ad presbyteros parochiae suae*. PL 105.191–208
– Second Diocesan Statute: C. De Clercq *La législation religieuse* 1.321–51
Turner, C.H. *Ecclesiae occidentalis monumenta iuris antiquissima. Canonum et
conciliorum graecorum interpretationes latinae* 2 vols, 4 parts. Oxford 1899–1913
Vives, J. *Concilios Visigóticos e Hispano-Romanos* Barcelona, Madrid 1963
Vulfodus of Bourges *Epistola pastoralis*. PL 121.1135–42
Waltcaud of Liége *Item alia capitula*: C. De Clercq *La législation religieuse* 1.363–6
Walter of Orleans *Capitula*. PL 119.725–46
Werminghoff, A. 'Verzeichnis der Akten fränkischer Synoden von 843–918'
Neues Archiv 26 (1901) 607–78
Zachary 'Gaudio magno' *Codex Carolinus* 479–87
– 'Susceptis sanctissimae' *Die Briefe des heiligen Bonifatius und Lullus* ed M. Tangl.
MGH *Epistolae selectae* 1, n 51

STUDIES

Adams, J.N. *The Latin Sexual Vocabulary* Baltimore 1982
Amann, E. 'Pénitence' DTC 12.749–948 (*Tables générales* 3558–69)
Aronstam, R.A. 'The Latin Canonical Tradition in Late Anglo-Saxon England:
the *Excerptiones Egberti*' PhD dissertation, Columbia University 1974. Xerox
University Microfilms 1981
Autenrieth, J. *Die Handschriften der Württembergischen Landesbibliothek Stuttgart* 2:
Die Handschriften der ehemaligen königlichen Hofbibliothek vol 3: *Codices iuridici et
politici* Wiesbaden 1963
Autenrieth, J. and R. Kottje *Kirchenrechtliche Texte im Bodenseegebiet. Mittelalter-
liche Überlieferung in Konstanz, auf der Reichenau und in St. Gallen* Sigmaringen
1975

Bailey, D.S. *Homosexuality and the Western Christian Tradition* London 1955

Bateson, M. 'The Supposed Latin Penitential of Egbert and the Missing Work of Halitgar of Cambrai' *English Historical Review* 9 (1894) 320–6

Berschin, W. *Bonizo von Sutri. Leben und Werk* Beiträge zur Geschichte und Quellenkunde des Mittelalters 2. Berlin, New York 1972

Bieler, L. 'The Irish Penitentials: Their Religious and Social Background' Studia Patristica vol 8 *Texte und Untersuchungen zur Geschichte der altchristlichen Literatur* 93 (1966) 329–39

Bischoff, B. and J. Hofmann *Libri sancti Kyliani Die Würzburger Schreibschule und die Dombibliothek im VIII. und IX. Jahrhundert* Würzburg 1952

Boswell, J. *Christianity, Social Tolerance, and Homosexuality. Gay People in Western Europe from the Beginning of the Christian Era to the Fourteenth Century* Chicago 1980

Bouchard, C.B. 'Consanguinity and Noble Marriages in the Tenth and Eleventh Centuries' *Speculum* 56 (1981) 268–87

Boyle, L. 'Summae confessorum' *Les genres littéraires dans les sources théologiques et phiiosophiques médiévales. Définition, critique et exploitation* Actes du colloque internationale de Louvain-la-Neuve 25–7 May 1981. Louvain-la-Neuve 1982. 227–37

Brommer, P. 'Die bischöfliche Gesetzgebung Theodulfs von Orléans' *ZSavRG.KA* 60 (1974) 1–120

– 'Die Rezeption der bischöflichen Kapitularien Theodulfs von Orléans' *ZSavRG.KA* 61 (1975) 113–60

– 'Die Quellen der "Capitula" Radulfs von Bourges' *Francia* 5 (1977) 27–43

– 'Capitula episcoporum. Bemerkungen zu den bischöflichen Kapitularien' *Zeitschrift für Kirchengeschichte* 91 (1980) 207–36

Browe, P. *Beiträge zur Sexualethik des Mittelalters* Breslau 1932

Brundage, J.A. 'Prostitution in the Medieval Canon Law' *Signs* 1 (1976) 825–45

– 'Rape and Marriage in the Medieval Canon Law' *RDC* 28 (1978) 62–75

Bullough, V. *Sexual Variance in Society and History* New York 1976

Cabrol, F. 'Jeûnes' *DACL* 7 (1939) 2488–91

Callam, D. 'The Origins of Clerical Celibacy' Dissertation, Oxford 1977

Callewaert, R.S. 'Les pénitentiels du moyen âge et les pratiques anticonceptionnelles' *La vie spirituelle. Supplément* 18 (1965) 339–66

Camelot, T. 'Le traités *De virginitate* au IVe siècle' *Mystique et continence* Travaux scientifiques du VIIe congrès international d'Avon *Etudes carmélitaines* 31 *Supplément* (1952) 273–92

Cantalamessa, R., ed *Etica sessuale e matrimonio nel christianesimo delle origini* Studia Patristica Mediolanensia 5. Milan 1976

'Censimento dei codici dei secoli X–XII' *Studi medievali* 3rd ser, 9 (1968) 1115–94, 11 (1970) 1013–1133

Chadwick, N. *The Age of the Saints in the Early Celtic Church* London 1961

Champeaux, E. 'Ius sanguinis. Trois façons de calculer la parenté au moyen âge' *RHDFE* 12 (1933) 241–90

Chelini, J. 'Les laïcs dans la société ecclésiastique carolingienne' *I laici nella 'societas christiana' dei secoli XI e XII* 23–50

Chevailler, L. 'Yves de Chartres' *DDC* 7 (1965) 1641–66

Coppens, J., ed *Sacerdoce et célibat: Etudes historiques et théologiques* Bibliotheca Ephemeridum theologicarum Lovaniensium 28. Gembloux-Louvain 1971

Crouzel, H. 'Le célibat et la continence ecclésiastique dans l'Eglise primitive: leurs motivations,' in J. Coppens, ed *Sacerdoce et célibat* 333–71

Deanesly, M. 'The Capitular Text of the "Responsiones" of Pope Gregory I to St. Augustine' *JEH* 12 (1961) 231–4

Deanesly, M. and P. Grosjean 'The Canterbury Edition of the Answers of Pope Gregory I to St. Augustine' *JEH* 10 (1959) 1–49

De Clercq, C. *La législation religieuse franque de Clovis à Charlemagne. Etude sur les actes de conciles et les capitulaires, les statuts diocésains et les règles monastiques (507–814)* Louvain 1936

– *La législation religieuse franque* Vol 2 *De Louis le Pieux à la fin du IXe siècle (814–900)* Anvers 1958

Devailly, G. 'La pastorale en Gaul au IXe siècle' *Revue d'histoire de l'église de France* 59 (1973) 23–54

Devisse, J. *Hincmar. Archevêque de Reims (845–882)* 3 vols. Geneva 1975–6

Díaz y Díaz, M.C. 'Para un estudio de los penitenciales hispanos' *Mélanges offerts à E.R. Labande* Poitiers 1974. 217–22

Dold, A. 'Eine alte Bussliturgie aus Codex Vaticanus latinus 1339' *Jahrbuch für Liturgiewissenschaft* 11 (1931) 94–130

Dubarle, A.M. 'La Bible et les pères ont-ils parlé de la contraception?' *La vie spirituelle. Supplément* 15 (1962) 573–610

– 'La contraception chez Césaire d'Arles' *La vie spirituelle. Supplément* 16 (1963) 515–19

Duby, G. and J. Le Goff, eds *Famille et Parenté dans l'occident médiéval* Collection de l'école française de Rome 30. Rome 1977

Duguit, L. 'Etude historique sur le rapt de séduction' *NRHDFE* 10 (1886) 587–625

Esmein, A. *Le mariage en droit canonique* 2nd edn. Vol 1 by R. Génestal. Paris 1929. Vol 2 by R. Génestal and J. Dauvillier. Paris 1935

Finsterwalder, P. 'Die sogenannte Homilia Leonis IV, ihre Bedeutung für Hinkmars Capitula und Reginos Inquisitio' *ZSavRG.KA* 27 (1938) 639–64

Flandrin, J.L. 'Contraception, mariage et relations amoureuses dans l'occident chrétien' *Annales. Economies, sociétés, civilisations* 24 (1969) 1370–90

Fleury, J. *Recherches historiques sur les empêchements de parenté dans le mariage canonique des origines aux Fausses Décrétales* Paris 1933

Fornasari, M. 'Un manoscritto e una collezione canonica del secolo XI provenienti da Farfa' *Benedictina* 10 (1956) 199–210

Forshaw, H.P. 'The Pastoral Ministry of the Priest-Confessor in the Early Middle Ages, 600–1100. A study of the origin and development of the role of the priest-confessor in the administration of private ecclesiastical penance in the West' PhD dissertation, London 1975

Foucault, M. *The History of Sexuality* Vol 1 *An Introduction* trans R. Hurley. New York 1978

Fournier, P. 'Les collections canoniques attribuées à Yves de Chartres' *Bibliothèque de l'école des chartes* 57 (1896) 645–98; 58 (1897) 26–77, 293–326, 410–44, 624–76

– 'De l'influence de la collection irlandaise sur la formation des collections canoniques' *NRHDFE* 23 (1899) 27–78

– 'Etudes sur les pénitentiels' *RHLR* 6 (1901) 289–317; 7 (1902) 59–70, 121–7; 8 (1903) 528–53; 9 (1904) 97–103
– 'De quelques collections canoniques issues du Décret de Burchard' *Mélanges Paul Fabre. Etudes d'histoire du moyen âge* Paris 1902. 189–214
– 'Le Liber ex lege Moysi et les tendances bibliques du droit canonique irlandais' *Revue celtique* 30 (1909) 221–34
– 'Etudes critiques sur le Décret de Burchard de Worms' *NRHDFE* 34 (1910) 41–112, 213–21, 289–331, 564–84
– 'Le Décret de Burchard de Worms. Ses caractères, son influence' *RHE* 12 (1911) 451–73, 670–701
– 'Un groupe de recueils canoniques italiens des xe et xie siècles' *Mémoires de l'institut national de France. Académie des inscriptions et Belles-Lettres* 40 (1916) 95–213
– 'Les sources canoniques du "Liber de vita christiana" de Bonizo de Sutri' *Bibliothèque de l'école des chartes* 78 (1917) 117–34
– 'Les collections canoniques romaines de l'époque de Grégoire VII' Extract from *Mémoires de l'Académie des inscriptions et Belles-Lettres* vol 41, 5(271)–131(397). Paris 1918
– 'L'œuvre canonique de Réginon de Prüm' *Bibliothèque de l'école des chartes* 81 (1920) 5–44
– 'Essai de restitution d'un manuscrit pénitentiel détruit' *Mélanges Mandonnet. Etudes d'histoire littéraire et doctrinale du moyen âge* 2.39–45. Paris 1930
Fournier, P. and G. Le Bras *Histoire des collections canoniques en occident depuis les Fausses Décrétales jusque'au Décret de Gratien* 2 vols. Paris 1931–2
Fransen, G. 'Principes d'édition des collections canoniques' *RHE* 66 (1971) 125–36
– *Les collections canoniques* Typologie des sources du moyen âge occidental 10. Turnhout 1973
– 'Le Décret de Burchard de Worms. Valeur du texte de l'édition. Essai de classement des manuscrits' *ZSavRG.KA* 63 (1977) 1–19
Frantzen, A. 'The Significance of the Frankish Penitentials' *JEH* 30 (1979) 409–21
– *The Literature of Penance in Anglo-Saxon England* New Brunswick NJ 1983
Freisen, J. *Geschichte des canonischen Eherechts bis zum Verfall der Glossenlitteratur* Paderborn 1893
Fuhrmann, H. 'Eine im Original erhaltene Propagandaschrift des Erzbischofs Gunthar von Köln (865)' *Archiv für Diplomatik* 4 (1958) 1–51
– *Einfluss und Verbreitung der pseudoisidorischen Fälschungen von ihrem Auftauchen bis in die neuere Zeit* Schriften der Monumenta Germaniae historica. Deutsches Institut für Erforschung des Mittelalters 24.1–3. Stuttgart 1972–4
Gaiffier, B. de 'Intactam sponsam relinquens. A propos de la vie de s. Alexis' *Analecta Bollandiana* 65 (1947) 157–95
Ganshof, F.L. *Recherches sur les capitulaires* Paris 1958
– *Droit romain dans les capitulaires.* 1 Le droit romain dans les capitulaires et dans la collection d'Ansegise. 2 Le droit romain dans la collection de Benoît le Lévite. Ius Romanum Medii Aevi I, 2 b cc α-β. Milan 1969
Gaudemet, J. 'L'apport de la patristique latine au Décret de Gratien en matière de mariage' *Studia Gratiana* 2 (1954) 49–81
– 'Elvire. II. Le concil d'Elvire' *DHGE* 15 (1963) 317–48
– 'Le pseudo-concile de Nantes' *RDC* 25 (1975) 40–60

- 'Les statuts épiscopaux de la première décade du IXe siècle' *Proceedings of the Fourth International Congress of Medieval Canon Law* ed S. Kuttner. Monumenta Iuris canonici series C: subsidia 5. Vatican 1976. 303–49
- 'Indissolubilité et consommation du mariage. L'apport d'Hincmar de Reims' *RDC* 30 (1980) 28–40
Gauthier, A. 'La sodomie dans le droit canonique médiéval,' in B. Roy, ed *L'érotisme au moyen âge* 109–22
Gilchrist, J.T. 'Canon Law Aspects of the Eleventh Century Gregorian Reform Programme' *JEH* 13 (1962) 21–38
- 'The Collection of Cod. Vat. lat. 3832, a Source of the Collection in Seventy-four Titles?' *Etudes d'histoire du droit canonique dédiées à Gabriel Le Bras* 1.141–56. Paris 1965
Giorgetti Vichi, A.M. and S. Mottironi *Catalogo dei manoscritti della Biblioteca Vallicelliana* Vol 1. Rome 1961
Gossman, F.J. *Pope Urban II and Canon Law* Washington 1960
Griffe, E. *La Gaule chrétienne à l'époque romaine* new edn. Vol 1. Paris 1964
- 'A propos du canon 33 du concile d'Elvire' *Bulletin de littérature ecclésiastique* 74 (1973) 142–5
Gryson, R. *Les origines du célibat ecclésiastique du premier au septième siècle* Recherches et synthèses, section d'histoire 2. Gembloux 1970
Haenni, G. 'Note sur les sources de la Dacheriana' *Studia Gratiana* 11 (1967) 1–22
Hägele, G. *Frühmittelalterliches Kirchenrecht in Oberitalien: Das Paenitentiale Vallicellianum Primum. Überlieferung, Verbreitung und Quellen* in press
Haggenmüller, M. and R. 'Ein Fragment des Paenitentiale Ps.-Bedae in der Ottobeurer Handschrift Ms. O.28' *Codices manuscripti* 5 (1979) 77–9
Haggenmüller, R. 'Eine weitere Überlieferung des Paenitentiale Burgundense: Anmerkungen zum Münchener Codex Clm 14780' *Bulletin of Medieval Canon Law* ns 10 (1980) 52–5
Hartmann, W. *Das Konzil von Worms 868: Überlieferung und Bedeutung.* Abhandlungen der Akademie der Wissenschaften in Göttingen, Philologisch-Historische Klasse, Dritte Folge 105. Göttingen 1977
Hefele, K.J. and H. Leclercq *Histoire des conciles* 8 vols. Paris 1907–21
Hellinger, W. 'Die Pfarrvisitation nach Regino von Prüm. Der Rechtsgehalt des 1. Buches seiner "Libri duo de synodalibus causis et disciplinis ecclesiasticis"' *ZSavRG.KA* 48 (1962) 1–116; 49 (1963) 76–137
Hertling, L. 'Hagiographische Texte zur frühmittelalterlichen Bussgeschichte' *Zeitschrift für katholische Theologie* 55 (1931) 109–22
- 'Hagiographische Texte zur Bussgeschichte des frühesten Mittelalters' *Zeitschrift für katholische Theologie* 55 (1931) 274–87
Hörmann, W. von 'Ueber die Entstehungsverhaltnisse des sogen. Poenitentiale Pseudo-Theodori' *Mélanges Fitting* 2.3–21. Montpellier 1908
Hoyt, F.S. 'The Carolingian Episcopate: Concepts of Pastoral Care as Set Forth in the Capitularies of Charlemagne and His Bishops (789–822)' PhD dissertation, Yale 1975
Hughes, K. *The Church in Early Irish Society* London 1966
I laici nella 'societas christiana' dei secoli XI e XII Miscellania del centro di studi medioevali 5. Milan 1968

Jaffé, P. *Regesta pontificum romanorum* 2nd edn, W. Wattenbach, S. Loewenfeld, F. Kaltenbrunner, P. Ewald. Vol 1 (to 1143). Leipzig 1885

Jungmann, J.A. *Die lateinischen Bussriten in ihrer geschichtlichen Entwicklung* Forschungen zur Geschichte des innerkirchlichen Lebens 3, 4. Innsbruck 1932

Kelly, W. *Pope Gregory II on Divorce and Remarriage. A canonical-historical investigation of the letter Desiderabilem mihi, with special reference to the response Quod proposuisti* Analecta Gregoriana 203. Series Facultatis Iuris canonici: sectio B 37. Rome 1976

Kenney, J.F. *The Sources for the Early History of Ireland. An Introduction and Guide.* 1 *Ecclesiastical.* Records of Civilization, Sources and Studies 11. New York 1929

Kerff, F. *Der Quadripartitus. Ein Handbuch der karolingischen Kirchenreform. Überlieferung, Quellen und Rezeption* Sigmaringen 1982
– 'Das Paenitentiale Pseudo-Gregorii III. Ein Zeugnis Karolingischer Reformbestregungen' *ZSavRG.KA* 79 (1983) 46–67

Kiefer, O. *Sexual Life in Ancient Rome* London 1934

Kottje, R. *Studien zum Einfluss des alten Testamentes auf Recht und Liturgie des frühen Mittelalters (6.–8. Jahrhundert)* 2nd edn. Bonn 1970
– *Die Bussbücher Halitgars von Cambrai und des Hrabanus Maurus. Ihre Überlieferung und ihre Quellen* Beiträge zur Geschichte und Quellenkunde des Mittelalters 8. Berlin, New York 1980
– 'Paenitentiale Theodori' *Handwörterbuch zur deutschen Rechtgeschichte* 3.1413–16
– 'Ehe und Eheverständnis in den vorgratianischen Bussbüchern,' in W. van Hoeck and A. Welkenhuysen, eds *Love and Marriage in the Twelfth Century* Louvain 1981. 18–40
– 'Überlieferung and Rezeption der irischen Bussbücher auf dem Kontinent,' in H. Lowe, ed *Die Iren und Europa im früheren Mittelalter* 1.511–24. Stuttgart 1982

Kunstmann, F. 'Das Eherecht des Bischofes Bernhard von Pavia mit geschichtlicher Einleitung' *AkK* 6 (1861) 3–14, 217–62

Kuttner, S. 'The Father of the Science of Canon Law' *The Jurist* 1 (1941) 2–19

Laeuchli, S. *Power and Sexuality. The Emergence of Canon Law at the Synod of Elvira* Philadelphia 1972

Lafontaine, P.H. 'Remarques sur le prétendu rigorisme pénitentiel du pape Sirice' *Revue de l'Université d'Ottawa* 28 (1958) 31*–48*

Laistner, M.L. 'Was Bede the Author of a Penitential?' *Harvard Theological Review* 31 (1938) 263–74

Le Bras, G. 'Les deux formes de la *Dacheriana*' *Mélanges Paul Fournier* Paris 1929. 395–414
– 'Alger de Liége et Gratien' *Revue des sciences philosophiques et théologiques* 20 (1931) 5–26
– 'Manuscrit vendômois du "Quadripartitus"' *RSR* 11 (1931) 266–9
– 'Notes pour servir à l'histoire des collections canoniques. v. Iudicia Theodori. vi. Pénitentiels espagnols' *RHDFE* 4th ser 10 (1931) 95–131
– 'Pénitentiels' *DTC* 12.1160–79

Leclercq, H. 'Pénitentiels' *DACL* 14 (1939) 215–51

Liebermann, F. 'Zum Poenitentiale Arundel' *ZSavRG.KA* 15 (1926) 531–2

Lindner, D. *Der usus matrimonii. Eine Untersuchung über seine sittliche Bewertung in der katholischen Moraltheologie alter und neuer Zeit* Munich 1929
Loew, E.A. *The Beneventan Script. A History of the South Italian Minuscule* 2nd edn, ed V. Brown. 1 *Text.* Rome 1980
Maassen, F. *Geschichte der Quellen und der Literatur des canonischen Rechts* Gratz 1870
Machielsen, L. 'Fragments patristiques non-identifiés du ms. Vat. Pal. 577' *Sacris Erudiri* 12 (1961) 488–539
– 'Les spurii de S. Grégoire le Grand en matière matrimoniale, dans les collections canoniques jusqu'au Décret de Gratien' *Sacris Erudiri* 14 (1963) 251–70
Makowski, E.M. 'The Conjugal Debt and Medieval Canon Law' *Journal of Medieval History* 3 (1977) 99–114
Manselli, R. *La religion populaire au moyen âge. Problèmes de méthode et d'histoire* Conférence Albert-Le-Grand 1973. Montreal 1975
– 'Il matrimonio nei penitenziali' *Il matrimonio nella società altomedievale* Settimane di studio del centro italiano di studi sull'alto medioevo 24. 1.287–315. Spoleto 1977
– 'Vie familiale et éthique sexuelle dans les pénitentiels,' in G. Duby and J. Le Goff, eds *Famille et Parenté dans l'occident médiéval* 363–78
May, G. *Social Control of Sex Expression* London 1930
McKitterick, R. *The Frankish Church and the Carolingian Reforms, 789–895* London 1977
McNeill, J.T. *The Celtic Penitentials and Their Influence on Continental Christianity* Paris 1923
McNeill, J.T. and H.M. Gamer *Medieval Handbooks of Penance. A translation of the principal libri poenitentiales and selections from related documents.* Records of Civilization, Sources and Studies 29. New York 1938
Meersseman, G.G. 'I penitenti nei secoli x e xii' *I laici nella 'societas christiana'* 306–39
Meyer, O. 'Überlieferung und Verbreitung des Dekrets des Bischofs Burchard von Worms' *ZSavRG.KA* 24 (1935) 141–183
Meyvaert, P. 'Les "Responsiones" de S. Grégoire le Grand à S. Augustin de Cantorbéry' *RHE* 54 (1959) 879–94
– 'Diversity within Unity, A Gregorian Theme' *The Heythrop Journal* 4 (1963) 141–62
– 'Bede's text of the *Libellus Responsionum* of Gregory the Great to Augustine of Canterbury' *England before the Conquest: Studies in Primary Sources presented to Dorothy Whitelock* ed P. Clemoes and K. Hughes. Cambridge 1971. 15–33
Mirbt, C. *Die Publizistik im Zeitalter Gregors vii* Leipzig 1894
Mordek, H. 'Kanonistische Aktivität in Gallien in der ersten Hälfte des 8. Jahrhunderts. Eine Skizze' *Francia* 2 (1974) 19–25
Morin, J. *Commentarius historicus de disciplina in administratione sacramenti poenitentiae* Venice 1702
Mortimer, R.C. *The Origins of Private Penance in the Western Church* Oxford 1939
Müller, M. 'Ein sexual-ethisches Problem der Scholastik' *Divus Thomas* (Freiburg) 12 (1934) 442–97

Noonan, J.T. *Contraception. A History of Its Treatment by the Catholic Theologians and Canonists* Cambridge Mass 1965

Oakley, T.P. *English Penitential Discipline and Anglo-Saxon Law in Their Joint Influence* Columbia University Studies in the Social Sciences 242. New York 1923

– 'The Cooperation of Mediaeval Penance and Secular Law' *Speculum* 7 (1932) 515–24

– 'Commutations and Redemptions of Penance in the Penitentials' *Catholic Historical Review* 18 (1932) 341–51

– 'The Origins of Irish Penitential Discipline' *Catholic Historical Review* 19 (1933) 320–32

– 'Cultural Affiliations of Early Ireland in the Penitentials' *Speculum* 8 (1933) 489–500

– 'Alleviations of Penance in the Continental Penitentials' *Speculum* 12 (1937) 488–502

– 'Celtic Penance. Its Sources, Affiliations and Influence' *Irish Ecclesiastical Record* 52 (1938) 147–64, 581–601

– 'The Penitentials as Sources for Medieval History' *Speculum* 15 (1940) 210–23

Payer, P. 'Early Medieval Regulations concerning Marital Sexual Relations' *Journal of Medieval History* 6 (1980) 353–76

Picasso, G. 'Atteggiamenti verso i laici in collezioni canoniche milanesi del secolo XII' *I laici nella 'societas christiana'* 722–32

Pierce, R. 'The "Frankish" Penitentials,' in *The Materials, Sources and Methods of Ecclesiastical History* ed D. Baker *Studies in Church History* 11 (1975) 31–9

Poschmann, B. *Penance and the Anointing of the Sick* trans and rev F. Courtney. New York 1964

Reynolds, R.E. '*Virgines subintroductae* in Celtic Christianity' *Harvard Theological Review* 61 (1968) 547–66

– 'Excerpta from the Collectio Hibernensis in three Vatican manuscripts' *Bulletin of Medieval Canon Law* ns 5 (1975) 1–9

– 'The "Isidorian" *Epistula ad Leudefredum*: an Early Medieval Epitome of the Clerical Duties' *Mediaeval Studies* 41 (1979) 252–330

– 'Canon Law Collections in Early Ninth-Century Salzburg' *Proceedings of the Fifth International Congress of Medieval Canon Law 1976* Vatican 1980. 15–34 (offprint)

Ritzer, K. *Le mariage dans les églises chrétiennes du Ier au XIe siècle* Paris 1970

Rosambert, A. *La veuve en droit canonique jusqu'au XIVe siècle* Paris 1923

Roy, B., ed *L'érotisme au moyen âge: études presentées au troisième colloque de l'Institut d'études médiévales* Montreal 1977

Ruggiero, G. 'Sexual Criminality in the Early Renaissance: Venice 1338–1358' *Journal of Social History* 8 (summer 1975) 18–37

Ryan, J.J. *Saint Peter Damiani and his Canonical Sources. A Preliminary Study in the Antecedents of the Gregorian Reform* Toronto 1956

Sauer, H. 'Zur Überlieferung und Anlage von Erzbischof Wulfstans "Handbuch"' *Deutsches Archiv* 36 (1980) 341–84

Schmidt, K. *Ius primae noctis. Eine geschichtliche Untersuchung* Freiburg im Breisgau 1881

Seckel, E. 'Studien zu Benedictus Levita II–v' *Neues Archiv* 29 (1904) 275–331

Taylor, G. Rattray *Sex in History* New York 1954

Thomas, W. *Der Sonntag im frühen Mittelalter mit Berücksichtigung der Entstehungsgeschichte des christlichen Dekalogs dargestellt* Göttingen 1929

Vaccari, P. 'La tradizione canonica del "debitum" coniugale e la posizione de Graziano' *Studia Gratiana* 1 (1952) 533–47

Van Balberghe, E. 'Les éditions du Décret de Burchard de Worms' *Recherches de théologie ancienne et médiévale* 37 (1970) 5–22

Van Hove, A. *Prolegomena ad codicem iuris canonici* 2nd edn. Malines, Rome 1945

Verbraken, P.P. *Etudes critiques sur les sermons authentiques de saint Augustin* Instrumenta patristica 12. Steenbrugge 1976

Vogel, C. *La discipline pénitentielle en Gaule des origines à la fin du VIIe siècle* Paris 1952

– 'La discipline pénitentielle en Gaule des origines au IXe siècle: le dossier hagiographique' *RSR* 30 (1956) 1–26, 157–86

– 'Composition légale et commutations dans le système de la pénitence tarifée' *RDC* 8 (1958) 289–318; 9 (1959) 1–38, 341–59

– 'Le péché et la pénitence. Aperçu sur l'évolution historique de la discipline pénitentielle dans l'Eglise latine' *Pastorale du péché* Bibliothèque de Théologie série 11, Théologie morale 8. Tournai 1961. 147–235.

– 'Le Pontifical romano-germanique du Xe siècle. Nature, date et importance du document' *Cahiers de civilisation médiévale* 6 (1963) 27–48

– 'Contenu et ordonnance primitive du Pontifical romano-germanique' *Atti del VI Congresso internazionale di archeologia cristiana* Rome 1965. 243–65

– 'Les rites de la pénitence publique au Xe et XIe siècles' *Mélanges offerts à René Crozet* ed P. Gallais and Yves-Jean Riou. 1.137–44. Poitiers 1966

– 'Pratiques superstitieuses au début du XIe siècle d'après le *Corrector sive medicus* de Burchard, évêque de Worms (965–1025)' *Etudes de civilisation médiévale (IXe–XIIe siècles). Mélanges offerts à E.R. Labande* Poitiers 1974. 751–61

– Les '*Libri Paenitentiales*' Typologie des sources du moyen âge occidental 27. Turnhout 1978

Vykoukal, E. 'Les examens du clergé paroissial à l'époque carolingienne' *RHE* 14 (1913) 81–96

Walter, C. *L'iconographie des conciles dans la tradition Byzantine* Archives de l'orient chrétien 13. Paris 1970

Watkins, O.D. *A History of Penance. Being a Study of the Authorities* 2 vols. London 1920

Wemple, S.F. *Atto of Vercelli. Church, State and Christian Society in Tenth Century Italy* Temi e Testi 27. Rome 1979

Werminghoff, A. 'Reise nach Italien im Jahre 1901' *Neues Archiv* 27 (1902) 567–604

Wilmart, A., E.A. Lowe [Loew], H.A. Wilson *The Bobbio Missal (MS Paris lat. 13246) Notes and Studies* Henry Bradshaw Society 61. London 1924

Tables of Reference

2 TABLE OF PENITENTIAL REFERENCES

3 TABLE OF MANUSCRIPT REFERENCES

General Index